AMERICAN PRESBYTERIANS:

A PICTORIAL HISTORY

JAMES H. SMYLIE

Philadelphia
Presbyterian Historical Society
1985

The *Journal of Presbyterian History* is published quarterly by the Presbyterian Historical Society (Department of History), 425 Lombard Street, Philadelphia, Pennsylvania, in cooperation with The Historical Foundation of the Presbyterian and Reformed Churches, Montreat, North Carolina and with the Historical Foundation of the Cumberland Presbyterian Church, Memphis, TN. The primary focus of the *Journal* is on American Presbyterian and Reformed history.

Subscription and Society Membership:

Subscription		$15.00
Society Membership including *Journal* (per year)	from	15.00
Single numbers of the *Journal* (except v. 63:1&2)		5.00
v. 63:1&2		12.95
Microfilm edition, 1901-1982, 14 rolls	per roll	28.00

Correspondence regarding the *Journal* should be sent to the Editor, 425 Lombard St., Philadelphia, Pa. 19147. The Society does not assume responsibility for statements of fact or of opinion made by the contributors to the *Journal*.

ISSN 0022-3883

© 1985 by the Presbyterian Historical Society

Second class postage paid at Philadelphia, Pa.

Contents

Preface		v
I	Presbyterian Roots	1
II	American Presbyterian Beginnings, 1700-1758	15
III	The Age of the American Revolution, 1758-1800	33
IV	Freedom's Ferment and the Evangelical Front, 1800-1838	53
V	Divisions, Expansion, and the Irrepressible Conflict, 1838-1861	81
VI	War, Reconstruction, and Fraternal Relations, 1861-1883	107
VII	The Age of Presbyterian Enterprise, 1883-1906	135
VIII	The Church's Work and Theological Conflict, 1906-1930	167
IX	From Depression to Global Responsibilities, 1930-1958	195
X	Confrontation, Reconciliation, and the Future, 1958-	225
Acknowledgments		251
Index		257

Preface

THE PRESBYTERIAN HISTORICAL SOCIETY through the editorial committee of the *Journal of Presbyterian History* projected this pictorial history of American Presbyterians several years ago, and now presents it to members of the Presbyterian Church (U.S.A.) and to others interested in our history. Our purpose has been to observe Presbyterians in action as well as to survey American Presbyterian life and witness from its roots through its many challenges and responses. We have tried to portray a variety of Presbyterian experiences and offer these pages for the nurture of the Church.

Many people have contributed ideas and illustrations to this volume, indeed, many more suggestions and photographs than we have been able to use, given limitations of space and the wealth of material. Some persons deserve special recognition.

Mrs. Mary Agnes Brown Groover and Mrs. Isabella Krey, members of the Bethesda Presbyterian Church in Maryland, took an early interest in this project. Because of their substantial financial assistance they made the publication possible.

Gerald W. Gillette, Manager of Research and Library Services of the Presbyterian Historical Society, served as the copy editor of this history through its various stages, and took the author's selections, text, and layout, and prepared it with wisdom, skill, and care for the printer. He also compiled the Index.

William B. Miller, Director of the Society, supported this work from the beginning, and handled the business arrangements for it with his usual kindness, efficiency, and effectiveness. Dorothy Kurtz, editorial assistant of the *Journal of Presbyterian History*, kept the record straight and helped us carry on the correspondence for photographs and copyright permissions. Members of the staff of the Society searched for material. Ruth See, Research Librarian of the Historical Foundation, Montreat, NC, provided many pictures from the collection of that repository.

Numerous members of the faculty, administration, and student body of Union Theological Seminary in Virginia, encouraged the author, commented upon and supported the project. Graduate students R. Milton Winter, James S. McClanahan, Jr., and Bruce L. Taylor offered drafts of texts for various chapters and made many useful suggestions. John N. Coffman, Jeffrey K. Keezel, and Roland G. Antonelli of the audio-visual department of the seminary supplied photographs, while Brenda Lee and Sally Hicks typed the text.

All of these persons, and many others, made contributions to this work. The author expresses appreciation to them. We have tried to acknowledge all whose pictures we decided to use, and we apologize to all whose favorite picture of American Presbyterians did not make it into this history. The author accepts responsibility for all problems with perspective and the narrative. Prints are individually numbered by chapter and their sources recognized in the Acknowledgments.

Elizabeth R. Smylie, wife and companion, deserves a special word of gratitude for her interest, insights, and patience while this project grew from its inception to final completion as a pictorial history of American Presbyterians.

1
PRESBYTERIAN ROOTS

PRESBYTERIANS IN AMERICA share with Christians through the ages and around the world, the Nicene Creed in which we confess the "one, holy, catholic, and apostolic Church," the head of which is Jesus Christ. This identification with the larger Christian family is symbolized in the religious backdrop designed by Henry Lee Willet, Willet Stained Glass Studio, Philadelphia, for the 1958 meeting of the National Council of Presbyterian Women's Organizations. Willet, a Presbyterian, focuses on Jesus Christ as Lord of all. The world wide Christian family waits the benediction of the Holy Spirit around the chalice of the Lord's Supper. The Hebrew letters for God are at the top of the glass; the circle represents God's love. The Maltese cross with eight points represents the beatitudes, while the vine and the grapes suggest a living relationship with Christ. The rays of light surrounding the dove remind of the fruits of the Spirit, and the waves represent a witness spreading into the world and every walk of life. Other Christian symbols and concerns, found in the outer medallions, tie Presbyterians to the whole human family.

The roots of American Presbyterians extend more immediately to the Protestant Reformation of the sixteenth and seventeenth century. This religious revolution took place along with other revolutions in science, politics, economics, discovery, and communication. While Martin Luther may be identified as the spiritual catalyst which shook both church and empire, other reformers had been at work in the Christian family before him, others carried on the work after his death. Presbyterians are part of what historians call the Reformed tradition, influenced chiefly by John Calvin of Geneva, but which spread widely to a number of countries all over the continent under numerous leaders. The Reformation was a religious movement. Those in the Reformed movement, building on Luther's experience, stressed God's sovereign rule of grace over the hearts and the common life of the people. Reading the Bible in a fresh light, and using the insights of the revival of learning of this period, the Reformed wrote national confessions of faith, rethought and reorganized the structures of the church along conciliar lines under presbyters, and participated in the political movement toward nation-states and constitutional monarchies. The Reformation also took place during a period when European nations stretched outward across the seas to build mighty empires. From Europe and from the British Isles, those in the Reformed tradition sailed to the American colonies where they found a fresh start and new challenges.

Iona Abbey

While recognizing the continuity of the Christian community throughout history, Presbyterians in America have been drawn to the traditions of Iona, an island off the coast of Scotland. Founded by St. Columba, the famous monastery there sent out missionaries to spread the faith among the nonChristians of Europe under the Celtic Cross. The adoption of the cross ties American Presbyterians to this past, and points ahead to the Reformation of the sixteenth century.

Peter Waldo (d.c. 1215) was one of the first medieval Christians to advocate a return to the lifestyle of the New Testament church. Formerly a wealthy Lyons merchant, he gave away his possessions and attracted others of like mind. Condemned by the church establishment because of their unauthorized and zealous preaching, evangelism, and use of scriptures in the vernacular, the Waldensians sought refuge in Lombardy and Provence. Despite persecution, Waldo's ideas spread to other parts of central Europe. The persecuted Christians enjoyed the fellowship of the Lord's Supper.

Peter Waldo

During the fifteenth century, the Waldensians had contact with other movements associated with similar innovative doctrines. The Council of Constance (1414-1418) condemned the English reformer John Wyclif and his Czech disciple, Jan Hus, both of whom emphasized the primacy and preaching authority of the Bible. Waldensians, Hussites, and Wycliffites were indistinguishable to those interested in eradicating "heresy." Hus was burned at the stake after the Council.

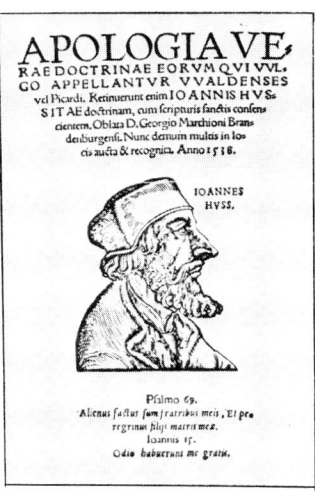

1517

Martin Luther (1483-1546), born in Saxony, was the towering figure of the Reformation in the sixteenth century. An Augustinian monk, biblical scholar, and theologian, he opposed the practice of indulgences on the basis of his insight into justification by faith which he gained from reading Paul's letter to the Romans. In 1517 he challenged church and empire with his Ninety-Five Theses and at the Diet of Worms. Interpreting Galatians on freedom, he gave to his followers a view of Christian liberty in his pamphlet of 1520 which strengthened their resolve.

Reformation Wall, Geneva

John Calvin (1509-1564) stood on Luther's shoulders as a successor to the German Reformer. He gave system to the insights of the Reformation and provided it with alternate ecclesiastical and political institutions. Born in Noyon, France, and never ordained, he was persuaded while travelling through Geneva to stay and assume the task of reshaping the city's life. His statue stands in Geneva along with others who were closely associated with him in his work, William Farel, Theodore Beza, and John Knox. Calvin, as the map of Europe indicates, had a widespread impact in the East, the North, and in the British Isles, especially in Scotland.

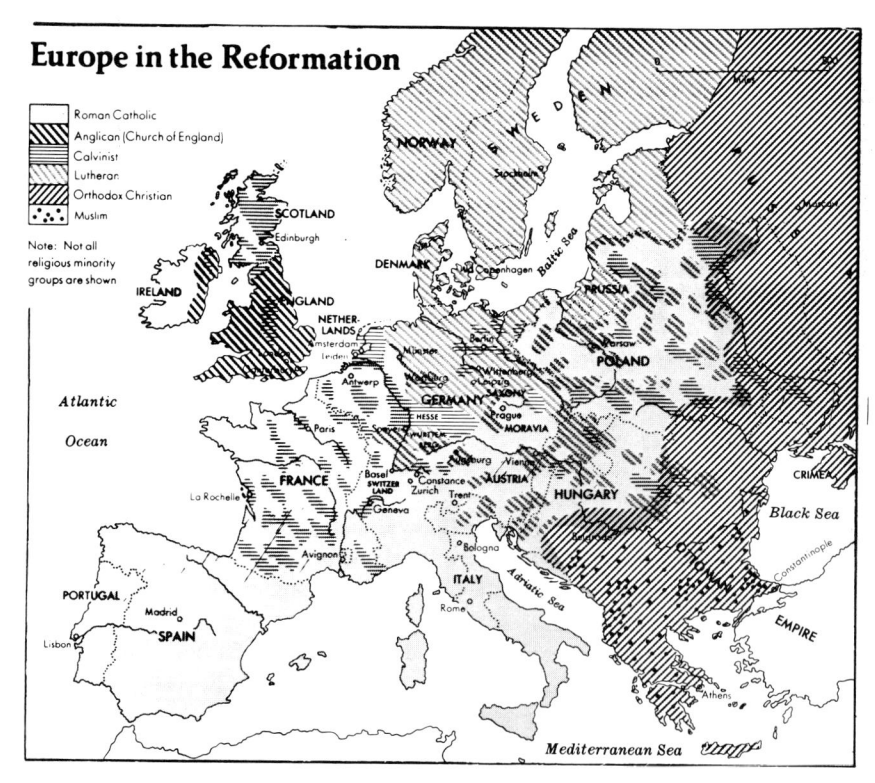

Europe in the Reformation

- Roman Catholic
- Anglican (Church of England)
- Calvinist
- Lutheran
- Orthodox Christian
- Muslim

Note: Not all religious minority groups are shown

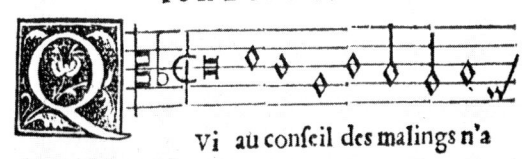

Calvin wrote: "We are God's: let us therefore live for him and die for him. We are God's: let his wisdom and will therefore rule all our actions. We are God's: let all the parts of our life accordingly strive toward him as our only lawful goal." With this focus on God, Calvin helped reshape the lives of people who heard him and the communities in which they lived. He was concerned not only about personal piety, but about every aspect of Genevan life—political, economic, social, as well as religious. The city became a haven for refugees from all over Europe.

Calvin encouraged singing. It is reported that people wept during the worship when they sang the Psalms which became so much a part of their lives.

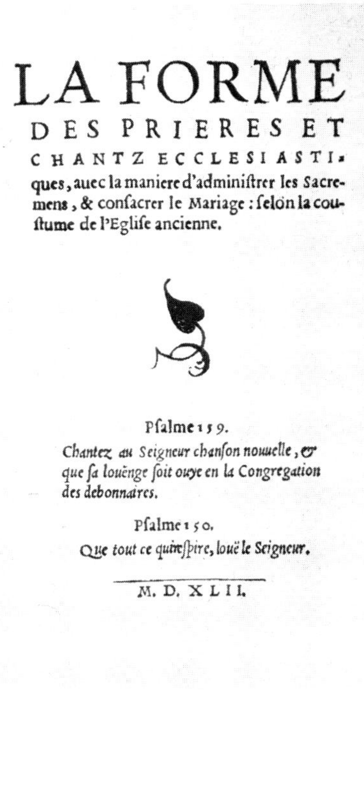

St. Peter's Cathedral, Geneva

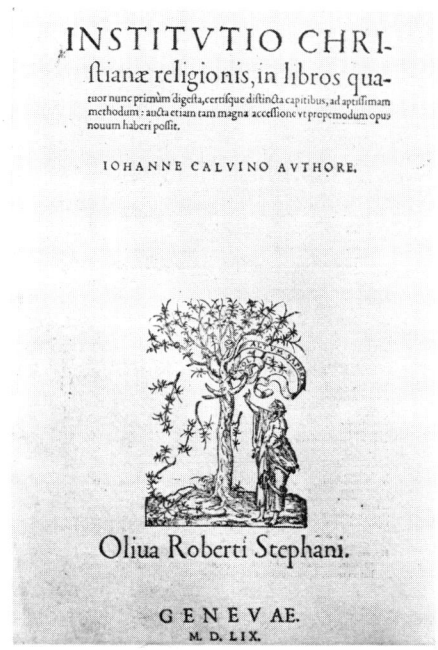

1536 Calvin was a preacher, and an exegete of the Scriptures. His many commentaries show him to be a brilliant interpreter. He wrote the first edition of the *Institutes of the Christian Religion* in 1536; it became the preeminent theological statement of the Reformed faith. Calvin continued to revise and expand the *Institutes*, based roughly on the articles of the Apostles' Creed, throughout his life. Concerned for educated Christians and citizens, he established the Geneva Academy. Theodore Beza became the first Rector. After its founding in 1559, the school trained pastors and laity who became the leaders of the Reformation.

In an age of intolerance Calvin condemned—and the civil magistrates burned—Michael Servetus at the stake in 1553 in Geneva. Servetus was a refugee from other Christian powers who sought to silence him for his unitarian and heretical views.

Geneva Academy

Servetus' Memorial

1560 John Knox (1515-1572) was attracted to Calvin's Geneva. Upon his return to Scotland, he commenced religious reform against the papacy and the mass, and railed against Mary of Guise and Mary Tudor. Scottish nationalism united with Protestantism to overthrow the government and religion of the country's rulers. In celebration of the Treaty of Edinburgh, under which French and English forces withdrew from Scotland, Knox conducted a service of thanksgiving at St. Giles Cathedral, July 15, 1560. Calvinism would not be conclusively established in Scotland, however, until the seventeenth century.

The principal statement of the Scottish Reformation was the *Confession of Faith* (1560), largely the work of Knox. Adopted by the Scottish Parliament, the Calvinistic document became the creed of the kingdom. Shortly thereafter, Parliament abolished papal jurisdiction and outlawed the mass.

Knox attacked the Catholic Queen Mary with a "trumpet blast," and demonstrated his own suspicions of women rulers.

St. Giles Cathedral   John Knox

The Swiss reform spirit was not confined to Geneva. Even before Calvin began his work on the shores of Lac Leman, Zurich was experiencing a scripturally-based reform under a patriotic Swiss humanist named Hildreich Zwingli (1484-1531). An ardent foe of Catholic practice, Zwingli's rejection of any physical presence of Christ in the sacrament of the Lord's Supper prevented uniting with the Lutherans.

Zwingli 21

1566 Zwingli's more ecumenically-minded successor was Heinreich Bullinger (1504-1575). Under his leadership, the Zurich Reformation was strongly influenced and modified by Calvinism. He and Calvin were able to agree on the interpretation of the Lord's Supper. Broader accord was achieved on the basis of the *Second Helvetic Confession* of 1566, written by Bullinger. It was accepted not only by the Swiss churches but also by a number of other Reformed churches in central Europe. Bullinger placed an emphasis on the covenants God has made with the people.

Bullinger 22

The Netherlands became Reformed in religion (1576) under William the Silent, also known as William of Nassau (1553-1584), after a struggle with Spain during which he commissioned the "sea beggars" to prey on Spanish shipping. Once an exile himself, he widened religious toleration and welcomed the persecuted to his country. Dutch Calvinism was expressed in the *Belgic Confession* (1561), the *Heidelberg Catechism* (1563), and the canons of the Synod of Dort (1619), and is represented in the U.S. by the Reformed Church of America.

William the Silent 23

Because of a controversy over the Lord's Supper, Frederick III, Elector of the Lutheran Palatinate in southwestern Germany, studied the issue himself. He was persuaded to reject the Lutheran for the Calvinist interpretation of Christ's presence, and he invited Reformed professors to teach at the University of Heidelberg. Two of these men, Zacharias Ursinus and Kaspar Olevianus, prepared the *Heidelberg Catechism* for use in the Elector's territories. Frederick adopted it in 1563, and soon Calvinists in different places found it useful and comforting.

Ursinus

Olevianus

The *Heidelberg Catechism* presents the essentials of the faith in question and answer form. It is a moderate and highly personal confession. The first question is:

Q. 1. What is your only comfort, in life and in death?
A. That I belong—body and soul, in life and in death—not to myself but to my faithful Savior, Jesus Christ, . . .

Calvin owed much to France, the land of his birth, where he was shaped by the humanistic and reforming leaven at work. The Huguenots, members of the French Reformed movement, were alternately tolerated and persecuted by the French monarchy. They had important supporters including Margaret DeValois, the Queen of Navarre. On St. Bartholomew's Day, 1572, Roman Catholics murdered thousands of Huguenots in a bloody massacre which was etched deeply on Protestant consciousness. The Huguenots were tolerated in France, but often harassed as they tried to worship God. By the end of the seventeenth century the French monarch revoked the Edict of Nantes under which Huguenots had gained some protection.

Margaret De Valois

Huguenots Worshipping in the Wilderness

Admiral Gaspar de Coligny, a Huguenot nobleman, promoted Huguenot colonies in America. A colony at the mouth of the St. John's River in Florida was destroyed by the Spanish in 1565, because of its threat to Spain's interests. The Huguenots were put to the sword after they were captured near an inlet still called Matanzas—meaning "slaughters."

Henry VIII of England broke with Rome in the 1530s, although reforms in religious life were few. Archbishop Cranmer invited a number of continental reformers to England, and Lutheran and Calvinist ideas shaped the British reformation as expressed in the *Thirty-nine Articles* (1563) and the *Book of Common Prayer*. When Queen Mary tried to restore Catholicism, a number of Protestants fled the country. Some went to Geneva where they produced a translation popularly known as the Geneva Bible (1560). They showed on the title page that they thought of their struggle as similar to Israel's plight and eventual deliverance from Egypt.

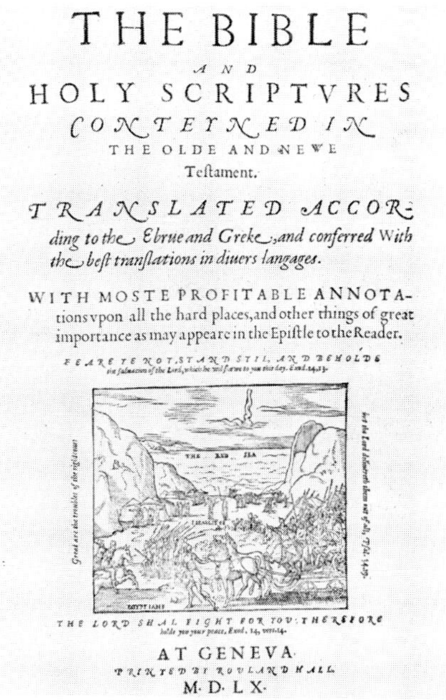

Thomas Cartwright

Some of the English, led by Thomas Cartwright (c. 1535-1604), a professor at Cambridge, advocated the Presbyterian form of church government as the true biblical expression, and opposed episcopacy and congregationalism as the polity for the British Isles. The church, according to this interpretation, should be governed by elders, ordained by the laying on of hands and prayer in the name of the Father, Son, and Holy Spirit.

Presbyterians in the British Isles were stirred by a strong piety, elements of which may be seen in the title page of this book showing the need for a broken and contrite heart.

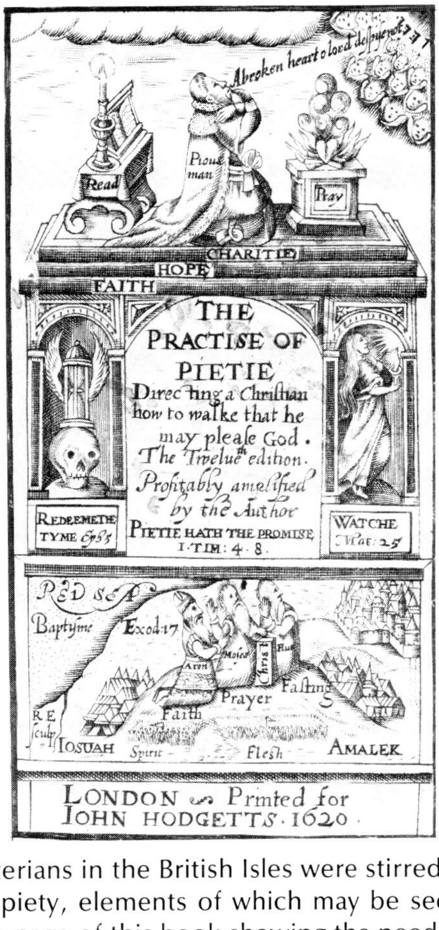

Greyfriars Church

Westminster Abbey

The Humble
ADVICE
Of the
ASSEMBLY
OF
DIVINES,
Now by Authority of *Parliament*
sitting at WESTMINSTER,
Concerning
A Confession of Faith:
With the QUOTATIONS and TEXTS of
SCRIPTURE annexed.

Presented by them lately to both Houses of Parliament.

Printed at LONDON;
AND
Re-printed at EDINBURGH by *Evan Tyler*, Printer to the Kings most Excellent Majestie. 1647.

The humble
ADVICE
OF THE
ASSEMBLY
OF
DIVINES,
Now by Authority of Parliament
sitting at WESTMINSTER,
CONCERNING
A shorter Catechism,
With the Proofs thereof out of the Scriptures,
Presented by them lately to both Houses of
PARLIAMENT.

A certain number of Copies are Ordered to be Printed onely for the use of the Members of both Houses and of the Assembly of Divines, to the end that they may advise thereupon.

LONDON,
Printed by *J. F.*

1646 Presbyterian discontent grew in the British Isles, especially in Scotland where they met at Greyfriars Church to defy attempts to press the Reformation in Scotland toward episcopacy. Samuel Rutherford, a Scottish leader, championed Presbyterianism and opposed political absolutism. His book *Lex Rex* set out the case for a constitutional monarchy. In the 1640s Parliament called an Assembly which met in Westminster Abbey. The Assembly of Divines, not all of them Presbyterian, wrote the *Westminster Confession* and *Larger* and *Shorter Catechisms* which shaped Presbyterianism from the time the *Confession* was adopted in 1648. The Assembly also proposed a *Directory of Worship* and Presbyterian polity.

The first question and response in the *Shorter Catechism* reflected the basic affirmation of Reformed faith:

Q. 1. What is the chief end of man?
A. Man's chief end is to glorify God, and to enjoy him forever.

1649 Civil War erupted between Parliament and King Charles I in 1642. The Puritan army under Oliver Cromwell was ultimately victorious over the royal forces, but during the course of the conflict it had become disenchanted with the conservative Presbyterian majority in Parliament. On December 6, 1648, the Puritan army expelled the Presbyterians from Parliament. The "Rump Parliament" tried and condemned the king and had him beheaded on January 30, 1649.

Beheading of Charles I

Early in his reign, Charles repressed Puritans. As their preachers were silenced, many Puritans sought religious freedom in America. John Winthrop (1587/88-1649) led a group of immigrants to Massachusetts Bay. They established a congregational polity and received pastoral leadership from men such as John Cotton (1584-1652) of the Boston church.

John Winthrop

John Cotton

Scottish Presbyterians attempted to establish the colony of Darien on the Isthmus of America in the middle of the seventeenth century. They founded communities called New Edinburgh and New Caledonia, as colonists founded New England far to the north. Francis Borland, a minister, preached in the Isthmus as well as in colonial America and Scotland, before the Spanish ended the experiment in colonization.

To try to solve the Irish question, the British monarchy settled English and many Scottish Presbyterians in Ireland. During the decades of the seventeenth and eighteenth centuries the friction between Presbyterians and Roman Catholics and Anglicans mounted. Much blood was shed during the turmoil. In the eighteenth century an estimated 250,000 people, many of them Presbyterian, emigrated from northern Ireland to America because of economic, political, and religious problems. Many also left Scotland for the same reasons to seek larger opportunities which they believed could be found in the New World.

Carncastle Meeting House

Londonderry

II
AMERICAN PRESBYTERIAN BEGINNINGS

1700-1758 The American Presbyterian community sprang from small plantings here and there in the American colonies beginning about the middle of the seventeenth century. The first sixty years of the eighteenth century were formative. Presbyterians took actions which determined the shape of the denomination for many years. Because of considerable growth in numbers and the need for some larger fellowship, discipline, and expression of unity, they organized the first presbytery in 1706 and the Synod of Philadelphia in 1716. Because of a need for an educated ministry and membership, they began to build academies and colleges near to churches they founded up and down the eastern seacoast and in the West. Because of a concern for theological standards, they agreed to the Adopting Act of 1729 by which Presbyterian ministers subscribed to the *Westminister Confession* and *Larger* and *Shorter Catechisms*, and yet allowed some freedom to disagree on nonessential and unnecessary articles of the faith as interpreted by the presbytery. Presbyterians split over the Great Awakening into New Side and Old Side factions, the first such division in American Presbyterian history. They had to learn during separation between 1741-1758 to accommodate the concerns of one another. During this period Presbyterian congregations were concentrated in New York, Pennsylvania, New Jersey, Delaware, and Maryland, but they began to push into the West and into the South with settlements. Out of this early period come the names of the colonial leaders who are still remembered because of their contributions to the Presbyterian family—Francis Makemie, Jonathan Dickinson, William and Gilbert Tennent, and Samuel Davies, among others who shaped the faith and life of the church.

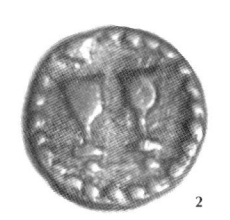

The elders of a Presbyterian congregation in the eighteenth century distributed communion tokens to church members judged as ready to come to the Lord's table. Tokens were made of various materials with the initials of a congregation or pastor stamped on them. The use of tokens followed the customs in Ireland and Scotland of "fencing the table" to uphold high standards of Christian faith and conduct. Footstoves or coalpans (above) kept worshipers warm when they congregated in unheated and drafty colonial churches of stone, brick, wood-frame, or log construction.

Makemie Statue, Makemie Park, VA

Minutes, The Presbytery

1706 The first presbytery in the Middle Colonies may have met in 1706 in Philadelphia. Seven ministers—Jedediah Andrews, PA; John Wilson, DE; Nathanial Taylor, MD; Samuel Davis, DE; John Hampton and George McNish, just arrived from the British Isles, and Francis Makemie, MD—probably gathered at that first meeting for fellowship, discipline, continuing education and edification in company with one another. While the first leaf of the minutes of the meeting is missing, the remaining record shows familiarity with Scottish ecclesiastical procedure. It also shows that the Presbyterians were shaping the structure of the church to deal with new problems in "the desolate places" on this side of the Atlantic. The March 22, 1707 meeting convened in Philadelphia, possibly at First "Old Buttonwood" Church, at which time elders as well as ministers were present. Makemie has been remembered with a statue as the father of organized American Presbyterianism. His handsome desk indicates a standing in the Maryland community as a gentleman.

Old Buttonwood

A NARRATIVE Of a New and Unusual AMERICAN Imprisonment Of Two PRESBYTERIAN MINISTERS: And Prosecution of Mr. Francis Makemie

One of them, for Preaching one SERMON at the City of NEW-YORK.

By a Learner of Law, and Lover of Liberty.

Printed for the Publisher. 1707.

1707 Lord Cornbury, Edward Hyde, governor of New York, charged and jailed Makemie in New York for preaching without a license. The governor called Makemie a "Jack of all Trades, a Preacher, a Doctor of Physick, a Merchant, an Attorney, or Counsellor at Law, and which is worst of all, a Disturber of Governments." Makemie argued that he had a license, that he had to obey God who called him to preach, and that he had religious and civil rights as an Englishman. The court acquitted Makemie. Cornbury assessed the Presbyterian court costs and for the time Makemie spent in jail.

Makemie's Trial

Jamaica First Church

Old Norriton

Dutch Reformed settlers organized the Old Norriton Church, PA, probably in the 1670s. English-speaking Calvinists brought the congregation into the Presbytery of Philadelphia in the early part of the eighteenth century. The present stone structure was built sometime between 1689-1698, and is the oldest known Presbyterian building in America. George Washington visited wounded who were kept here during the American Revolution.

The Jamaica Presbyterian Church, NY, traces its origins back to 1662. In 1699 the town constructed the old stone building which stood at the center of the village until 1813. It was forty feet square with a pyramidal roof and a belfry and bell in the middle. A primitive imitation of a dove was mounted on a weathervane of sheet-copper, according to descriptions of the church.

The Southampton Presbyterian Church, Long Island, formed in 1640, is the oldest Presbyterian congregation in America. It was also a part of the oldest English settlement in New York. Under the ministry of Abraham Pierson it grew. The print here shows the church building, which was erected in 1707. Sexes were segregated. Men and boys sat on one side while the women and girls occupied the other.

Southampton Church Communion Cups

Southampton Church

Rehoboth Church

Francis Makemie served the Presbyterian congregation at Rehoboth, MD, which still stands near a tributary of the Pocomoke River. Makemie lived on the river and he and other Presbyterians used it for transportation to meetings.

As early as the 1650s a Dutch Reformed congregation worshiped at New Castle in Delaware. After 1664 when the British took over the Dutch colonies, the church began to represent that fact and included English, French Huguenot, and Scottish elements. By 1698 the people had called a Presbyterian pastor, and they entered the Presbytery formed in 1706. The gambrel-roofed building was erected in 1707, and has been restored to its original design in recent years.

New Castle Church

Calvinists in the New World took seriously the need to reflect on Christian faith and life. Samuel Willard (1640-1707) was the teacher at South Church in Boston. He gave a series of two hundred and fifty lectures to his people on the *Westminster Shorter Catechism*; these lectures were published after his death as *A Compleat Body of Divinity* (1726). Willard's work, the largest ever printed in America to that time and the first American systematic theology, showed the author to be an imaginative and sensitive thinker who asked how human beings might express their dignity as children of God. Children studied the catechism found in *The New-England Primer,* published first in the seventeenth and well into the nineteenth century.

A COMPLEAT
Body of Divinity
IN
Two Hundred and Fifty
EXPOSITORY LECTURES
ON THE
Assembly's Shorter Catechism
WHEREIN
The DOCTRINES of the CHRISTIAN RELIGION are unfolded, their Truth confirm'd, their Excellence display'd, their Usefulness improv'd; contrary Errors & Vices refuted & expos'd, Objections answer'd, Controversies settled, Cases of Conscience resolv'd; and a great Light thereby reflected on the present Age.

By the REVEREND & LEARNED
SAMUEL WILLARD, M. A.
Late Pastor of the *South Church* in *Boston*, and Vice-President of Harvard College in Cambridge, in New-England.

Prefac'd by the Pastors of the same Church.

HEB. xiii. 7. *Remember Them — who have spoken to you the Word of* GOD: *Whose Faith follow, considering the End of their Conversation.*
HEB. xi. 4. *By Faith — He obtained witness, that He was Righteous*; GOD *testifying of his Gifts: And by it He being dead, yet speaketh.*
II. TIM. i. 13. *Hold fast the Form of sound Words, which thou hast heard of Me, in Faith & Love which is in* CHRIST JESUS.

BOSTON in NEW-ENGLAND:
Printed by B. GREEN and S. KNEELAND for B. ELIOT and D. HENCHMAN, and Sold at their Shops.
MDCCXXVI.

Samuel Willard

In Adam's Fall
We sinned all.

Thy Life to mend,
God's Book attend.

The Cat doth play,
And after slay.

A Dog will bite
A Thief at Night.

The Eagle's Flight
Is out of Sight.

The idle Fool
Is whipt at School.

New-England Primer

William Tennent

Log College Lock

William Tennent (1673-1746) undertook the task of theological education at the "Log College," Neshaminy, PA, near his home and church. The school was dubbed the "Log College" by Tennent's detractors because of the modest building in which he conducted classes. Born in Ireland, Tennent immigrated to Philadelphia in 1717. He educated his sons and a number of other young men who became leaders in the Presbyterian Church and in the Great Awakening. The "Log College" generated support and stimulated the interest which led to the establishment of the College of New Jersey in the 1740s in Princeton.

THE TRUE
SCRIPTURE-DOCTRINE
Concerning Some
Important Points
OF
Christian Faith,
Particularly
ETERNAL ELECTION, | Justification by FAITH,
ORIGINAL SIN, | And the
GRACE IN CONVERSION, | SAINTS PERSEVERANCE.
Represented and *Apply'd*
In five DISCOURSES.
By *Jonathan Dickinson*, A.M.
Minister of the Gospel at Elisabeth-Town, N. Jersey.
With a PREFACE by Mr. FOXCROFT.

BOSTON, Printed by G. ROGERS, for S. ELIOT
in Cornhill. 1741.

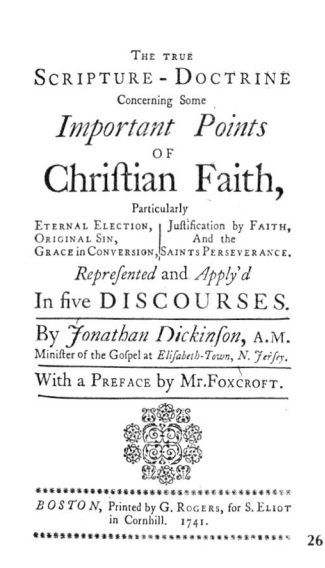

Jonathan Dickinson

1729 Blown by the winds of doctrine in the eighteenth century, the Presbyterian Synod, organized in 1716, took steps to adopt the *Westminster Confession of Faith* with the *Larger* and *Shorter Catechisms* as the theological standard for the denomination. Jonathan Dickinson (1688-1747), a New Englander called to the Elizabethtown Presbyterian Church in New Jersey, opposed the adoption of such a standard at first. He thought confessions tended to take the place of the Bible in the life of the church and set tradition above the Word. He helped Presbyterians work out the Adopting Act of 1729.

They agreed to accept the Westminster documents as being "in all the essential and necessary articles, good forms of sound words and systems of Christian doctrine," to allow for disagreement in nonessentials, and to submit to a method of dealing with such disagreements while preserving unity. Thus, they provided a standard, and yet allowed freedom in the church.

The Adopting Act

George Whitefield

Old South Meeting House

According to tradition, George Whitefield (1714-1780) could wring tears from the eyes in the way in which he pronounced "Mesopotamia." A brilliant English pulpiteer, part Calvinist, part Anglican, part Methodist, he crossed the Atlantic a number of times and stirred people with the Gospel. In his travels from Boston to Georgia so many people turned out to hear him that he had to deliver his messages in the fields or streets, or build larger buildings to accommodate the people. He was accused of being "censorious," an "itinerant," and an "enthusiast"—all those things of which people who were against the Great Awakening were suspicious. He preached for a number of Presbyterian churches, and he lies buried in the Newburyport (Old South First) Presbyterian Church in Massachusetts. While at first favorably impressed, Dickinson grew cautious about Whitefield's impact upon Presbyterians.

1741 Whitefield made a lasting impression on Gilbert Tennent (1703-1763), eldest son of William, as did Theodore Frelinghuysen, a deeply pious Dutch pastor of the Raritan Valley, NJ. An awakening broke out under Tennent's preaching at his New Brunswick Presbyterian Church in the latter part of the 1720s. He gained notoriety when he preached his sermon entitled, "The Danger of an Unconverted Ministry" (1740) in which he attacked unconverted clergy as being "Pharisee-teachers, having no Experience of a special Work of the Holy Ghost. . ." and as blind men leading the blind. New Englander John Hancock warned against "The Danger of an Unqualified Ministry" (1743) in response to Tennant's outburst. Being unable to contain the tension, the Presbyterians divided into Old Side and New Side Synods in 1741, a split which lasted until 1758. Tennent moved to the Second Presbyterian Church in Philadelphia in 1743, where he was considerably more disciplined and irenic.

Gilbert Tennent

THE OLD TENNENT CHURCH.

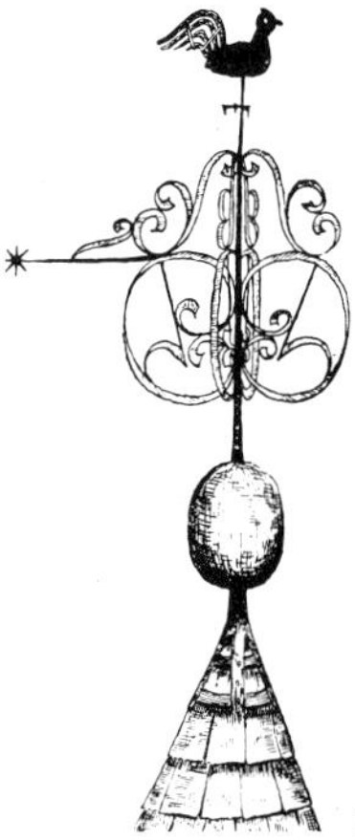

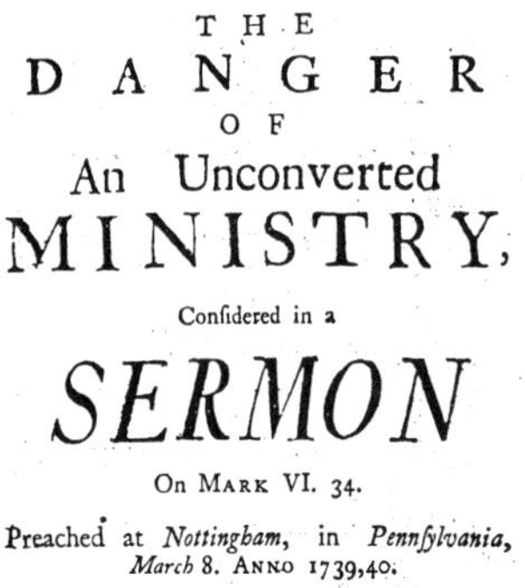

THE
DANGER
OF
An Unconverted
MINISTRY,
Considered in a
SERMON
On Mark VI. 34.

Preached at *Nottingham*, in *Pennsylvania*,
March 8. Anno 1739,40.

By GILBERT TENNENT, A.M.
And Minister of the Gospel in *New-Brunswick*,
New-Jersey.

Jerem. V. 30, 31. *A wonderful and horrible Thing is committed in the Land: The Prophets prophesy falsely, and the Priests bear Rule by their Means, and my People love to have it so; and what will they do in the End thereof?*

PHILADELPHIA:
Printed by BENJAMIN FRANKLIN,
In *Market-street*, 1740.

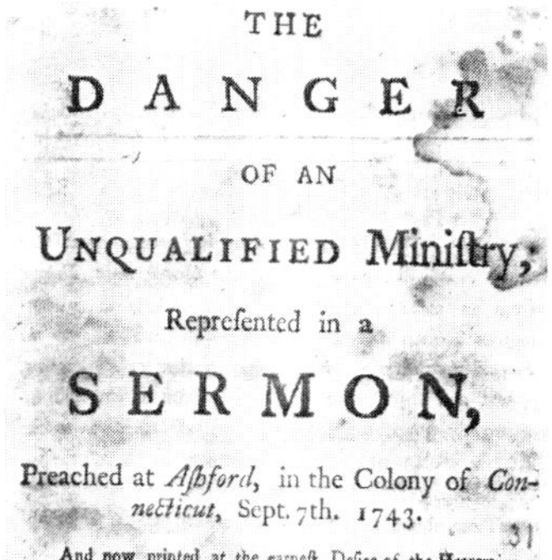

THE
DANGER
OF AN
UNQUALIFIED Ministry;
Represented in a
SERMON,
Preached at *Ashford*, in the Colony of *Connecticut*, Sept. 7th. 1743.

And now printed at the earnest Desire of the Hearers.

By *John Hancock*,
Pastor of the first Church in BRAINTREE.

Mal. ii. 7. *The Priest's Lips should keep Knowledge, and they should seek the Law at his Mouth; for he is the Messenger of the LORD of Hosts.*
Rom. xi 13.——*I magnify mine Office.*

BOSTON, Printed and Sold by ROGERS and FOWLE in Queen Street, next to the Prison. 1743.

Jonathan Edwards   Sarah Edwards

Jonathan Edwards (1703-1758), one of the greatest American theologian-philosophers, started his ministry in the Presbyterian Church of New York City in the 1720s before going to Northampton, MA, where he served until 1750 when he became a missionary to Indians in western Massachusetts. Edwards was deeply involved in the Great Awakening, defending it in his great work on *Religious Affections* as well as doctrines such as *Original Sin*. While he became known for his sermon about "sinners in the hands of an angry God," he was a preacher of God's sovereign grace and justification by faith, the principal hinge of the Reformation. He owed much to his wife, Sarah, from whom he gained spiritual inspiration. The New Side College of New Jersey in Princeton elected Edwards president in 1757, but unfortunately he died shortly after taking up his duties. He had been innoculated for smallpox, yet died of the disease.

A
TREATISE
Concerning
Religious Affections,
In Three PARTS;

PART I. Concerning the Nature of the *Affections*, and their Importance in *Religion*.
PART II. Shewing what are *no certain Signs* that religious *Affections* are *gracious*, or that they are *not*.
PART III. Shewing what *are distinguishing Signs* of truly gracious and *holy Affections*.

By *Jonathan Edwards*, A.M.
And Pastor of the *first* Church in *Northampton*.

THE
Great Christian Doctrine
OF
ORIGINAL SIN
defended;
Evidences of it's *Truth* produced,
AND
Arguments to the *Contrary* answered.
Containing, in particular,
A Reply to the Objections and Arguings of Dr. JOHN TAYLOR, in his Book, Intitled, " The Scripture-Doctrine of *Original Sin* pro- " posed to free and candid Examination, &c.

By the late Reverend and Learned
JONATHAN EDWARDS, A.M.
President of the College of *New-Jersey*.

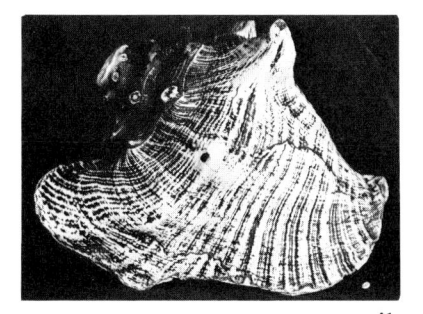

David Brainerd (1718-1747) once accused an instructor at Yale of having no more grace than a chair. Brainerd did not graduate. He became a missionary to Indians in Pennsylvania and New Jersey, traveling over 3000 miles in his ministry. Overcome with tuberculosis, he died at the age of thirty in the arms of the daughter of Edwards, to whom he was engaged. Edwards edited Brainerd's *Journal*, which motivated many to accept the call as missionaries during the eighteenth and nineteenth centuries. Brainerd used the conch shell, now in the Presbyterian Historical Society, to call Indians to worship.

Francis Alison (1705-1779) immigrated to America from his native Ireland when he was thirty years old and after study at the University of Glasgow. After a brief time in Maryland, where he was ordained to the ministry, he was installed as pastor of the New London, PA, congregation. In 1743 he opened a classical academy which was taken over and supported by the Old Side Synod of Philadelphia. As one of the most noted classical scholars in the colonies, he trained not only ministers but also many who became physicians and prominent in the political life of the colonies. Two signed the Declaration of Independence.

Francis Alison

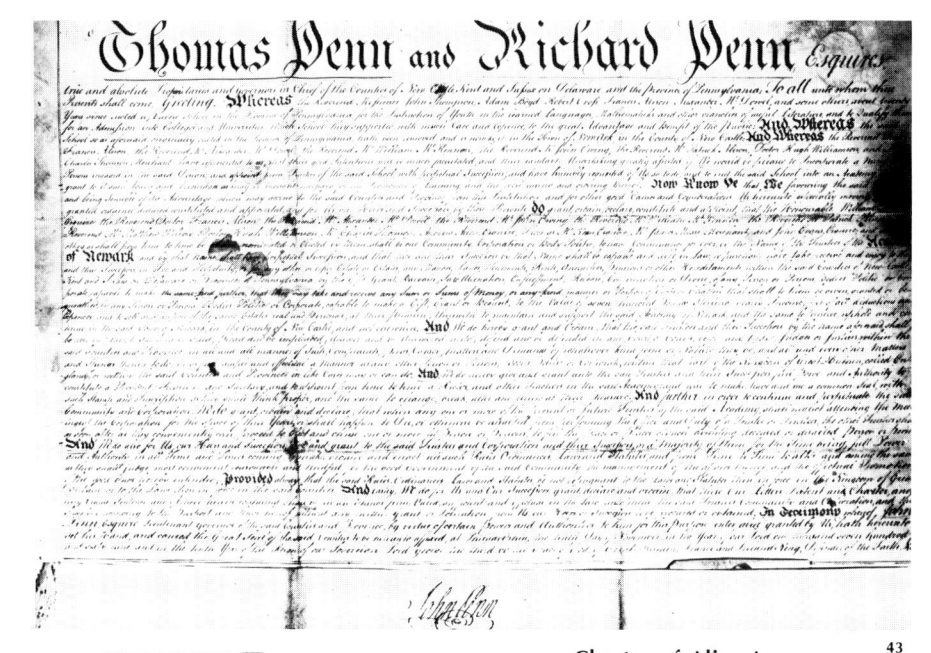

Charter of Alison's Academy, New London

After Benjamin Franklin failed to get an Anglican to be the rector of the Philadelphia Academy, he turned to Alison for help. The latter had established himself as a leading educator in the Middle Colonies. When the academy was chartered as a college, Alison became vice provost and professor of moral philosophy, positions he held until his death. He was also able to give direction to Presbyterian causes as co-pastor of the First Presbyterian Church in the city.

THE OLD ACADEMY.

Esther Burr

Samuel Finley

1746 New Side Presbyterians of the Synod of New York gained a charter for the College of New Jersey in 1746 shortly after the "Log College" was closed. It was first located in the home of Jonathan Dickinson in Elizabethtown, NJ, Dickinson serving as its first president. After a time in Newark, the school was moved to Princeton in 1756, where it occupied Nassau Hall, one of the largest buildings in colonial America at the time. The New Side provided its trustees and president, including Aaron Burr (1715-1757), Samuel Davies (1723-1761), and Samuel Finley (1715-1766). Edwards served in that capacity for several months in 1758. A student poked fun at Finley in the cartoon of the college leader.

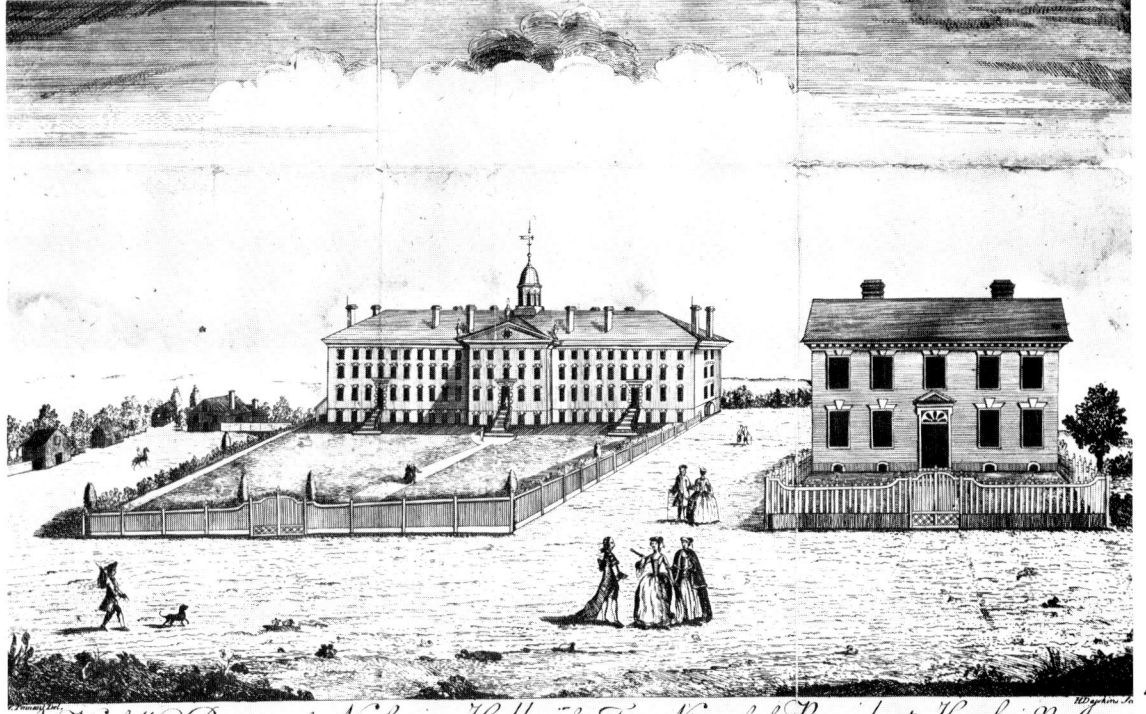

A North-West Prospect of Nassau-Hall, with a Front View of the Presidents House, in New Jersey

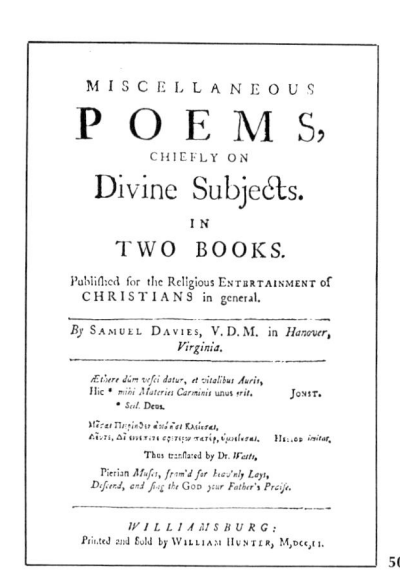

1755 Samuel Davies studied in Samuel Blair's academy at Faggs Manor, PA, and then went south into Virginia as an evangelist of the Synod of New York in 1747. So successful was he in his preaching that he was able to organize the Hanover Presbytery in 1755 which embraced much of the South. He was an eloquent preacher, a poet, and an educator, who gave much attention to teaching slaves under his charge. He also pleaded for the rights of dissenters in Virginia to their own churches, despite the wishes of the Anglican establishment. In 1759 he succeeded Jonathan Edwards as president of the College of New Jersey. Davies founded the Providence Presbyterian Church in Gum Spring, VA, in 1747.

Providence Presbyterian Church, Gum Spring, VA

Middle Octorara Convenanter United Presbyterian Church

Scottish Covenanters, who had suffered for the faith during the Restoration in the 1660s, and Seceders, who protested the patronage system in Scotland in the 1730s, were among the immigrants who came to America. They organized Reformed and Associate presbyteries, and sometimes cooperated with one another.

Alexander Gellatly organized the Octorara congregation and the Associate Presbytery in 1753. The church building, still standing, was erected in 1754 with an entrance at both the east and west ends and an aisle wide enough for members to be seated and served by elders at communion tables.

Guinston United Presbyterian Church

Old Guinston, formerly Old Muddy Creek Church, York County, PA, was also a part of the Associate Presbytery. It was organized in 1754, and was the oldest congregation with a continuous history of the United Presbyterian Church of North America. The building is still standing and used.

A Communion Gathering

Because of the isolation of churches in colonial America, the Lord's Supper was usually observed only twice a year during a communion season lasting three to five days, according to Scottish custom. The season included singing, preaching, praying, fasting, and an examination of church members for their readiness to receive the sacrament. The Lord's Supper was served on long tables placed in the aisles of churches or outside in the open. Samuel Davies used the communion pewter pictured here.

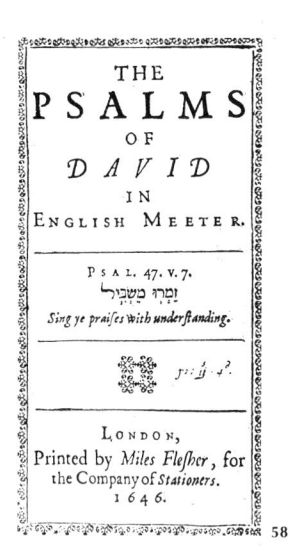

Presbyterians sang the Psalms in worship because they were the divinely inspired hymns. They used *The Whole Psalms of David in English Metre* by Francis Rous, a Puritan member of the Long Parliament. A precentor led the singing by lining out the Psalms, "Old One Hundred" being one of the favorites. Gradually some Presbyterians began to use the paraphrases of the Psalms by Isaac Watts as well as some of his own hymns.

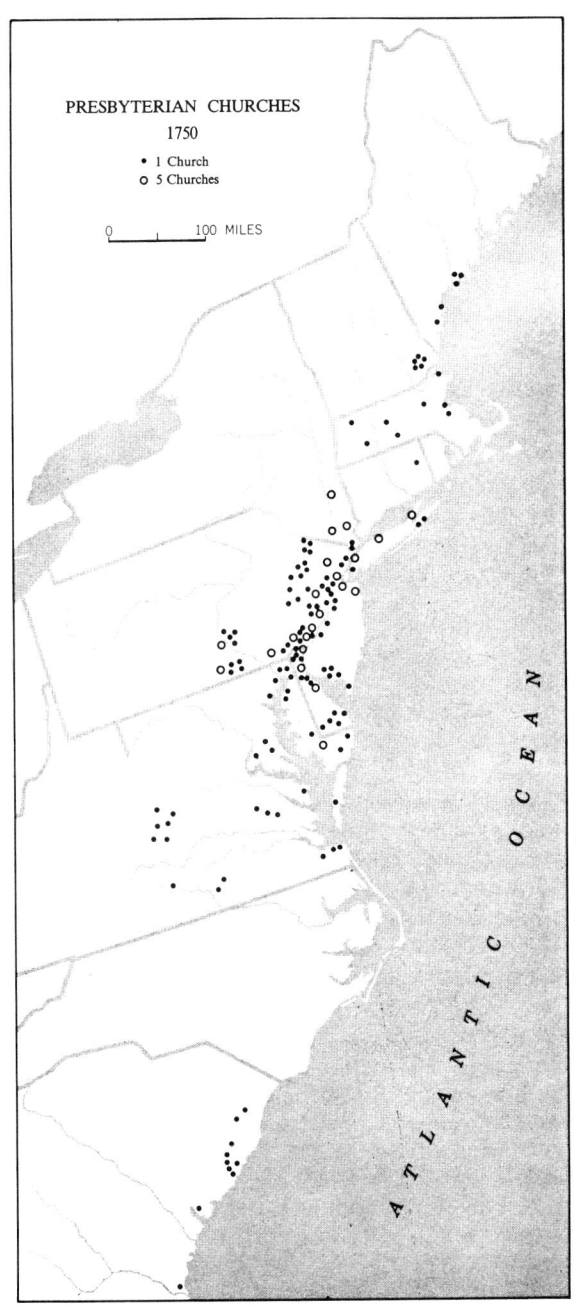

PRESBYTERIAN CHURCHES
1750
• 1 Church
○ 5 Churches

0 100 MILES

ATLANTIC OCEAN

Presbyterians increased in numbers during the eighteenth century. By 1750 Presbyterian congregations existed in most of the colonies, a few in New England and in South Carolina, most in the colonies of New York, New Jersey, Pennsylvania, Delaware, and Maryland. Moreover, a few Presbyterians organized congregations on the frontier, often very isolated from the life of other Christians. During this period New Side congregations increased more than did those of the Old Side.

Samson Occum (1723-1792), a Mohegan Indian born in Connecticut, was converted along with his mother during the Great Awakening. He studied theology with Eleazer Wheelock and was ordained to the ministry. He preached in England to raise funds for Wheelock's school and collected some £10,000 for the cause. After his ordination, Occum worked among the Indians in New York. As a Presbyterian, he did not like the Anglicans, and he commented once that he thought the English bishops did not want Indians to go to heaven with them.

DR. JOHN REDMAN.

1757 The Synod of Philadelphia under the leadership of Francis Alison and physician John Redman grew increasingly concerned about the support of ministers and their families. The "small and uncertain stipends of ministers and the poverty and distress of their widows and children" turned out to be "great discouragements to many pious and able men" who might enter the ministry. So the Synod established a charitable corporation named "Corporation for ye Relief of poor & distressed Pennsylvania Ministers & their Widows & children in the Province of Pensilvania. . . ." This corporation grew into the Presbyterian Ministers' Fund, the first life insurance company in America.

Know all Men by these Presents That we William Humphries and William Allen both of the City Philadelphia Merct. are held and firmly bound to the Corporation for Relief of poor and distressed Presbyterian Ministers and of the poor and distressed Widows and Children of Presbyterian Ministers for the Province of Pennsylvania and Counties of New Castle Kent and Sussex upon Delaware in the full and just Sum of Two thousand Pounds current Money of the Province aforesaid to be paid to them their Successors and Assigns To the which Payment well and truly to be made and done we bind ourselves our Heirs Exors and Admors and each and every of them jointly and severally firmly by these Presents Sealed with our Seals and dated the Sixteenth Day of July in the Year of our Lord One Thousand Seven hundred and Sixty

III
THE AGE OF THE AMERICAN REVOLUTION

1758-1800 Presbyterians seeking the "peace of Jerusalem," as Gilbert Tennent put it, reunited in 1758 to form the Synod of New York and Philadelphia out of New Side-Old Side factions. They did so during the conflict known as the French and Indian War fought by Old World powers in the New World, and as tensions mounted to bring on the American Revolution and independence. Presbyterians joined other Protestant dissenters opposing the consecration of an Anglican bishop for this side of the Atlantic. Such an episcopacy represented both political and economic power. Moreover, some Presbyterians participated in outbreaks of violence in Pennsylvania, North Carolina and South Carolina, and in New York as Sons of Liberty—discontent with the treatment colonists received from colonial governments. Moreover, they raised questions about the Quebec Act of 1774 which seemed to give Canadian Catholics privileges not enjoyed by dissenters to the South. Although divided by the call for independence, most Presbyterians supported the revolutionary cause. John Witherspoon, immigrant from Scotland in 1768 and president of the College of New Jersey, signed the Declaration of Independence and participated in the Continental Congress. He was symbolic of Presbyterian involvement. The denomination planted churches and schools on the frontiers as Americans pressed westward. Moreover, Presbyterians, concerned for religious and civil liberty, gave support both for a wider religious liberty for all, and proposed gradual, but eventual elimination of slavery. With some exceptions, they saw these liberties being protected under the new constitutions of the Presbyterian Church in the United States of America and that of the nation, both of which were ratified and went into effect in 1789. In 1789 the General Assembly met in Philadelphia and George Washington was inaugurated President in New York.

James Lyon (1735-1794), a Presbyterian minister, published the first Psalter of tunes composed by an American in *Urania* (1761). While dependent upon eighteenth century English volumes, Lyon included some tunes of his own. Early in the eighteenth century, Irish immigrants were the most numerous. Then Scottish immigration increased during the second half of the century. The picture of Scottish worship in the eighteenth century, with the "Stool of Repentance," indicates the traditions these newcomers brought with them.

1758 Old Side Presbyterians accused New Side Presbyterians of censoriousness, itineracy, and enthusiasm during the Great Awakening, and a split occurred among Presbyterians about 1741. As early as 1749 Gilbert Tennent, whose preaching had fired the controversy, made conciliatory approaches to the Old Side. He was now a pastor in Philadelphia and wrote *Irenicum Ecclesiasticum, or a Humble Impartial Essay upon the Peace of Jerusalem*. In 1758 the two sides organized the Synod of New York and Philadelphia based on the acceptance of the *Westminster Confession of Faith* and by developing procedures to deal with earlier complaints. The Synod also required that ministers be sound in doctrine and have an "experimental acquaintance" with religion. Gilbert Tennent was elected moderator of the new synod.

Philadelphia was a center of Presbyterian as well as national life. John Ewing (1732-1802) studied under Francis Alison and at the College of New Jersey. He taught mathematics and philosophy at the College of Philadelphia and was its provost during the American Revolution. He was active in Philadelphia politics as well as in the second Philadelphia Presbytery. Signaling their growth in numbers, Presbyterians built the Third Presbyterian Church (Old Pine Street) in 1768. Thomas Read (1746-1823), shown here with his grandson, also studied under Francis Alison. After receiving his degree from the College of Philadelphia, he was ordained and served churches in Delaware. He also taught at the Newark Academy.

John Ewing

Old Pine St. Church

Thomas Read

William Livingston

As soon as religious controversy among Presbyterians calmed down, political controversy boiled up. In New York, another center of Presbyterians, the laity were in the middle of the turmoil. King George III, Parliament, and the English heated tensions with new taxes, regulations, and with rumors of an episcopate for the colonies. Presbyterian lawyers, William Livingston—related to a long line of Dutch Reformed settlers, William Smith and John Morin Scott, gained a reputation as the "New York Triumvirate," editing *The Independent Reflector* to fight against an Anglican establishment.

The cartoon of 1769 showing colonists hurling the works of John Calvin and John Locke at an Anglican bishop suggests the continued unrest of British citizens in America, as rumors of the arrival of such an officer of the crown and of Canterbury persisted. That unrest grew even stronger in the next decade.

Paxton Church

1764 Presbyterians and Quakers did not get along well in Pennsylvania as the pamphlet attack on Francis Alison and John Ewing, "A Vindication of Quakers," suggests. John Elder, minister of the Paxton Presbyterian Church near Harrisburg, PA, organized a ranger troop known as the "Paxton Boys" in 1763 to offer protection, he thought, from the Indians. The frontier settlers felt they could not count on the government in Philadelphia. The "Paxton Boys" stirred up Pennsylvania by murdering several Indians in Conestoga Manor and at the Lancaster workhouse, and by threatening Lancaster and Philadelphia. Benjamin Franklin persuaded Elder and his rangers to put down their arms, to submit their grievances to the Assembly, and to resolve their problems without resort to violence.

Alarm in Philadelphia

Rittenhouse Orrery

14

John Witherspoon

13

John Witherspoon (1723-1794) had already made a reputation for himself in Scottish ecclesiastical affairs. He immigrated to New Jersey in 1768 to be president of the College of New Jersey. He brought his clock with him. Almost immediately upon arrival he purchased the orrery of scientist David Rittenhouse for instruction at the college. New Jersey citizens elected him to public office and sent him to the Continental Congress where he was the only active minister to sign the Declaration of Independence. He was also active in ecclesiastical affairs, as pastor of the Princeton Presbyterian Church and in the process of organizing the General Assembly of the denomination.

Nassau Hall

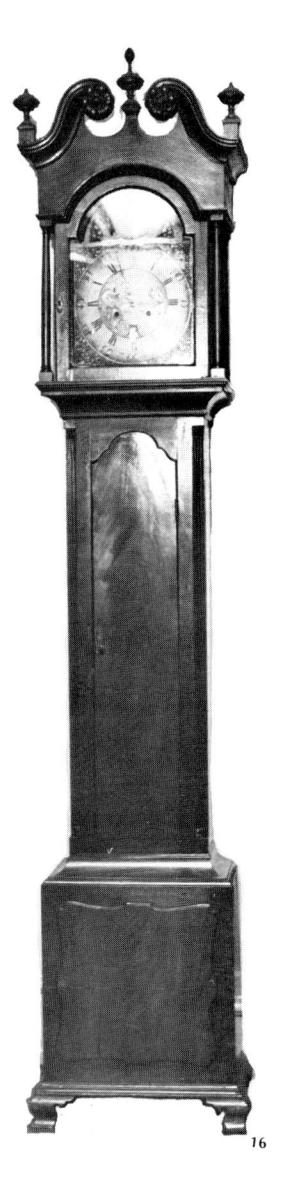

15

16

1774-1775 In the cartoon a Dutch barber, Jacob Vredenburgh, refuses to complete the shave of a British sea captain in 1774 upon hearing that the British closed Boston harbor. Wig boxes carry the names of American patriots, including a number of the "Sons of Liberty," showing the Presbyterian-Dutch-Reformed connection in the Hudson valley.

In 1775, citizens including numerous Presbyterians passed resolves against what were perceived to be oppressive acts of the British Parliament in Hanover, Lancaster County, PA; Fincastle County, VA; and Charlotte, Mecklenburg County, NC. In Augusta County, VA, where Presbyterians worshipped in the Augusta Stone Presbyterian Church, the citizens passed a resolution in favor of freedom of conscience, a gift from heaven, which they intended to defend as a God given right in support of the Continental Congress. The Augusta church stands very much as it did when it was built in 1749.

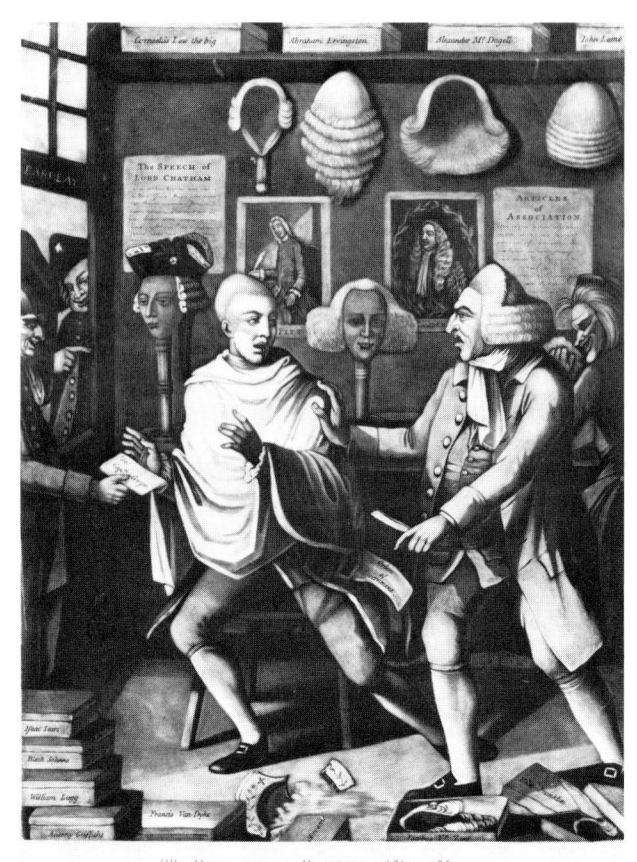

Augusta Stone Church

The Declaration of Independence by John Trumbull

THE LAW OF LIBERTY.
A SERMON
ON
AMERICAN AFFAIRS,
PREACHED
AT THE OPENING OF THE PROVINCIAL
CONGRESS OF GEORGIA.
ADDRESSED
TO THE RIGHT HONOURABLE
THE EARL OF DARTMOUTH.
WITH AN APPENDIX,
GIVING A CONCISE ACCOUNT OF THE STRUGGLES OF
SWISSERLAND TO RECOVER THEIR LIBERTY.
BY JOHN J. ZUBLY, D.D.
IS. XI: 13. EPHRAIM SHALL NOT ENVY JUDAH,
AND JUDAH SHALL NOT VEX EPHRAIM.
PHILADELPHIA:
PRINTED BY HENRY MILLER. MDCCLXXV.

1776 Until the writing and signing of the Declaration of Independence, Americans, including Presbyterians, professed allegiance to the King of England. Talk of independence finally lead to the resolve, and a committee of the Congress began to write a declaration in June 1776. Although Thomas Jefferson penned the first draft, a committee refined it and presented it to members who approved it on July 4, 1776. Benjamin Rush, James Smith, George Taylor, James Wilson, Thomas McKean, William Floyd, Philip Livingston, Richard Stockton, John Witherspoon, John Hart, Abraham Clark, and Matthew Thornton, all sometime Presbyterians, signed the document, although not all of them made it into John Trumbull's famous painting of the presentation of the Declaration to the Congress in 1776.

John Joachim Zubly (1724-1781), pastor of the Independent Presbyterian Church in Savannah, GA, sympathized with American grievances but opposed separation from England and revolution. He cautioned calm in a sermon about the "law of liberty" in 1775, a work which caused his banishment for a time from Georgia, the lost of half of his estate, and much sadness until his death toward the end of the war.

Liberty Hall Ruins

1776 In Virginia, Presbyterians continued their interest in education during the American Revolution. William Graham, Presbyterian minister, became rector of Liberty Hall in 1776, an institution which had begun as a classical school in the middle of the century. Across the Blue Ridge mountains from Liberty Hall, Presbyterians organized Hampden-Sydney College in the same year. Although an ecumenical adventure, two brothers, Samuel Stanhope Smith and John Blair Smith, both Presbyterian ministers, served as president of the institution.

In 1776, Hanover Presbytery wrote its first memorial to the Virginia legislature in support of Thomas Jefferson's Act for Religious Liberty.

Samuel S. Smith

John B. Smith

Hanover Presbytery Memorial

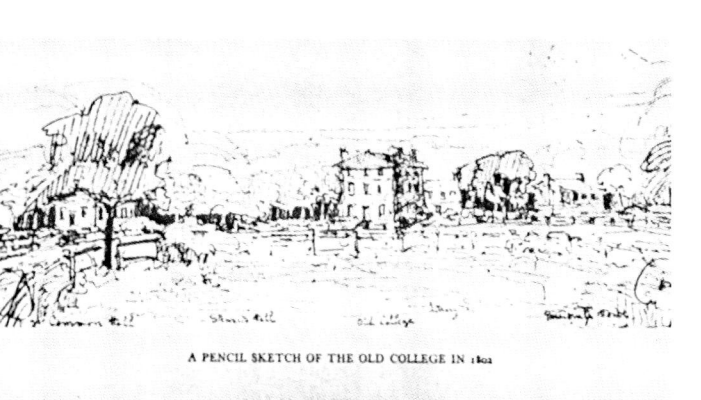

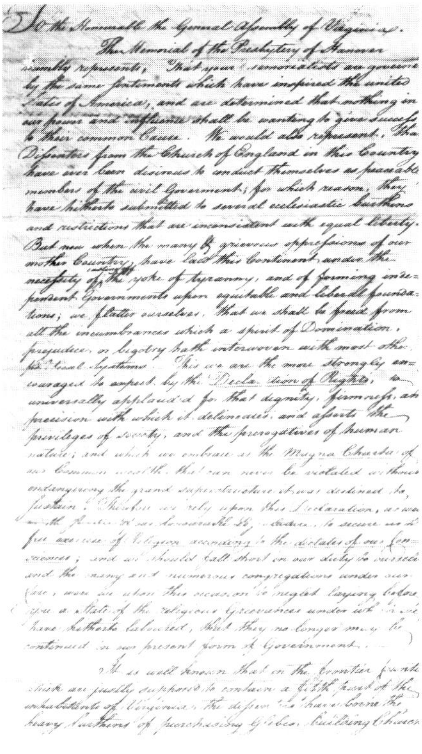

Hampden-Sydney College

Benjamin Rush

Julia Stockton

Many Presbyterians participated in public affairs during this era. Benjamin Rush, a Philadelphia physician and Presbyterian, signed the Declaration of Independence, as did lawyers James Wilson and Thomas McKean, who were destined to play a large part as lawyers and jurists in early Pennsylvania and national life. Rush was married to Julia Stockton, daughter of Richard Stockton, in Princeton, NJ, at which service John Witherspoon presided. Stockton and Witherspoon were also signers of the Declaration. Charles Thomson, a student of Francis Alison and a Presbyterian, served as Secretary of the Continental Congress from 1774 to 1789.

James Wilson

Charles Thomson

Thomas McKean

41

Caldwell at Battle of Springfield

Some Presbyterians fought in the thick of the battle. Chaplain James Caldwell, known as the fighting parson, rushed into church when the soldiers were running short of gun wadding, grabbed some of the Psalm books, and gave them to the troops with the exhortation: "Put Watts into them, boys." General Alexander McDougall, a Presbyterian, gained famed before the revolution as a "son of liberty," by attacking the governor of New York for furnishing supplies to British troops at taxpayers expense. He spent eleven months in jail for his trouble. He was already a hero before he rose in the army ranks to be general in George Washington's army. General Daniel Morgan, a hero of the battle of Saratoga, served in northern Virginia.

General Morgan

Alexander McDougall

Jane McCrae, daughter of the Rev. James McCrae, was killed on the New York frontier by Indians paid by the British. She was on her way to a rendezvous with an English soldier. Despite the ambiguity in this situation, Americans celebrated her as a martyr to the brutality of the British and of the revolutionary cause.

William Smith

Edward Shippen

Some Presbyterians found themselves in awkward positions for not supporting the revolution. William Smith of New York City worked long for reconciliation between Britain and America, until his loyalty to the crown forced him and his family behind the British lines in 1780. Edward Shippen was one of a number of very prominent Presbyterians in First Church, Philadelphia, who were loyalists during the conflict. Flora MacDonald arrived in America from Scotland in 1775. She and her family became a part of the Barbecue congregation in North Carolina. She worked for the crown in the South, while her soldier husband fought. He was captured and imprisoned by the Americans, and she had to return to Scotland in 1779.

The Battle of King's Mountain (below) pitted Loyalist Scot and Scotch-Irish patriots against one another. The Americans won this crucial battle of the war in the South.

Flora MacDonald

Gathering of Overmountain Men at Sycamore Shoals

George Duffield

1782-1783 When peace and independence finally came, George Duffield (1732-1790), preached an eloquent sermon comparing the American colonies to God's Israel of old. He proclaimed America "banner of civil and religious liberty," an "asylum for the poor and oppressed from every part of the earth," in a word, God's American Zion. Duffield, pastor of Philadelphia's Third Presbyterian Church, acted as chaplain to the Continental Congress for a time. The Presbytery to the Eastward was not so sure about America's prospects. In *Bath-Kol, A Voice from the Wilderness*, the presbytery in New England warned about how the Old World had already sown seeds of corruption in the New in the immorality and profiteering, for example, which had been a part of the war.

Congress fled to Princeton in 1783, it should be noted, when soldiers rioted in Philadelphia for their back pay. Despite the reason, John Witherspoon was happy about the presence of the illustrious company, including Washington and foreign diplomats from other countries, at the College of New Jersey.

Continental Congress at Nassau Hall

1782 Two small Presbyterian bodies, known as Covenanters and Seceders, began the process of organizing on a national basis after the war. The Reformed Presbytery of America and the Associate Presbytery of Pennsylvania formed the Associate Reformed Church in 1782. In the same year, Robert Aitken, a printer and elder in the Associate Church in Philadelphia, shown here, brought out one of the first American printings of the Bible commended to the public by Congress and the Presbyterian churches. John Mitchell Mason, minister of New York City, gave leadership to the new denomination.

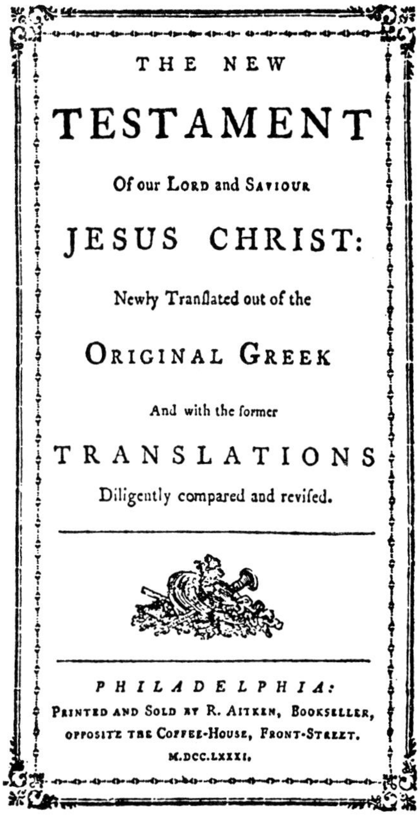

One of the first women's missionary societies met in Chartiers, PA to make clothes for young men studying for the ministry.

John McMillan

McMillan chair & saddle bags

Presbyterians pushed westward as did many other Americans. John McMillan (1752-1833), after study at Princeton, planted churches in Maryland, western Virginia, and western Pennsylvania. This early apostle to the West established the school which became Jefferson College. Samuel Doak planted churches and schools in Tennessee after his ministerial training at the College of New Jersey and ordination to the ministry. McMillan, Doak, and many other Presbyterians rode the circuit to offer preaching, pastoral care, and education to frontier communities.

Samuel Doak

Samuel Kirkland (1741-1808), also a student at Princeton in the 1760s, worked among the Oneida Indians in New York for forty years. In cooperation with Alexander Hamilton he secured lands on which to build an academy for Indians, which served them and also white settlers in the Oneida territory. The academy evolved into Hamilton College.

Samuel Kirkland

First Church, Newark, NJ

Old Stone Church, Lewisburg, WV

Presbyterians built churches in this revolutionary era, some of which are still standing. The congregation of Lewisburg, WV, built the Old Stone Church in 1796, after its organization in 1783, a building that has been in continuous use since its construction. Presbyterians in Newark, NJ, erected the First Church's third building in 1791. The congregation was organized in 1666 and was growing with the times. Scottish pioneers built the Old Presbyterian Meeting House in 1774 when toleration allowed dissenters to have their own houses of worship. George Washington attended services here. The congregation installed one of the first pipe organs in use in a Presbyterian church in the early 1780s. The Independent Presbyterian Church, Savannah, GA, was founded in 1755 before the revolutionary era. Its pastor at the time of the Revolution, John Joachim Zubly, was a loyalist, and the church was used as a stable during the war. The congregation began to readjust and rebuild its life after the conflict in which it had been caught between Loyalist and Patriot sympathies.

Old Presbyterian Meeting House, Alexandria, VA

Independent Presbyterian Church, Savannah, GA

47

David Ramsay

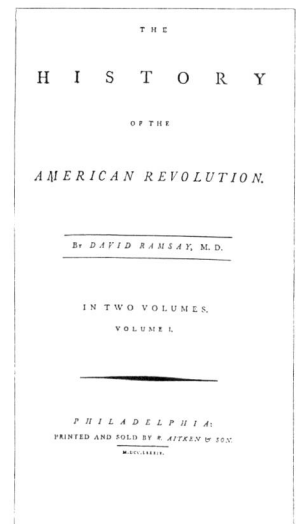

David Ramsay, a physician, wrote one of the earliest interpretations of the era in volumes entitled *History of the American Revolution* (1789). Although he took much of his material from British sources, he interpreted the event in providential terms. God championed the colonial struggle for "life, liberty, and the pursuit of happiness." Ramsay was a member of the Independent Church of Charleston, SC, made up of Congregationalists and many others with Presbyterian leanings. Its pastors were often Presbyterian. Ramsay's third wife, Martha Laurens, was a deeply spiritual woman who was under the influence of the teachings of John Witherspoon and her ministers, William Hollinshead and Isaac Stockton Keith, the latter a Presbyterian.

Martha Ramsay

Other Presbyterians in Charleston, SC, formed a congregation as early as 1685. They held services intermittently during the war, then incorporated in 1784, erecting the present building in the early decades of the nineteenth century as the First (Scots) Presbyterian Church.

First (Scots) Church

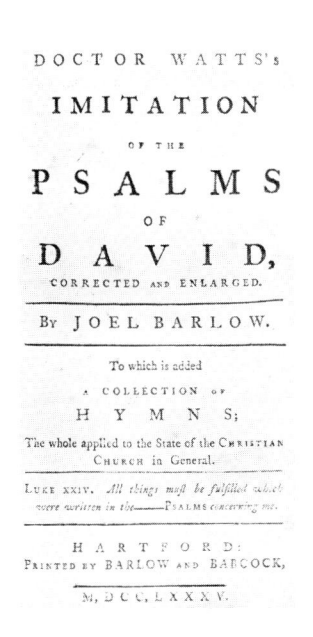

1787-1788

Joining the trend toward national organization, the Synod of New York and Philadelphia began a restructuring process in the early 1780s. Presbyterians drew up a *Constitution* which included the *Westminster Confession,* the *Larger* and *Shorter Catechisms* (with amendments about the civil magistrate which brought these statements into conformity with American reality), a *Form of Government and Discipline,* and a *Directory For Worship.* They also organized four synods and sixteen presbyteries in a rearrangement of boundaries and then called a General Assembly which would exercise oversight and give direction to the denomination. At the time of this organization there were 177 ministers and 420 congregations. In 1787 the Synod approved the use of Joel Barlow's revisions of the Isaac Watts' *Psalms of David* in the churches. The same Synod condemned slavery in evangelical and rational terms, and called for its gradual elimination.

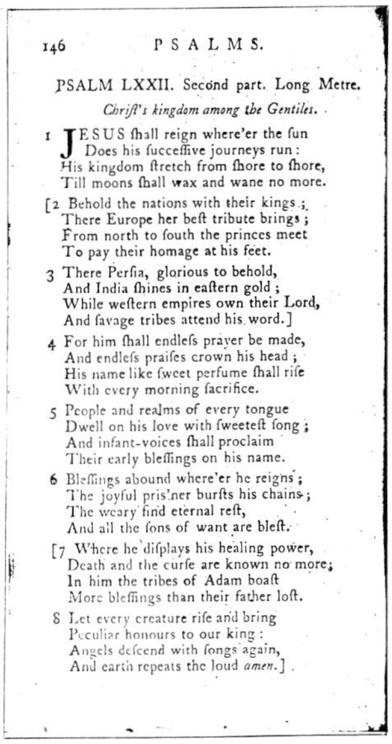

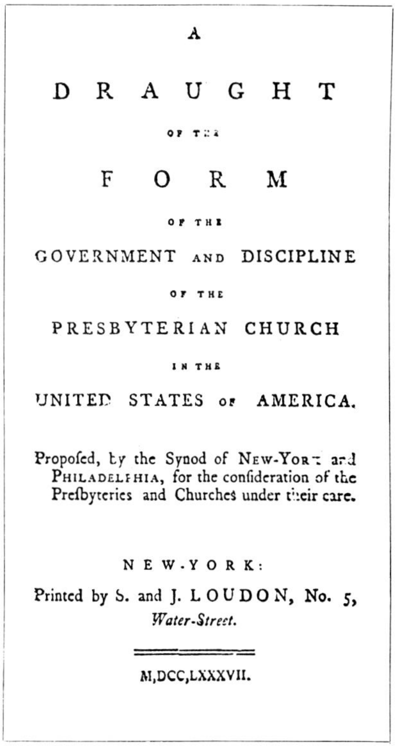

Lamp. First Presbyterian Church, Philadelphia, PA

Pew and collection bag. Old Stone Church, Lewisburg, WV

1789 The first General Assembly of the Presbyterian Church in the United States of America met in the Second Presbyterian Church of Philadelphia (below) in May 1789. On the occasion, John Witherspoon, aging revolutionary, nearly blind, convened the Assembly and preached the opening sermon on the text, I Corinthians 3:7: "So then neither is he that planteth anything, neither he that watereth; but God that giveth the increase." Witherspoon preached from that text twenty years before when he became pastor of the Presbyterian Church in Princeton. John Rodgers (1727-1811), a Bostonian by birth, and a New York pastor, was elected moderator of the first Assembly. A patriot, he preached a thanksgiving sermon in 1784 entitled "The Divine Goodness Displayed in the American Revolution."

John Rodgers

Philadelphia, PA. Second Church spire

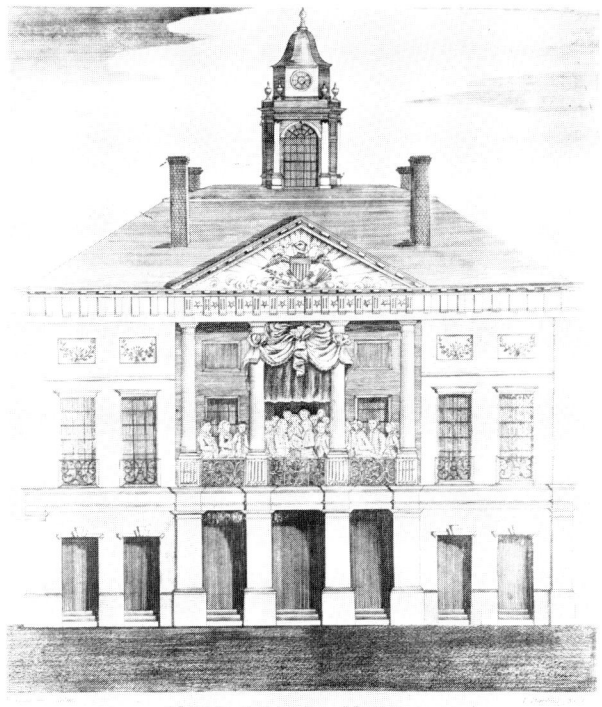

1789 In the same year the first General Assembly met, the nation inaugurated George Washington first President of the U.S.A. in a ceremony which took place in New York City. The occasion symbolized the high hopes and promise of the New Republic. The General Assembly addressed a congratulatory letter to the chief executive expressing support of him as he took up his office. In 1791 during Washington's first term, the country ratified ten amendments to the Constitution including the first which summarized the religious and civil rights of Americans: "Congress shall make no law respecting an establishment of religion, or prohibiting the free exercise thereof; or abridging the freedom of speech, or of the press; or the right of the people peaceably to assemble, and to petition the government for a redress of grievances."

Washington found it necessary to use troops to put down the "Whiskey Rebellion" in western Pennsylvania, when citizens, Presbyterians among them, revolted against tax policies of the government in 1794.

When the capitol moved to Washington, Presbyterian stone masons from Scotland used the carpenter's shop on the grounds of the White House for worship. From this small beginning the First Presbyterian Church of Washington was organized.

> In memory of George Bryan, who died 27th of January aged sixty years. Mr. Bryan was among the earliest and most active and uniform friends of the rights of man before the Revolutionary War. As a member of the Assembly of Pennsylvania, and of the Congress of New York in 1765, and as a citizen, he was conspicuous in opposition to the Stamp Act, and other acts of British tyranny. He was equally an opponent of domestic slavery. The emancipation of the people of color engaged the feelings of his heart and energies of his mind, and the Act of Abolition (which) laid the foundation of their liberation issued from his pen. He filled several important offices during the Revolutionary Contest and for the last eleven years of his life he was one of the judges of the Supreme Court. In his private deportment he was exemplary, — a Christian in principle and practice.

George Bryan (1761-1791) was a prominent merchant and Philadelphia Presbyterian. He also gave of his time in public service in support of the colonial cause, and in opposition to domestic slavery which he helped to end in Pennsylvania. John Ewing preached his funeral service and survivors inscribed his tombstone in the churchyard of the Second Presbyterian church with a brief statement of his life in a revolutionary age.

Elias Boudinot (1740-1821), of Huguenot ancestry and a resident of New Jersey, served under the Articles of Confederation as "President of the United States in Congress Assembled" in 1783 after the war. A lawyer and business man, he was deeply interested in the prophecies of the Bible about the coming of Christ's kingdom. He was also a member of the Corporation for Relief of Poor and Distressed Ministers, and the first president of the Board of Trustees established by the General Assembly of 1799 to administer the properties of the whole church. This board now serves as the trustees of the Presbyterian Church (U.S.A.).

Elias Boudinot

Act of Incorporation

An Act for incorporating the Trustees of the Ministers and Elders, constituting the General Assembly of the Presbyterian church, in the United States of America.

52

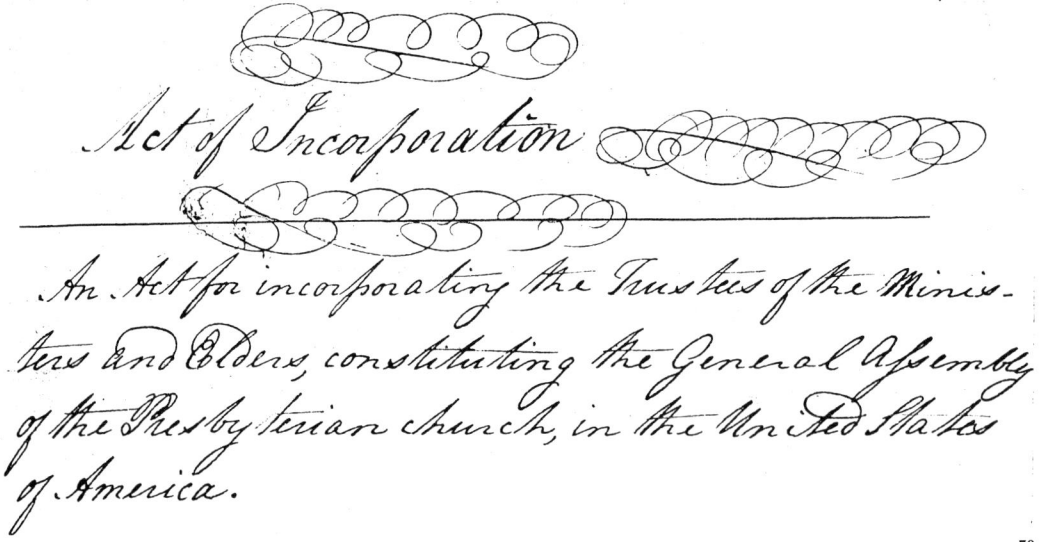

IV FREEDOM'S FERMENT AND THE EVANGELICAL FRONT

1800-1838 In the first third of the nineteenth century, Presbyterians shared with other Protestants the enthusiasm and the challenge of building a new nation. The newly formed Presbyterian denomination cooperated with other Christians, especially with those who shared a similar Reformed and evangelical outlook. The ecumenical ties with the Congregationalists were particularly strong after the Plan of Union of 1801. The two denominations agreed to plant churches together in the westward movement of America. While supporters of revivals, Presbyterians who appreciated decency and order were suspicious of the theological assumptions of revivalists. Therefore, they tried to discipline enthusiasm. Moreover, they threw their weight behind various ecumenical, mission, educational, and reforming enterprises which blossomed during this period, at the same time establishing Presbyterian agencies in these areas. Through various movements, Presbyterians tried to exercise some influence in the voluntary sector over the direction in which the nation moved. They could not avoid the overriding moral issue, slavery, because of the black presence in the church itself, and because of the conflict of conscience among whites in the denomination. Some were slaveholders, others abolitionists. American Presbyterians suffered divisions; the first, the organization of the Cumberland Presbyterian Church, the second, the split between Old School-New School which came at the end of the 1830s.

A winged cherubim keeps watch over the grave of Jeptha Bryan who died in 1801, and who lies buried in the Sparta, NJ, Presbyterian Church graveyard. The stone warns the visitor of the frailty of life:

> Behold and see, as you pass by,
> As you are now, so once was I,
> As I am now, so you must be
> Prepare for death, and follow me.

Presbyterians pointed beyond themselves and to their hope in God as they participated in the life of the new nation. The open book tombstone in the same cemetery suggests that the deceased was remembered as being faithful to the Word unto death.

1800 Presbyterian life was marked by revivals of religion in the early days of the Republic. James McGready, a Presbyterian, joined Baptist, Methodist and other ministers in what has been called a Second Great Awakening. The awakenings were tumultuous social and personal events for whole communities and persons. People responded to powerful exhortations, some swooning with religious excitement. The revival at Cane Ridge drew thousands of people. The painting of 1839 by English caricaturist, J. Maze Burbank depicts explicitly the ecstatic throng at one of the revival meetings characteristic of these years.

Barton W. Stone

Barton Warren Stone (1772-1844), converted by James McGready, preached at Cane Ridge. Opposition to his eccentric religious practice, caused him and others to leave the PCUSA and establish their own denomination. Stone and his followers took the name Christian, claiming no creed but the Bible. Stone later joined another ex-Presbyterian, Alexander Campbell, to form the Disciples of Christ which had as one of its purposes the end of divisions among Christians. Stonites and Campbellites multiplied steadily. Presbyterians continued to worry about decency and order among unruly pioneers pushing westward.

Cane Ridge, KY
Meeting House

55

Samuel Hopkins

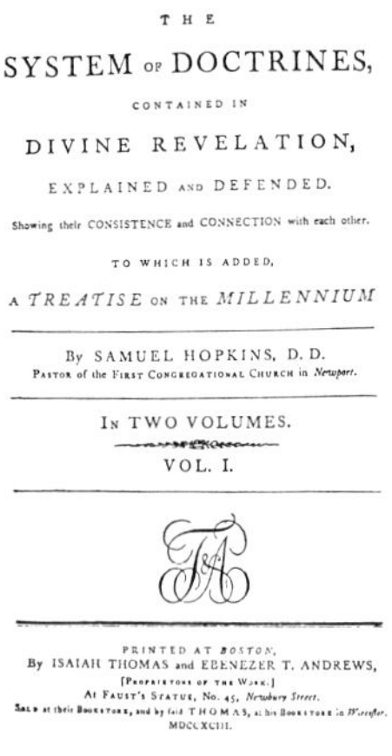

THE
SYSTEM OF DOCTRINES,
CONTAINED IN
DIVINE REVELATION,
EXPLAINED AND DEFENDED.

Showing their CONSISTENCE and CONNECTION with each other.

TO WHICH IS ADDED,
A TREATISE ON THE MILLENNIUM

By SAMUEL HOPKINS, D.D.
Pastor of the First Congregational Church in Newport.

IN TWO VOLUMES.
VOL. I.

PRINTED AT BOSTON,
By ISAIAH THOMAS and EBENEZER T. ANDREWS,
[Proprietors of the Work.]
At Faust's Statue, No. 45, Newbury Street.
Sold at their Bookstore, and by said THOMAS, at his Bookstore in Worcester.
MDCCXCIII.

1801 Motivated by kinship and eagerness to plant churches, Presbyterians and New England Congregationalists cooperated in the Plan of Union of 1801. The Plan allowed people of both denominations to form congregations, and to follow the polity arrangements at the local level of the majority of the people. Numerous churches were formed in New York, Ohio, Indiana, Illinois, Michigan, and Wisconsin under this plan, one which the Congregationalists argued, increased Presbyterians the most. New England Calvinists, Samuel Hopkins (1721-1803) and Timothy Dwight (1752-1817), president of Yale, had a considerable impact upon some Presbyterians, theologically. Dwight, a president-preacher-poet, wrote the hymn, "I Love Thy Kingdom, Lord." New York City was a center of Presbyterian activity and of cooperation with the New Englanders.

Timothy Dwight

First Presbyterian Church, New York, NY

1802 The General Assembly established a Standing Committee on Missions in 1802, the first such agency of the denomination, and among Protestants in general, to encourage national missions. Ashbel Green (1762-1848), who as a student at Princeton addressed Congress assembled there in 1783, served as chairman of this committee, and later of the Board of Missions. Green's ministry spanned fifty-five years.

Ashbel Green

Gideon Blackburn

Salmon Giddings

Presbyterian ministers moved west with the growing American populations to plant churches. Gideon Blackburn, a missionary among the Cherokees in eastern Tennessee, founded Presbyterian churches in Nashville and northern Alabama. Salmon Giddings, a Connecticut Yankee, became a Presbyterian, and organized churches in St. Louis, and in other places in Missouri and Illinois. Giddings planted the first Presbyterian church west of the Mississippi River. James Kemper settled north of the Ohio River as the first Presbyterian in that territory, and became an important influence in the Buckeye state. Isaac Reed travelled to Indiana and founded congregations throughout that area. His journal, *The Christian Traveler*, tells the tales of a Presbyterian circuit rider in the Hoozier Zion.

James Kemper

Isaac Reed

William McWhir

Government St. Church, Mobile, AL

In St. Augustine William McWhir organized the first Presbyterian Church in Florida in 1824. As the only Protestant minister in the whole territory for many years, he spent his energies until his death at age ninety-three, in evangelism and educational work. John B. Warren organized the Mobile, AL, Government Street Presbyterian Church in the 1800s. The congregation completed the Greek Revival building in 1837.

1810 Gradually Presbyterians began to make a greater distinction between national and foreign missions. In 1810, they cooperated with Congregationalists and others in forming the American Board of Commissioners for Foreign Missions, the first of such national boards to be established in the United States. Pressed for support by Williams College students who committed their lives to the mission field, the Board participated in the ordination and dedication of its first missionaries in 1812. Presbyterians, such as Ashbel Green, Samuel Miller, and Elias Boudinot, a layman, sat on the Board. The General Assembly recommended support of the agency among the constitutency.

1810 During the religious excitement of the Second Great Awakening, Presbyterians divided once again. Finis Ewing (1773-1841), joined by Samuel King and Samuel McAdow, organized the Cumberland Presbytery on February 4, 1810, independent of the PCUSA. The division occurred because of conflict over the requirements for the education and licensure of candidates for the ministry, disagreement over Calvinist doctrine of predestination, and a falling-out over revivalistic methods. The new denomination was organized in the log home of McAdow, Dickson, TN. Ewing was elected moderator in 1812 and 1818 as the church grew and spread rapidly in Kentucky and Tennessee.

Finis Ewing [18]

Samuel McAdow's home, Dickson, TN [19]

Sumner Bacon [20]

Sumner Bacon (1790-1844), a native of MA, worked in the South as a distributor of Bibles and tracts. Ordained in Louisiana because of his effectiveness as an exhorter and for his prayer meetings, he headed west to Texas. As a Cumberland Presbyterian minister he organized the first church in that area. "The Apostle of Texas," in a picture allegedly of him with Bible in one hand and gun in another, played a leading role in organizing the Presbytery of Texas in 1837.

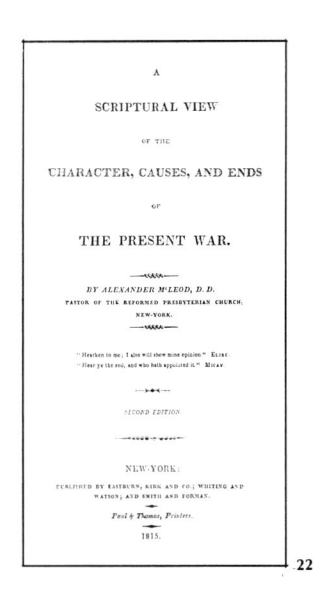

David Low Dodge

1812 The War of 1812 with Great Britain badly divided the new nation. Presbyterians, in the just war tradition, also debated the issue. As early as 1808 David Low Dodge, a well-to-do New York merchant, expressed his opposition to war. In a tract, *Observations on the Kingdom of Peace,* he promoted the concerns of those who formed the New York Peace Society in 1815 and the American Peace Society in 1828. Another Presbyterian minister, Alexander McLeod, argued in favor of the conflict in a tract entitled, *A Scriptural View of the Character, Causes, and Ends of the Present War* (1815), building on the statement in the *Westminster Confession of Faith* that Christians may make war on "just and necessary occasions."

The British focused attention on Baltimore. The congregation of the First Presbyterian Church lived through the turmoil which led to the burning of the White House just a few miles away in the capitol.

First Presbyterian Church, Baltimore

FIRST INFANT SCHOOL IN GREEN STREET NEW YORK.

VIEW FROM THE ROSTRUM
Moniter Nine & Six? Scholars Fifteen! &c.

VIEW FROM THE GALLERY. 
The Children Marching & Reciting aloud, "Twice two's Four &c."

Presbyterians gave increasing attention to education during these years, to provide schooling for the youngest children in the society. In New York City, for example, the Orange St. Presbyterian Church opened its basement for educational purposes. In 1816 Isabella Graham and her daughter, Joanna Bethune, founded a Female Society for the Promotion of Sabbath Schools in the city. In Philadelphia, Alexander Henry, a Presbyterian layman, started a Sunday and Adult School Union which became the American Sunday School Union in 1817.

Isabella Graham

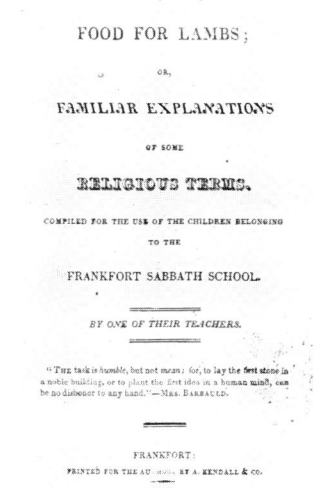

FOOD FOR LAMBS;
OR,
FAMILIAR EXPLANATIONS
OF SOME
RELIGIOUS TERMS.

COMPILED FOR THE USE OF THE CHILDREN BELONGING TO THE
FRANKFORT SABBATH SCHOOL.

BY ONE OF THEIR TEACHERS.

"The task is humble, but not mean; for, to lay the first stone in a noble building, or to plant the first idea in a human mind, can be no dishonor to any hand."—Mrs. BARBAULD.

FRANKFORT:
PRINTED FOR THE AUTHOR BY A. KENDALL & CO.
1824.

Service Seminary

Archibald Alexander

In the early part of the nineteenth century Presbyterians stood for a well-educated ministry. They gave considerable attention to establishing theological seminaries to provide for such leadership. The Associate Reformed Presbyterian Church organized the first seminary in 1794 in Service, PA, on the western frontier. Later, the General Assembly of the PCUSA founded the Theological Seminary at Princeton, NJ, under the professorship of Archibald Alexander (1772-1851), a native of Virginia, a prominent Philadelphia pastor, and one who exercised decisive influence over the shape of the ministry among Presbyterians throughout the century. Samuel Miller and Charles Hodge soon joined Alexander to offer instruction at the new institution, adding to its prestige.

Princeton Theological Seminary

John Holt Rice (1777-1831), a close friend of Alexander, helped the Synod of Virginia establish Union Theological Seminary at Hampden-Sydney in 1812, an institution which took its name in 1828 when the Synod of North Carolina joined the enterprise. Rice, a prominent pastor in Richmond, VA, before his appointment as professor of theology at the seminary, believed that the whole Presbyterian Church was a missionary society with responsibility to aid in the conversion of the world. Theological education was a means to help the members of the church fulfill that aim. Columbia Theological Seminary was organized at Columbia, SC, illustrating the interest of an educated ministry in the region.

John Holt Rice

Columbia Theological Seminary

Calvin Stowe   Lyman Beecher   Dinarca Allen

As the Old School-New School controversy continued, the New School group founded seminaries in this era. Lane Theological Seminary was founded in 1829. Lyman Beecher, of Boston, was called to the leadership of Lane in Cincinnati in 1832, and was embroiled in various controversies having to do with theology, polity, and slavery. In 1836, Presbyterians with decided New School sympathies founded Union Theological Seminary in New York. They began to train ministers with more liberal sympathies than those at several of the other schools, thus aggravating the tensions mounting among the factions in the denomination. The picture is from a catalogue of 1854.

Union Theological Seminary
New York

Davidson College

Centre College

Wherever Presbyterian ministers went they established schools, education being the handmaiden to religion. In cooperation with others, especially Congregationalists, they believed that such schools were essential for the Christianizing and civilizing of the West into which Americans were swarming. By one count, Presbyterians had organized forty-nine colleges and universities in twenty-one of the thirty-four states, thus taking a key place in higher education in the period.

George Junkin
Founder of Lafayette College

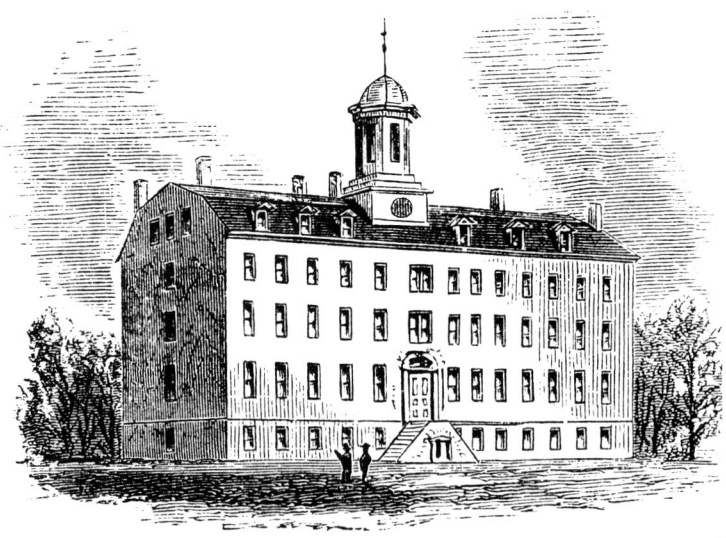

LaFayette College

Isaac Anderson

Caleb Mills

Presbyterians founded Lafayette College, Easton, PA (1826), which grew under its president, minister George Junkin. They also established Davidson College, Davidson, NC (1838), Maryville College, Maryville, TN (1819), Centre College, Danville, KY (1819), and Muskingum College, OH (1837). Isaac Anderson started teaching in Maryville, Edward Beecher served as President of Illinois College (1829), and Caleb Mills founded Wabash College (1833) in Indiana. Presbyterians continued interest in higher education throughout the century by building more colleges where they felt they were needed.

Edward Beecher

Muskingum College

Union College Revival

The religious life in the residential colleges founded by Presbyterians, sometimes in association with Congregationalists and others, was marked by revivals. At Union College, Schenectady, NY, often presided over by Presbyterian presidents, a revival broke out among the students on the occasion of a death of one of their number.

Some members of the denomination maintained that they should help in the development of higher education in the public sector. So Presbyterians pioneered in the establishment of state universities. Ministers, Philip Lindsley, Robert H. Bishop, and John Monteith, helped to found the University of Tennessee, Miami University, OH, and the University of Michigan, respectively. Sometimes Presbyterians could not agree among themselves about the best educational strategy, and they were often in conflict with members of other denominations who believed they were taking over the public system.

Philip Lindsley

Robert H. Bishop

John Monteith

Because of the need for literate Christians and citizens, Presbyterians joined other Christians in forming societies to provide the population with appropriate literature. Thus, they hoped to contribute to a "righteous empire." The American Bible Society began in 1816 after the pattern of local organizations, and the American Tract Society in 1825. The societies printed and distributed through colporteurs, Bibles and pious pamphlets and books across the nation to the godly, to keep them so, and the ungodly, to help them change their ways. Presbyterians supported these educational societies and a number of others to promote Sabbath observance and many other reforms.

46 American Bible Society logo

47

48

49

Americans drank too much alcohol, according to Lyman Beecher. While still in New England, he preached "Six Sermons on Intemperance" which lead to the organization of a Society for the Reformation of Morals. As a result the American Temperance Society started its work in 1833. Presbyterians believed in temperance, but many of them could not sign the pledge to stop drinking altogether. Total abstinence, as one minister put it, was not biblical, nor necessary for his piety, sobriety, nor for the eventual reformation of society.

John
Gloucester

John Gloucester (1776-1822) was Gideon Blackburn's slave, and served under Blackburn as a missionary to Cherokees in Tennessee. He was befriended by Archibald Alexander in Philadelphia, and was licensed to preach by the presbytery there. He organized the first Presbyterian church for blacks in the city which grew to a congregation of three hundred members. His son, Jeremiah, succeeded him in the pulpit in Philadelphia, while his son James organized the Siloam Presbyterian Church, Brooklyn, NY. Son Stephen was a lay evangelist and educator in Philadelphia.

First African Church, Philadelphia

Samuel Cornish

Samuel Cornish (1793-1855) helped to found the first Negro newspaper, *Freedom's Journal* (1827), the motto of which was "Righteousness exalteth a nation." Cornish, a free-born black from Delaware, enrolled in John Gloucester's school in Philadelphia. After ordination, he became the pastor of the First Colored Presbyterian Church in New York City. He along with another Negro minister, Theodore Wright, a graduate of Princeton Theological Seminary, attacked the idea of sending blacks back to Africa as colonizers to convert the continent. These Presbyterian pastors supported the antislavery societies which were organized in various communities around the nation.

Robert Finley

1817 Slavery! It was America's great moral problem. It represented a dilemma many began to sense between what America professed as a nation and what it practiced in its institutions. Robert Finley, a Presbyterian minister, faced the issue by proposing to send blacks to Africa to evangelize and civilize while transporting Africans back to the place of their origin. In 1817 he helped to organize the American Colonization Society. With government support the society purchased land which became the republic of Liberia, settled by transplanted freedmen. The General Assembly of the PCUSA supported this effort.

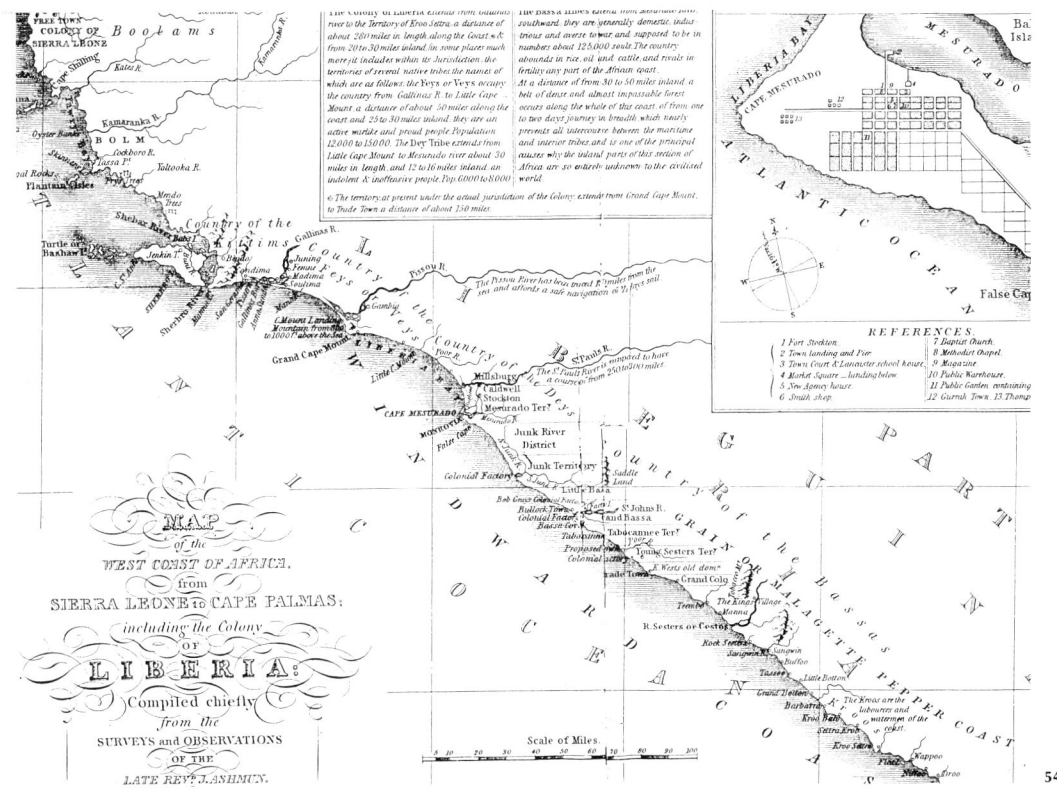

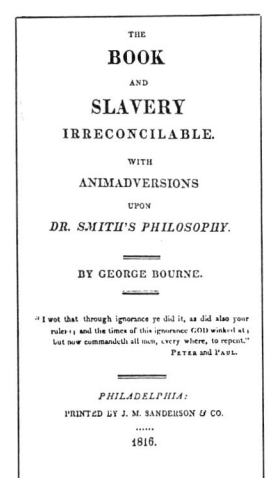

1818 Not all Presbyterians agreed with Finley and the colonization efforts. George Bourne, of the Presbytery of Lexington, VA, published a book entitled, *The Book and Slavery Irreconcileable* (1815) in which he condemned the institution on biblical grounds. The presbytery finally deposed him. In 1818, the General Assembly issued its strongest antislavery statement condemning the institution on grounds similar to those used by Bourne, but calling for gradual emancipation, for kind treatment of those in bondage, and support of colonization. The Assembly asked Presbyterians not to use the "plea of necessity" as an excuse for not facing the issue and eventually doing away with the institution.

Samuel Miller

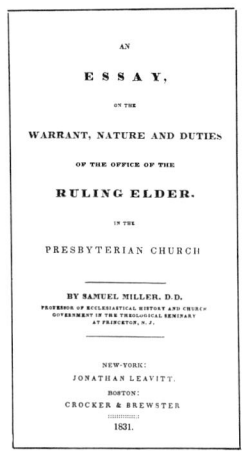

Although the laity always have been considered as essential and integral to Presbyterian faith and polity, Samuel Miller (1769-1850), New York pastor, Princeton professor, and author, wrote a volume which gave the elder a more prominent place in the life of the denomination. Reflecting anxiety of the period about the democratic ferment, Miller argued in the *Essay on the Warrant, Nature, and Duties of the Office of the Ruling Elder in the Presbyterian Church* (1831) that by strengthening the eldership Presbyterians would avoid a rude mobocracy threatening to undermine the church, and a clerical caste which would lord it over the laity. He tried to strike a balance of power which he described as "Presbyterian Republicanism."

Two laymen, Arthur (1786-1865) and Lewis (1788-1873) Tappan, wealthy New York merchants, supported a great number of social reform movements, illustrating the importance of the laity in the age of Jackson.

Philadelphia Presbyterian Matthias W. Baldwin pioneered in locomotive building which revolutionized travel, and helped Americans push westward.

Arthur Tappan

Lewis Tappan

Matthias Baldwin

Old Ironsides

Andrew Jackson

Rachel Jackson

1828 The American people elected lawyer, planter, major-general, hero of the Battle of New Orleans, Andrew Jackson, President of the United States in 1828 and again in 1832. Born in South Carolina with Scotch-Irish ancestry, he was the first person elected to the office from west of the Appalachians. In his later years he was a member of the First Presbyterian Church, Nashville, TN, with his beloved wife, Rachel.

Ezra Stiles Ely, pastor of the Old Pine Street Church, Philadelphia, preached a sermon on Independence Day, 1827, entitled "The Duty of Christian Freemen to Elect Christian Rulers." He urged all true Christians to join a "Christian Party." Ely supported Jackson for the presidency against John Quincy Adams', and his sermon created a furor in the city. While Ely's attempt to form a political party did not get off the ground, the General Assembly of the denomination elected him moderator in 1828.

Ezra Stiles Ely

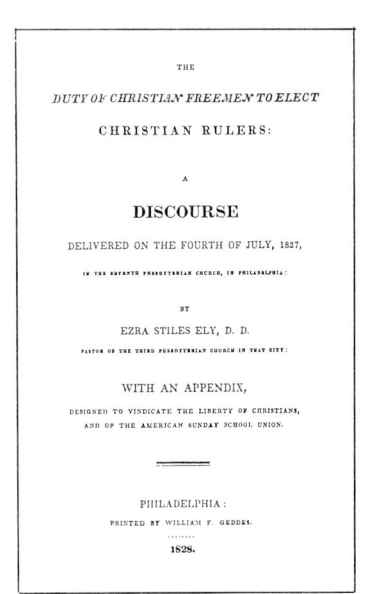

71

"Old Hickory," as Jackson was called, made a good many enemies during his terms in office. Because he pushed democratic policies, one cartoonist drew a caricature of him as "King Andrew the First." The controversy over Peggy Eaton, the wife of Secretary of War John H. Eaton, a woman whose reputation made her *persona non grata* among the wives of other cabinet members, also caused a national stir and the resignation of some of Jackson's cabinet. Jackson died in 1845 surrounded by his children and friends.

THE CELESTIAL CABINET.

DEATH OF GENL ANDREW JACKSON.

William Wirt

Vermonter, Samuel Austin Worcester travelled south to Georgia in 1825 to work among the Cherokee Indians as a missionary of the American Board of Commissioners for Foreign Missions. He fought against white encroachment on Indian lands and went to jail in a case of civil disobedience. In 1833 William Wirt, a Presbyterian lawyer and one-time attorney general of the United States, took the side of the Cherokees and won the case in the Supreme Court against the state of Georgia. Andrew Jackson would not enforce the decision and the Cherokees were forced on their Trail of Tears, finally settling in Oklahoma. Worcester, a missionary for thirty-four years, accompanied them on their trek.

The Dwight Indian Mission at Sallisaw Creek, AK, began its mission in 1832 and continued until 1948.

Samuel & Erminia Worcester

Dwight Mission

Elizabeth Beach Swift

Elijah Pope Swift

Elijah Pope Swift (1792-1865) and his wife, Betsy wanted to be missionaries, and placed themselves under the ABCFM. Thwarted in this effort, Swift moved to Pittsburgh where he became pastor of the Second Presbyterian Church. There he was elected the first secretary of the Western Missionary Society in 1831, a Society which evolved into the Board of Foreign Missions of the PCUSA.

Elder and merchant, David W. C. Olyphant, involved in the China trade, provided Robert Morrison of Scotland passage to the orient on one of his ships in 1807, thus facilitating the start of Protestant missions in China. Olyphant supported mission work in the Far East. Peter Parker, an ophthalmologist, went to Canton in 1834 under the American Board, and established a hospital there.

Peter Parker

Joseph Eastburn founded the Mariner's Church in Philadelphia about 1820 to minister to sailors in a busy port. "We procured a sail loft," he reported, "and on the Sabbath hung out a flag. As the sailors came by, they hailed us, 'Ship ahoy.' We answered them. They asked us, 'Where we were bound?' We told them 'to the port of the New Jerusalem—and they would do well to go in the fleet.' 'Well,' they said, 'we will come in and hear your terms.'"

Robert Ralston, a Philadelphia merchant who made a fortune in the East India trade, supported Eastburn in his efforts. Ralston, an elder in Second Church, Philadelphia, also gave to missions, education, and the Philadelphia Bible Society of which he was the founder.

Robert Ralston

Joseph Eastburn

Mariners' Church

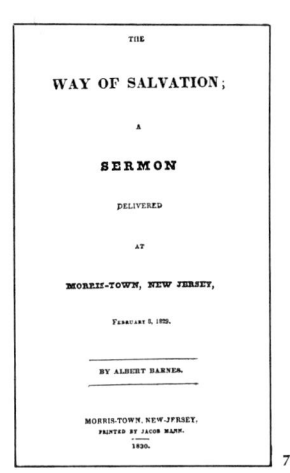

Albert Barnes

In 1836 the New School leader Albert Barnes (1798-1870) won acquittal at a second heresy trial at which he was accused by Old School Presbyterians of unsound doctrine and lax polity. Barnes, a graduate of Princeton Theological Seminary, preached a sermon "The Way of Salvation" (1829), in which he challenged some of the tenets of his opponents. He was able to disseminate his ideas as pastor of the First Presbyterian Church, Philadelphia, where he served from 1830-1867. A bold preacher and biblical commentator, he championed education, temperance, antislavery causes, and was one of the best known ministers in America.

First Presbyterian Church, Philadelphia

Charles Hodge (1797-1878) started his career as teacher at Princeton Seminary in 1820 where he lectured and wrote until his death in 1878. While moderate in spirit, he emerged as a champion of Old School Presbyterians against the New School theology of his popular contemporary, Barnes.

Charles Hodge

1835 Charles Grandison Finney once said that there was a jubilee in hell when the Old School General Assembly met. A lawyer, converted in 1821, ordained by the Presbyterian Church in 1824, Finney became the most famous revivalist in the United States. While a pastor at Second Presbyterian Church, New York City, he delivered his *Lectures on Revivals* (1835) which became the guide book for evangelicals who championed the "new measures," such as the anxious bench, anxious meetings, and protracted periods of revival preaching. Finney also taught at Oberlin College, OH. He aggravated Old School-New School friction.

Charles Finney

Broadway Tabernacle

William Sprague also gave *Lectures on Revivals* (1832), representing Old School concerns for spiritual awakening, but cautioning about careless theology and methods. The Tappan brothers helped to finance Broadway Tabernacle where Finney conducted his urban revivals.

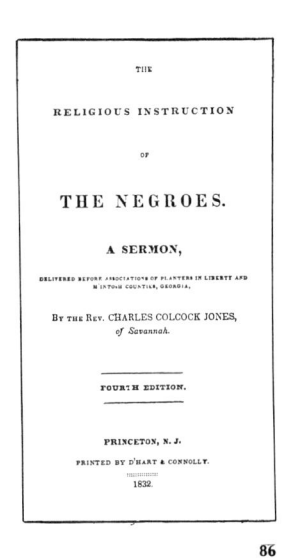

Charles Colcock Jones

Midway Church

Some Presbyterians began to argue that slavery was a positive good. Charles Colcock Jones (1804-1861), Presbyterian pastor in Midway, GA, and a large slave holder, showed some desire to do away with the institution. He later became an apostle to the slaves in his community, attempting to convert, catechize, and care for them, not only to make them Christians, but also to make them content with the role God gave to them. His book was entitled *A Catechism . . . For the Oral Instruction of Colored Persons* (1834). Old Quarterman was a black slave who assisted Jones in his ministry.

Old Quarterman

Churches of New York City joined in a call to Thomas Hastings to help in improving congregational singing beginning in the 1830s. He did so as choirmaster of the Bleeker Street Presbyterian Church, from which position he became a noted American composer, compiler, and hymnwriter. With Lowell Mason he issued *Spiritual Songs for Social Worship* in 1832. Hastings composed over a thousand hymn tunes, the most famous being "Toplady" to which "Rock of Ages" is sung.

Thomas Hastings

Robert J. Breckinridge 90

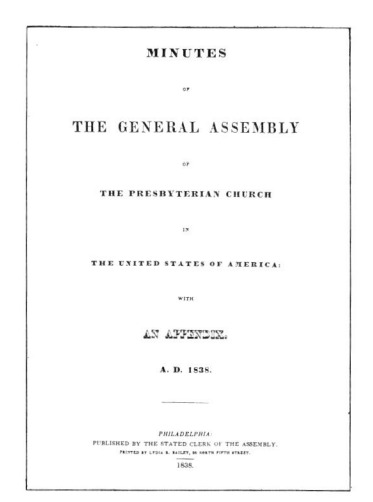

William S. Plumer 92

91

1837 The Presbyterian Church split into Old School and New School branches in 1837-1838. Differences over theology, polity, and slavery aggravated tensions and caused the division. The Old School charged that the New School was less Reformed, congregationalist, and abolitionist in sympathies. Having the majority in the General Assembly of 1837, the Old School abrogated the Plan of Union of 1801, and exscinded the synods of western New York and Ohio. Robert J. Breckinridge, of Baltimore's Second Presbyterian Church, and William Plumer of Richmond's First Presbyterian Church, led the Old School faction, Plumer being elected moderator. Nathan S. S. Beman of the First Presbyterian Church, Troy, NY, organized the New School. The Rev. Samuel Fisher, of the Presbytery of Newark, was elected New School moderator.

Nathan S. S. Beman 93

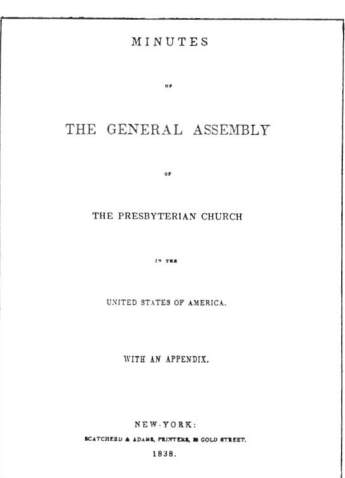

Samuel W. Fisher 95

94

While Old and New School constituents fought, layman William Caldwell of Maryville, TN, attempted to help New School members in the South sing praises in greater harmony.

96

Des Peres Presbyterian Church

1837 Originally from Maine, Elijah Parish Lovejoy (1802-1837) moved west to St. Louis where he worked as a journalist. After conversion he began to preach at the Des Peres Presbyterian Church. As a journalist and antislavery leader, he turned the *St. Louis Observer* into a noted abolitionist paper. Attacked by the pro-slavery faction, he moved his press to Alton, IL. Rioters destroyed three of his presses, and finally shot him to death after he had established himself for a fourth time. Lovejoy's martyrdom alerted antislavery proponents that their own freedoms were at stake in the civil conflict. Edward Beecher, president of Illinois College, gave Lovejoy strong support.

The Alton Riot

V
DIVISIONS, EXPANSION, AND THE IRREPRESSIBLE CONFLICT

A favorite gesture of the preacher of the Port Gibson, MS, Presbyterian Church was a finger pointing toward heaven. In 1829 it was carved in wood, gold-leaved, and put on top of the steeple.

1838-1861

The Old School-New School division among Presbyterians occurred during a time of vitality among American Christians. Robert Baird wrote about American evangelicalism, a term he used to describe a broad range of Protestant denominations, whose lives were marked by revivalism and voluntarism. Presbyterians reached out often in competition with other Protestants, to plant churches in the Northwest, in California, in Texas, as the United States incorporated more and more territory. It was our "manifest," or as Lyman Beecher put it, our "providential destiny." German Presbyterians organized in the Great Plains area, and Presbyterians of the Scottish covenanter tradition organized the United Presbyterian Church of North America in Pittsburgh. According to some, Catholic immigrants did not fit well into American religious, political, or economic life. Presbyterians who expressed hostility to them may have stimulated some of the "nativist" riots which marked this era. Presbyterians could not avoid the influences flowing from what has been called the Romantic movement in theology, in worship, or in architecture, nor the growth of lay influences within the churches as represented in the Fulton Street Revival in the latter part of the 1850s. Neither could they repress the slavery controversy. Presbyterians were reminded of this moral problem by their own black abolitionist members. Cyrus McCormick once said that Old School Presbyterianism was that bond which held the nation together. Finally that bond snapped in 1861 as war clouds gathered and Presbyterians attempted to sort out their loyalties. American Presbyterians split another time in 1861 into one branch loyal to the Union blue, and another, to the Confederate gray.

Presbyterians raised funds for benevolent causes in various ways. Mrs. Susan Bott (left), of the Tabb Street Presbyterian Church, Petersburg, VA, sold homemade wax flowers (right) and pincushions to raise almost seven thousand dollars for Presbyterian educational enterprises.

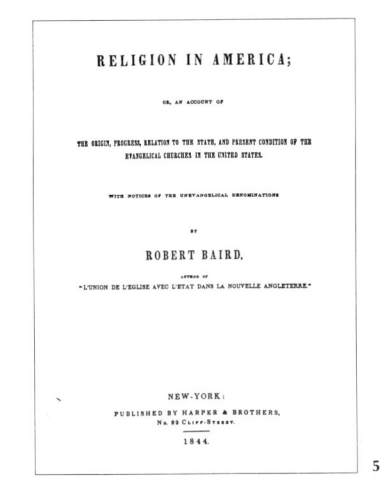

1843 In 1843 Old School Presbyterian Robert Baird (1798-1863) published *Religion in America,* one of the first and most important histories of the subject. He was serving in Europe as a missionary to Catholics and an interpreter of American life. Baird focused his attention on American evangelicals, members of Protestant denominations, characterized by concern for revivalism and voluntary associations. He had very little to say about Unitarians or Roman Catholics in America, although the latter denomination had become the largest single body in the United States by 1850.

Presbyterians had established churches in every state except North Dakota, Utah, and Arizona between 1837 and 1870, as indicated by this map of the nation which by the end of this period embraced the continent.

EXPANSION OF THE PRESBYTERIAN CHURCH
1837-1870

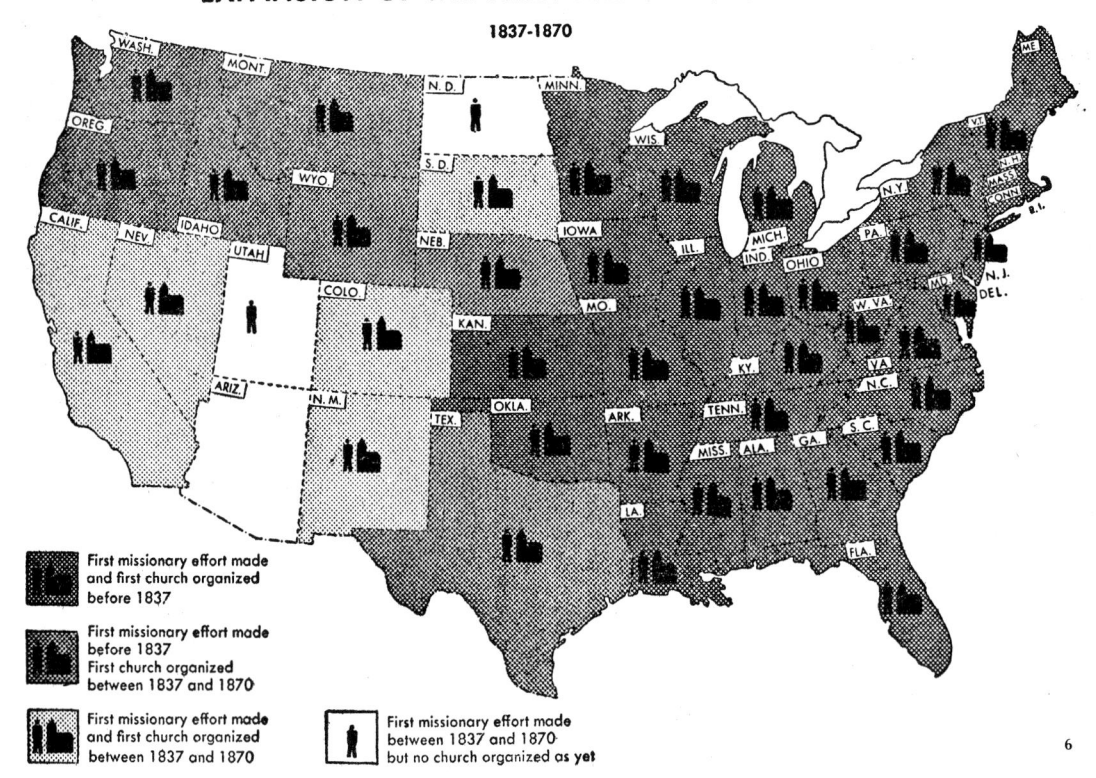

First missionary effort made and first church organized before 1837

First missionary effort made before 1837
First church organized between 1837 and 1870

First missionary effort made and first church organized between 1837 and 1870

First missionary effort made between 1837 and 1870 but no church organized as yet

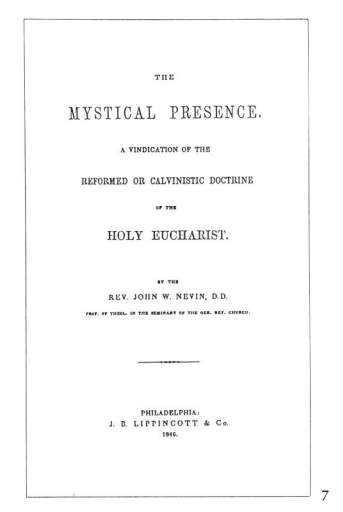

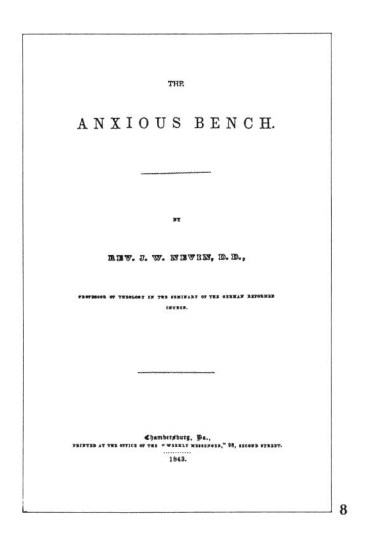

John W. Nevin

In the 1840s a fresh current in American theology flowed from the small German Reformed Seminary at Mercersburg, PA. Philip Schaff (1819-93), a native of Prussia and a product of German universities, and John Williamson Nevin (1803-86), a Presbyterian by birth and a student of Charles Hodge at Princeton, shaped the "Mercersburg Theology," ecumenical and sacramental in its emphases. Through books such as *The Anxious Bench* (1843), *The Principle of Protestantism* (1844) and *The Mystical Presence* (1846), Schaff and Nevin attempted to "reform" American evangelicalism with the philosophical tools of German Idealism. Attracted to the *Heidelberg Catechism* of Schaff's tradition, Nevin wrote a commentary on it (1847). In later years Schaff became a Presbyterian and taught at Union Theological Seminary in New York.

Philip Schaff

Through the pages of *The Theological Medium* Cumberland Presbyterians articulated their own moderate Calvinism. This publication was instrumental in the development of a full-bred Cumberland Presbyterian theology.

Theodore Dwight Weld (1803-95) was an antislavery disciple of Charles Finney. As an agent for the American Anti-Slavery Society, Weld influenced Henry Ward Beecher, James G. Birney and Harriet Beecher Stowe to join the antislavery cause. In 1839, Weld published a composite picture of slave treatment in America. *Slavery As It Is* was a source for Charles Dickens' chapter on slavery in *American Notes* and for Stowe's *Uncle Tom's Cabin*.

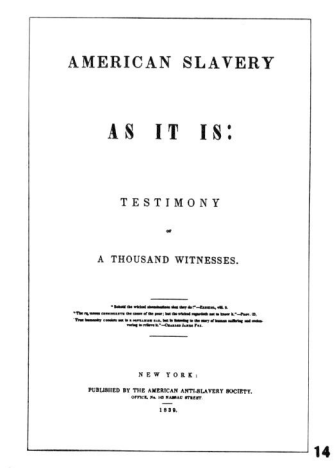

Theodore D. Weld

James Gillespie Birney (1792-1857), a prominent Presbyterian lawyer, was twice the presidential candidate of the antislavery Liberty Party. While in England as Vice-President of the World Anti-Slavery Convention, Birney penned his indictment of the close-mouthed attitude of American churches to the evils of slaveholding.

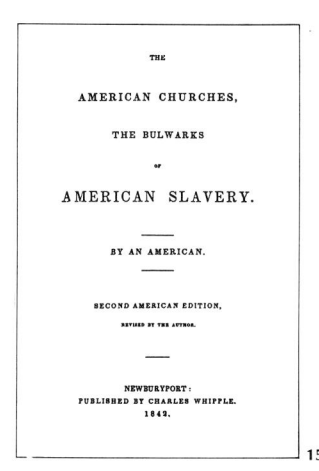

James G. Birney

Presbyterian pastor John Rankin hid slaves fleeing North on the underground railroad, and supplied Harriet Beecher Stowe with the story of Eliza leaping across the Ohio River on ice for *Uncle Tom's Cabin*. Here Rankin is pictured with his large family.

1843 Henry Highland Garnet (1815-82), a freed slave, was licensed by Troy (NY) Presbytery in 1842, where he preached, edited a weekly paper and served the American Anti-Slavery Society. In 1843 he made a firey address to the National Congress of Colored Americans, warning that Negroes might revolt against the brutal injustice of slavery. In 1865 he preached before the U.S. House of Representatives to commemorate passage of the Thirteenth Amendment of the Constitution abolishing slavery. Garnet ended his career as U.S. Ambassador to Liberia. He maintained that blacks were in America to stay and would be free.

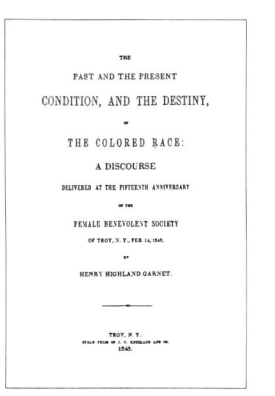

Henry Highland Garnet

Outstanding among early Negro Presbyterian ministers, J. W. C. Pennington was pastor of the First Colored Presbyterian Church in New York City, 1848-1856. He visited Europe three times to lecture on slavery and received an honorary degree from the University of Heidelberg. Pennington wrote the story of his life in *The Fugitive Blacksmith,* and a *Text Book of the Origin, and History . . . of the Colored People,* in which he tried to refute prejudices and misconceptions about Negroes.

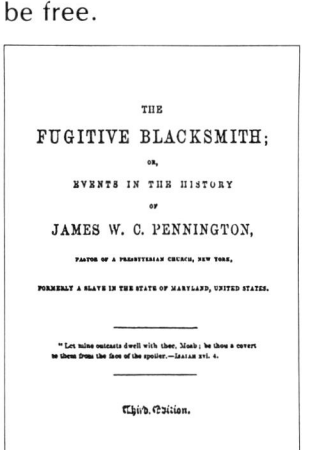

James W. C. Pennington

One of the largest American Presbyterian congregations was the predominantly black Zion church in Charleston, SC. The first floor seated a thousand Negroes and a balcony accommodated 250 whites. Time and again pastor John L. Girardeau declined calls from prominent white churches that he might serve his "brother in black."

Zion Presbyterian Church

Nicholas Murray

23

24

Aroused by a rapid influx of immigrants from Ireland, Germany and the southern European countries, anti-Catholic feeling grew strong across the U.S. Nicholas Murray, pastor of the Presbyterian Church at Elizabethtown, NJ, moderator of the 1849 Old School Assembly, was one of the chief crusaders against Rome. Irish-born, of Catholic parentage, Murray felt specially fitted to expose the evils of Popery. He addressed weekly letters through the New York *Observer* to Bishop John Hughes of New York, signing them "Kirwan" in honor of Dean Walter Blake Kirwan, a famed 18th century Irish convert from Catholicism. The invectives were quite popular and were reprinted in book form. "Nativist" controversies often led to violence as in the Philadelphia riot of July 7, 1844.

RIOT IN PHILADELPHIA
JULY 7th 1844.

25

Joseph Henry

Joseph Henry (1799-1878), a Presbyterian, was the first Director of the Smithsonian Institution. A prolific inventor, he was President of the American Association for the Advancement of Science and the National Academy of Science. A leading intellectual of the period, Joseph LeConte (1823-1901) wrote as philosopher, popular scientist and educator. A Harvard graduate, who taught in southern colleges and later at the University of California, LeConte was a Presbyterian champion of Darwin's ideas, attempting to reconcile the theory of evolution with Christian orthodoxy. In 1838 Hampden-Sydney College of Virginia opened a medical department in Richmond. With state assistance a massive building in the Egyptian style was built for the medical school in 1845. After 1866 the medical building was supported by the Commonwealth of Virginia.

Hampden-Sydney College—Medical College of Virginia

1847 A friendly rivalry existed between the theologians of Princeton and Columbia seminaries, and in 1846 and 1847 Charles Hodge and James Henley Thornwell took turns in the moderator's chair at General Assembly. Hodge, the moderator of the 1846 meeting in Philadelphia, was at Princeton Theological Seminary. Thornwell (1812-62), moderator of the 1847 Assembly in Richmond, served as Pastor of the Columbia, SC, First Church and as Professor of Theology in Columbia Seminary. The intellectual leader of the Presbyterians, in the South, Thornwell was a noted apologist for slavery. His discussions with Hodge over the nature and mission of the church culminated in a great debate in 1860. Hodge contended that Thornwell's views represented a "hyper-hyper-High Church Presbyterianism," Thornwell responded that Hodge's principles led to "no *no* No Presbyterianism!"

The popularity of Romanticism as a cultural and intellectual movement inspired a succession of Gothic and pseudo-Gothic meetinghouses across America's Presbyterian landscape. Wrote Moses D. Hoge of Richmond's Second Church, "I go in for Gothic, rubble walls, crevices for moss and ivy: holes where old Time may stick in his memorials: cozy loopholes of retreat, where the sparrow may find a house. . . ."

Charles Hodge

James H. Thornwell

Second Presbyterian Church
Richmond, VA

Sarah Childress Polk

First Presbyterian Church
Nashville, TN

Until the 1840s, few Americans foresaw that the population of their country would advance beyond the upper Mississippi Valley into the supposedly barren regions west of the Missouri. Others talked of the nation's "manifest destiny" to expand westward to the Pacific. James K. Polk of Tennessee was elected President on a platform advocating acquisition of new territory in Oregon and the annexation of Texas. In 1846 the U.S. went to war with Mexico, resulting in the cession to the U.S. of a vast territory in the Southwest, including California. Sarah Childress Polk was a devout and active Presbyterian. In later years the Polks lived in Nashville, where the First Presbyterian Church dedicated an Egyptian Revival sanctuary in 1851.

Daniel Baker

A pioneer PCUSA minister to be heard in the valley of the Rio Grande, the Reverend Daniel Baker, became known as the apostle of Presbyterianism in Texas. A native of Georgia, Baker responded to a call for missionaries to Texas. Landing at Galveston in 1840, he preached over the entire region. He was instrumental in establishing Austin College and served as its first president.

Narcissa Whitman

Marcus Whitman

Whitman Statue, Washington

Whitman Massacre

Henry H. Spalding

1847

In 1836, just thirty-one years after Lewis and Clark explored the Columbia River, Marcus Whitman, M.D. and his bride, along with the Reverend and Mrs. Henry H. Spalding risked the Oregon Trail to set up a mission station among the Cayuse Indians. Narcissa Whitman and Eliza Spalding were the first white women to cross the Continental Divide. Whitman, whose statue stands in the National Capitol and at the Presbyterian Historical Society was the first medical missionary to the American Indians. In 1847 an epidemic of measles ravaged the Indians, doing little harm to the whites. As a result, the Whitmans were accused of sorcery and massacred with twelve others, the first Protestant martyrs on the Pacific coast. Spalding and Eliza continued their mission in the West.

**Oregon Territory Stamp
1936**

The pictorial chart was made about 1845 by Eliza Spalding as an aid in teaching Christian history to the Indians of Oregon. The Presbyterian Stairway to Heaven and Hell starts at the bottom with the Old Testament and moves up chronologically, forming a "learning ladder." Painted on a six-foot-long, two-foot-wide roll, the ladder is marked by two vertical columns, the narrow one on the right representing the way of salvation, the broader path on the left, the way of damnation. Between them is the crucifixion of Jesus, with the twelve disciples dressed in variations of Henry Spalding's best suit.

Sylvester Woodbridge

Albert Williams

James Woods

1848 Americans cried "Gold," and Presbyterians recognized California as a new frontier. The first full time Presbyterian minister in California was Timothy Hunt, who sailed from Honolulu as soon as word of the gold strike was received. Hunt served as chaplain of San Francisco and held interdenominational services in a schoolhouse. Meanwhile other Presbyterian missionaries were on the way. Three Old School ministers, who organized the Presbytery of California were long known as the "three Ws." In April 1849, Sylvester Woodbridge organized a church at Benicia, the first Presbyterian Church in San Francisco. As with many western churches, the pioneer congregation held initial services in a tent. Albert Williams and James Woods founded churches in the territory also.

In 1846, William Speer of Pittsburgh obeyed an urgent call from the Board of Foreign Missions to go to China. After learning the language, Speer and his family returned home, victims of an unfriendly climate. When Chinese poured into California, Speer worked among them. He established the first Chinese Presbyterian church in the state on 6 November 1853. That same year Speer published a lecture arguing the special obligation of California whites to provide for the spiritual welfare of the Chinese who lived in their midst.

Among the Presbyterian missionaries to the Hawaiian islands were the Reverend and Mrs. William Patterson Alexander. Born in Kentucky and educated at Centre College and Princeton Seminary, Alexander (1805-84) and his wife arrived at Honolulu in May 1832. An eloquent preacher and expert linguist, Alexander established a theological school for the Hawaiians in 1863. He died in 1884. Mrs. Alexander continued her work in Maui. A ship, the Morning Star I, paid for in part by contributions of New School Presbyterian children to the American Board of Commissioners for Foreign Missions, carried missionaries, Bibles and tracts to the Hawaiians.

William and Mary Alexander

Alexander preaching

Packet "Morning Star"

Adrian Van Vliet [50]

German Presbyterian Church, Dubuque [51]

German Presbyterian congregations were founded in the Midwest in the middle of the 19th century. Adrian Van Vliet, a native of Holland who settled near Dubuque, served as minister of a German Presbyterian church there. Van Vliet helped form separate German judicatories in the Presbyterian Church, U.S.A., as well as a theological school at Dubuque which eventually became the Theological Seminary of the University of Dubuque. The German church is typical of many which were built across the Midwest. The Female Seminary in Dubuque illustrates the growing interest in women's education. Originally built by the Congregationalists under the leadership of Catharine Beecher, the Seminary building became the home of the German Presbyterian Theological School of the Northwest.

German Presbyterian Theological School of The Northwest [52]

The stages of a woman's life in the nineteenth century are portrayed in this artist's drawing—as a pilgrimage from cradle to old age.

Catharine Beecher (1800-78), was an advocate of higher education for women. She collaborated with William McGuffy on his *Eclectic Fourth Reader* (1837) and with her sister Harriet Beecher Stowe, published *The American Woman's Home* in 1869. Late in life she expressly rejected the "soul withering doctrines" of Presbyterianism and joined the Episcopal Church. Augusta Female Seminary in Staunton, VA, the forerunner of Mary Baldwin College, was established in 1842 as a Presbyterian women's school. Joseph R. Wilson, father of the Presbyterian President, was pastor of the Presbyterian Church in Staunton (1855-58) and served for one year as principal of the seminary. Woodrow Wilson was baptized in the Staunton church, which adjoined Augusta Seminary.

Catharine Beecher

Augusta Female Seminary

Horace Bushnell (1802-76), leading New England "Presbygationalist" minister rejected revivalism's storm and stress, holding that under normal circumstances conversion was educative, rather than emotional. The death of an infant daughter led Bushnell to put his thoughts in print, and his *Christian Nurture* was published in 1847. The influential book underlined the organic nature of family and church. A properly nurtured person need never have a "conversion" experience—and might never remember being other than a child of God.

Horace Bushnell [56]

1850 Cortlandt Van Rensselaer (1808-60), Secretary of the Board of Education of the Old School Assembly, was instrumental in establishing and was first President of the Presbyterian Historical Society at the 1852 Assembly meeting at Second Presbyterian Church, Charleston, SC. The Publications Building of the Presbyterian Church in the United States of America in Philadelphia was built in 1850 at Van Rensselaer's urging.

Cortlandt Van Rensselaer [57]

Second Presbyterian Church, Charleston [58]

Presbyterian Board of Publication [59]

96

1851 Presbyterians continued to sing the praises of God during these years, using the officially adopted *Hymns and Psalms* (1843). But in 1851 Harriet Beecher Stowe and Stephen Colwell called attention to two serious challenges to Christian piety. Stowe, daughter of Lyman Beecher, sister of Catherine, and wife of Calvin Stowe, published *Uncle Tom's Cabin; or Life among the Lowly*. Using the form of the family novel, she focused attention on the impact of slavery on the lives of blacks and whites, raised questions about the defense of slavery by people such as Charles Colcock Jones and James Smylie, and called on Christians to show the sympathies of Christ in dealing with the great moral issue. Colwell, a Philadelphia manufacturer, thought Presbyterians ought to be doing more to help what some people called the wage slaves of the North's growing industrial system. We have, he told his readers of *New Themes for the Protestant Clergy*, "creeds without charity," "theology without humanity," and "Protestantism without Christianity."

Harriet Beecher Stowe

Stephen Colwell

Charles W. Baird

1855 Charles W. Baird, the son of evangelical missionaries to European Catholics, was deeply touched by the liturgical worship of the continental Reformed churches. His *Eutaxia, or the Presbyterian Liturgies* (1855), created quite a stir. In this work, Baird collected the liturgies of Calvin, Knox, Richard Baxter, the French Huguenots, the Dutch and German Reformed churches. His efforts helped redirect American Presbyterians to their rich heritage of liturgical worship.

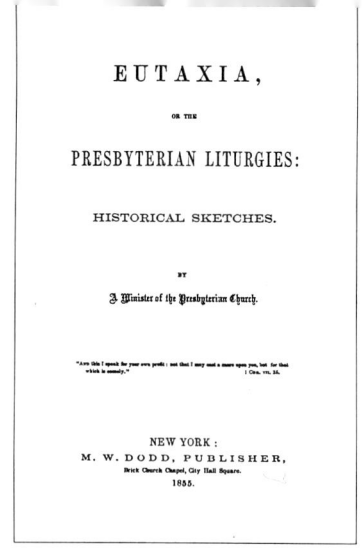

Levi A. Ward, a wealthy Presbyterian businessman in Rochester, NY, built a magnificent new church opposite his estate in 1853. The handsome Romanesque building, rebuilt and enlarged in 1868, was distinctive for its architecture. To encourage congregational participation, Ward prepared a servicebook with forms for weddings, funerals and the administration of the sacraments, as well as for ordinary Sunday services.

Levi A. Ward

St. Peter's Presbyterian Church
Rochester, NY

Wheatland, Buchanan's Home

1856 James Buchanan (1791-1868) was the nation's second Presbyterian President. Born near Mercersburg, PA, Buchanan was educated at Dickinson College and served with distinction in the U.S. House of Representatives, the Senate, and as ambassador to Russia and England. He was Secretary of State under President Polk. Buchanan presided over the breakup of the Union, leaving the inevitable military contest to be decided under another Presbyterian President, Abraham Lincoln.

James Buchanan

THE GREAT PRESIDENTIAL SWEEPSTAKES OF 1856.

Henry Ward Beecher (1813-87), son of Lyman Beecher, became one of the most influential Protestant leaders of his time. He was refused ordination by the Miami (OH) Presbytery of the Old School church. After serving two pastorates in New School churches in Indiana, Beecher became pastor of the prestigious Plymouth Congregational Church in Brooklyn, NY. The cartoon (above) shows Beecher supporting Buchanan with rifles for Kansas abolistionists.

Henry Ward Beecher

Donald C. McLaren   Joseph T. Cooper   John T. Pressly

1858 A new day dawned for descendants of the Scottish dissenting churches in America with the formation of the United Presbyterian Church of North America. On 26 May 1858, commissioners of the General Synod of the Associate Reformed Presbyterian Church (Covenanters) met their fellows from the Synod of the Associate Presbyterian Church (Seceders) at Seventh and Springfield Streets in what is now Pittsburgh's "Golden Triangle" and marched together to the old City Hall to consummate the union of the two churches. The Reverend D. C. McLaren was the final moderator of the ARP synod, and the Reverend Joseph T. Cooper had the corresponding honor in the Associate synod. John Pressly of the ARP Allegheny Seminary was unanimously elected the first moderator of the new church. The new UPCNA was a Psalm singing church as indicated by the program of the union meeting.

The 1858 Union

ORDER OF EXERCISES

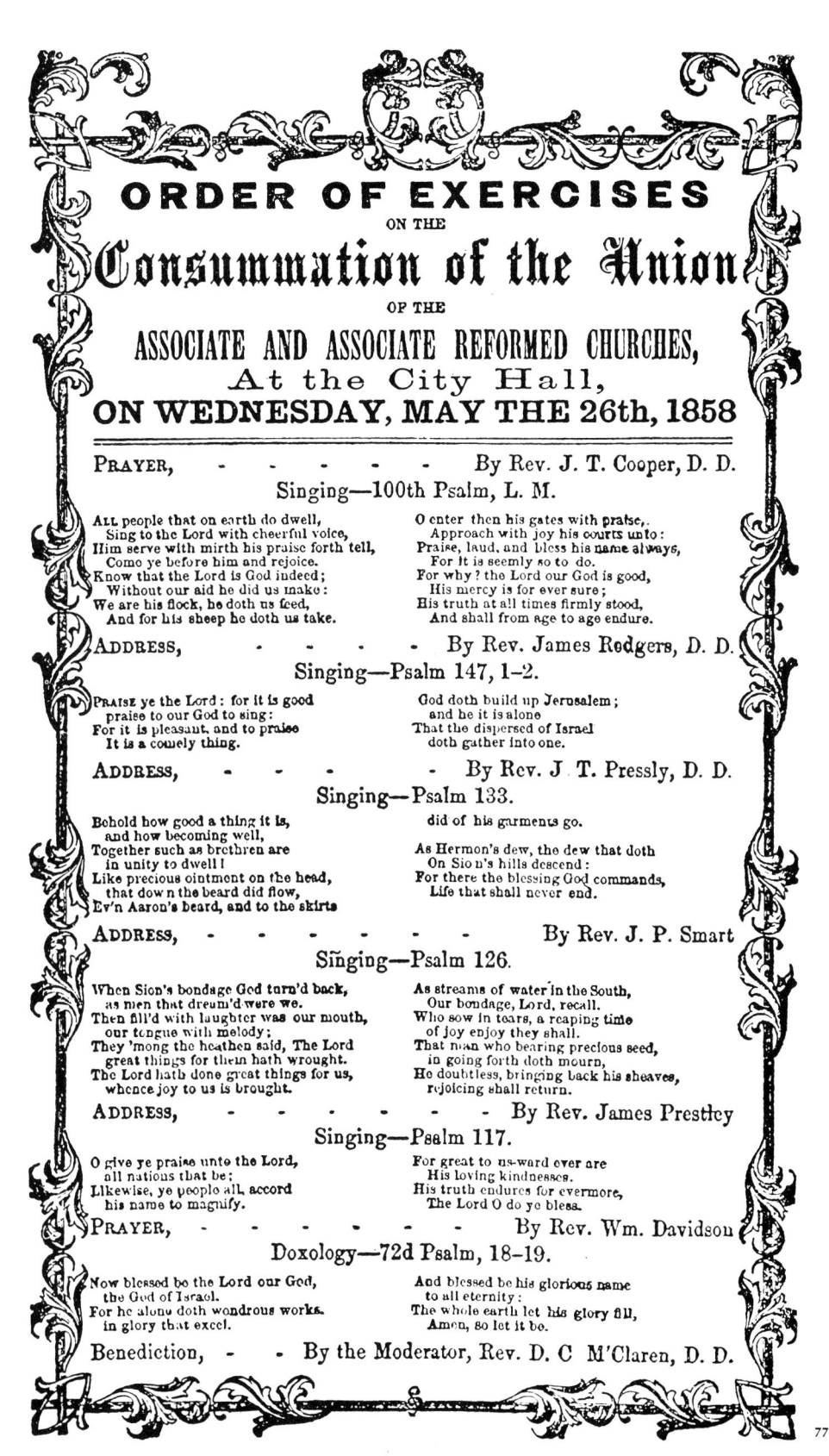

ON THE

Consummation of the Union

OF THE

ASSOCIATE AND ASSOCIATE REFORMED CHURCHES,

At the City Hall,

ON WEDNESDAY, MAY THE 26th, 1858

PRAYER, - - - - - By Rev. J. T. Cooper, D. D.

Singing—100th Psalm, L. M.

All people that on earth do dwell,
　Sing to the Lord with cheerful voice,
Him serve with mirth his praise forth tell,
　Come ye before him and rejoice.
Know that the Lord is God indeed;
　Without our aid he did us make:
We are his flock, he doth us feed,
　And for his sheep he doth us take.

O enter then his gates with praise,
　Approach with joy his courts unto:
Praise, laud, and bless his name always,
　For it is seemly so to do.
For why? the Lord our God is good,
　His mercy is for ever sure;
His truth at all times firmly stood,
　And shall from age to age endure.

ADDRESS, - - - - - By Rev. James Rodgers, D. D.

Singing—Psalm 147, 1-2.

Praise ye the Lord: for it is good
　praise to our God to sing:
For it is pleasant, and to praise
　It is a comely thing.

God doth build up Jerusalem;
　and he it is alone
That the dispersed of Israel
　doth gather into one.

ADDRESS, - - - - - By Rev. J. T. Pressly, D. D.

Singing—Psalm 133.

Behold how good a thing it is,
　and how becoming well,
Together such as brethren are
　in unity to dwell!
Like precious ointment on the head,
　that down the beard did flow,
Ev'n Aaron's beard, and to the skirts

did of his garments go.

As Hermon's dew, the dew that doth
　On Sion's hills descend:
For there the blessing God commands,
　Life that shall never end.

ADDRESS, - - - - - - By Rev. J. P. Smart

Singing—Psalm 126.

When Sion's bondage God turn'd back,
　as men that dream'd were we.
Then fill'd with laughter was our mouth,
　our tongue with melody;
They 'mong the heathen said, The Lord
　great things for them hath wrought.
The Lord hath done great things for us,
　whence joy to us is brought.

As streams of water in the South,
　Our bondage, Lord, recall.
Who sow in tears, a reaping time
　of joy enjoy they shall.
That man who bearing precious seed,
　in going forth doth mourn,
He doubtless, bringing back his sheaves,
　rejoicing shall return.

ADDRESS, - - - - - - By Rev. James Prestley

Singing—Psalm 117.

O give ye praise unto the Lord,
　all nations that be;
Likewise, ye people all, accord
　his name to magnify.

For great to us-ward ever are
　His loving kindnesses.
His truth endures for evermore,
　The Lord O do ye bless.

PRAYER, - - - - - By Rev. Wm. Davidson

Doxology—72d Psalm, 18-19.

Now blessed be the Lord our God,
　the God of Israel.
For he alone doth wondrous works,
　in glory that excel.

And blessed be his glorious name
　to all eternity:
The whole earth let his glory fill,
　Amen, so let it be.

Benediction, - - By the Moderator, Rev. D. C M'Claren, D. D.

The Presbyterian Family Almanac of 1858 encouraged Bible reading, praise and prayer around the family table every season of the year with the father of the household acting as priest. The scythe and the hour glass remind Presbyterian readers soberly of finitude and the frailty of life.

In western Pennsylvania, artist David Gilmore Blythe, who grew up in a strict Presbyterian family and showed vision in his art, pokes fun at family worship. Excited by the little boy, a goat disrupts devotions with a butt, and the lad pretends innocence in the whole affair. Blythe painted these scenes of domestic turmoil in 1856.

George Duffield (1818-1888) was the pastor of the First Presbyterian Church in Detroit. In 1858 a dying friend called upon Christians to stand up for Jesus. Duffield, son of the revolutionary war pastor, wrote the hymn in his friend's honor:

Stand up, stand up for Jesus,/Ye Soldiers of the Cross;
Lift high His royal banner,/It must not suffer loss:
From victory unto victory/His army shall He lead,
Till every foe is vanquished,/And Christ is Lord indeed.

Collegiate Reformed Church New York City 82

83

Prayers & Exhortations
Not to exceed 5 minutes, *in order to give all an opportunity.*

NOT MORE than 2 CONSECUTIVE PRAYERS OR EXHORTATIONS.

NO CONTROVERTED POINTS DISCUSSED.

84

Samuel Irenaeus Prime 85

1858 The Fulton Street revival started in the Collegiate Reformed church in New York City. It touched many Presbyterians, and spread throughout the country as people found religious solace in prayer. Largely a lay movement and ecumenical in character, the participants did not hesitate, as the sign suggests to instruct one another about what was expected with regard to length, number, and content of prayers. Samuel Irenaeus Prime (1854-1885), a minister-editor of *The New York Observer,* was caught up in the revival and described it in *Power of Prayer*. He continued to follow the prayer meeting in his writings for twenty-five years.

86

Susan B. Warner

Anna B. Warner

1859 Susan Bogert Warner (1819-1885) and Anna Barlett Warner (1827-1915) were New Yorkers who wrote sentimental and moralistic novels about Christian experience, and taught a Sunday school class for years at West Point. One editor dismissed Susan's *The Wide, Wide World* (1851) as "Fudge," yet it sold widely in the era. The Warners were Presbyterians although Anna, shown here with some of her West Point cadets, showed Methodist sympathies toward the end of her life. In her novel, *Say and Seal*, (1859) a Sunday school teacher sang to a child who lay dying in his arms the words which became the hymn of the American Sunday school movement:

Jesus loves me, this I know,/For the Bible tells me so;
Little ones to him belong,/They are weak but he is strong.

1861 Gardiner Spring (1785-1873) was pastor of the Brick Presbyterian Church in New York City from the time of his ordination in 1810 to his death. He helped to organize numerous voluntary societies, including the American Bible Society, the American Tract Society, and the American Home Missionary Society. At the 1861 General Assembly (OS) he introduced the resolution which, when amended, called for the support of the federal government formed under the constitution to which Presbyterians had given allegiance since 1789.

Gardiner Spring

General Assembly
Old School
1861, Philadelphia

The General Assembly (OS) met in Philadelphia during May, 1861. Lincoln presided in the White House. South Carolinians had already fired on Fort Sumter. Secession had begun. Just a few Presbyterians from the South managed to attend the Assembly which admonished Presbyterians to remain loyal to the Union on the biblical grounds found in Romans 13. Charles Hodge and others protested and argued that the ecclesiastical court was trying to determine a political question. New School Presbyterians divided in 1858 over the question of slavery.

John C. Backus (right), pastor of the First Presbyterian Church of Baltimore, MD was elected moderator of the Assembly.

Benjamin
M.
Palmer 93

First Presbyterian Church, Augusta

1861 Southern presbyteries withdrew from the Old School Assembly. In December, 1861, commissioners met in Augusta, GA, at the First Presbyterian Church to form the Presbyterian Church in the Confederate States of America. Benjamin M. Palmer (1818-1902), a pastor of the First Presbyterian Church, New Orleans, was elected moderator, and theologian James Henley Thornwell exerted power over the deliberations of the new General Assembly. The body sent out the "Address of the Southern General Assembly to all the Churches of Jesus Christ" which explained the reasons for the division of Presbyterians and made a vigorous defense of slavery as well as the "spirituality" of the church, not preserved by former colleagues in the North. Presbyterians in the South asked for prayers for the Confederate cause.

VI
WAR, RECONSTRUCTION, AND FRATERNAL RELATIONS

Romney Church bier

1861-1883 Philip Schaff, who observed the fratricidal bloodletting at Gettysburg, called the Civil War a baptism of blood for the nation. Presbyterian fought Presbyterian. Each, as Lincoln said, read the same Bible and prayed to the same God, for fulfillment of the purposes of the conflict. While the North was victorious, both sides suffered. During years of Reconstruction Yankee and Cavalier nursed wounds with considerable mutual bitterness. The postwar years were marked by ecumenical endeavors among Protestants and Presbyterians. Old School-New School reunited in the South during the war, while in the North, Old School and New School came together in a notable gathering in Pittsburgh in 1869. Presbyterians participated in the meetings of the Evangelical Alliance and in the formation of their own Alliance of Reformed Churches throughout the World which included Presbyterians, North and South. During these years home mission work continued to expand westward, and foreign missionaries pressed outward to carry the Christian witness to peoples of six continents. Educational work grew not only within the Sunday schools of the churches, but also in the public schools in which William McGuffey's readers shaped the mind of young America. Samuel Clemens, alias Mark Twain, poked fun at Presbyterians among whom he grew up in Hannibal, MO, for "preforeordestination," and the intellectual ferment of the age, including the theory of evolution, caused new tensions. Gradually, the PCUS emerged from regional captivity, and after long negotiations entered into fraternal relations with the PCUSA in 1883, and started the slow process of reuniting American Presbyterians, divided in 1861.

Sidney Lanier

Influenced by James Woodrow, Presbyterian minister and professor at Oglethorpe College, Midway, GA, Sidney Lanier became one of America's leading poets. In "Psalm of the West" (1876) he spoke of the nation's "Onward-ache." The nation was baptized in the blood, death, and destruction of the Civil War as it pushed onward in the 1860s and 1870s. The funeral bier (above) was used by the congregation of the Presbyterian church in Romney, WV.

1861 When Abraham Lincoln was inaugurated as President of the United States, March 1861, seven southern states had already seceded from the Union. Four more followed suit when Lincoln issued a call for troops to suppress the "rebellion" at Fort Sumter, South Carolina. Old School Presbyterians waited until their Assembly in May, 1861, before they divided. In Washington, DC, President and Mrs. Lincoln worshipped at the New York Avenue Presbyterian Church.

Mary Todd Lincoln

Phineas D. Gurley

New York Ave. Church

Pastor and friend to the Lincolns, Phineas D. Gurley (1816-68) was the minister of the F Street Church which in 1859 united with Second Presbyterian to form New York Avenue Church. Chaplain of the Senate in 1858, Gurley officiated at Lincoln's funeral. In 1867, he was chosen moderator of the General Assembly which met in Cincinnati.

Long Lincoln a Little Longer

Gen. George B. McClellan

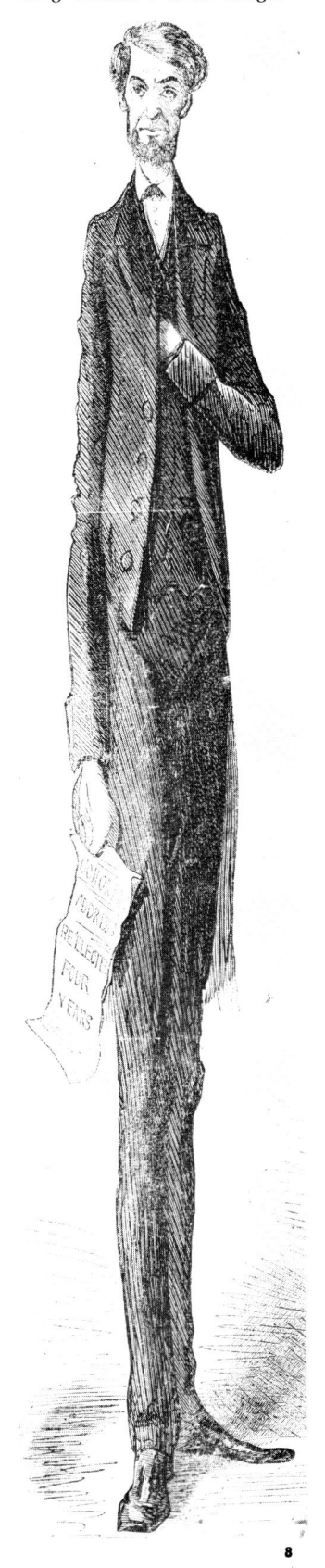

Presbyterians met and fought each other at assemblies and on battlefields during the war years 1861-65. Gen. George B. McClellan, 34, won overall command of the Union armies in July 1861. Son of a Philadelphia Presbyterian surgeon, "Little Mac" graduated second in the 1846 West Point class, won distinction in the Mexican War. An able organizer, he won the confidence and affection of his Army of the Potomac. As an elder, he attended the Pan-Presbyterian Council which met in Philadelphia in 1880.

Robert L. Dabney   **Gen. Stonewall Jackson**

The "right arm" of Confederate Gen. Robert E. Lee, Gen. Thomas J. "Stonewall" Jackson was a deacon in the Lexington, VA, Presbyterian Church and regularly taught a Sunday school class for Negroes. He persuaded Robert L. Dabney of Union Seminary in Virginia to serve for a time as his personal secretary. Jackson was mortally wounded at Chancellorsville. His last words were, "Let us cross the river and rest under the shade of the trees."

James R. Miller

Christian Commission Headquarters Washington, DC

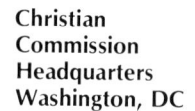

Christian Commission on the Pamunkey

The Civil War was enormously costly in human life and resources, as Americans fought Americans. One of the ways Christians provided for the spiritual welfare of the soldiers was through the United States Christian Commission. The Christian Commission had headquarters in Washington, DC, set up camps with chapels and reading rooms and ministered to soldiers wounded in the field. Presbyterian layman, George Stuart, helped to found the Christian Commission, and James R. Miller served as a field agent during the war. Presbyterian sisters Abby Howland, Jane Stuart, and Georgeanna Woolsey rendered service as Civil War relief and hospital workers in connection with the Sanitary Commission.

U.S. Christian Commission Station, General Hospital, City Point, VA

Samuel B. McPheeters, pastor of the Pine St. Church in St. Louis, aroused sectional feelings among border state Presbyterians. Complaints about his loyalty to the Union were raised when he baptized a child in 1862 named for a Confederate general. Banished from Missouri by the Army, McPheeters carried his appeal to Lincoln who intervened on his behalf and rescinded the order. The government could not undertake "running the churches." Suspicions of disloyalty by a rump presbytery kept him out of his pulpit for several years. He moved to Kentucky, in 1868, and was received into the PCUS in 1869.

Samuel B. McPheeters [15]

Isaac W. K. Handy was pastor of the First Church at Portsmouth, VA. The Federals captured the area in 1861. Imprisoned for fifteen months, refusing to take the oath of allegiance to the Union, Handy taught theology to interested fellow Confederate prisoners.

[16]

Francis L. Cardozo

Elizabeth Keckley

Presbyterianism among Negroes is represented here by Elizabeth Keckley, Francis L. Cardozo, and a Sunday school class in Liberty Co., GA. Keckley, a Virginia-born slave for thirty years serving Mrs. Jefferson Davis and then Mrs. Lincoln in the White House, was a member of a Washington, DC, Presbyterian Church. Cardozo, a South Carolina Presbyterian minister, principal of Avery Institute, served as secretary of state (1868-72), treasurer (1872-78), and was the first black state cabinet officer in America. The members of the class pictured below were former parishioners of Georgia minister Charles C. Jones, a leader in organizing Presbyterian missions to slaves. He died during the war. Former slaves of Jones, Charles and Lucy, stand by Jones' grave after the war.

Charles and Lucy at Jones' Grave

Liberty Co., GA, Sunday School Class

Wylie Memorial Church

George H. Stuart

1867 A Pan-Presbyterian Convention meeting in the First Reformed Presbyterian Church of Philadelphia on November 8, 1867, discussed Presbyterian union. An elder in that church, businessman and philanthropist, George H. Stuart was the proponent of the convention which brought together Old and New School, Reformed, United Presbyterian, Dutch, Cumberland, and Presbyterians in the South to consider the subject.

The ecumenical spirit was furthered by two Union Theological Seminary (NY) professors, Henry Boynton Smith and Philip Schaff. Leading New School theologian, Smith (1815-77) was chairman of the Evangelical Alliance executive committee, moderator of the 1863 Assembly (NS), and was instrumental in the 1869 reunion of the PCUSA. Schaff (1819-93) came into the PCUSA from the German Reformed Church. His *Creeds of Christendom* (1877) contributed greatly to the ecumenical spirit.

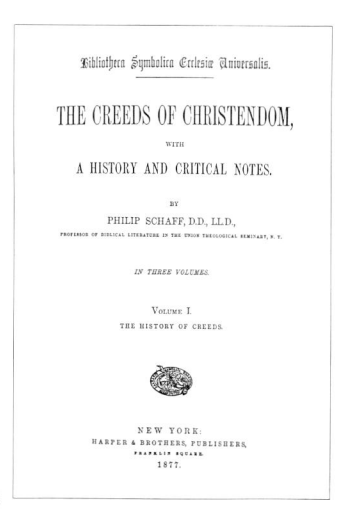

Henry B. Smith

113

First Presbyterian Church (O.S.)

Third Presbyterian Church (N.S.)

Old School-New School Reunion

J. Trumbull Backus

1869 Meeting separately for the last time, Old and New School Presbyterians of the PCUSA held their Assemblies in the First and Third churches of Pittsburgh where they approved reunion. Consummation took place on 12 November 1869, with the two Assemblies forming a procession which moved through the streets. *Harper's Weekly* called it "the greatest and most sublime spectacle ever witnessed in the ecclesiastical history of America." The first moderator of the reunited church was J. Trumbull Backus, pastor of the Schenectady, NY, First Church. The former New School minister, was elected unanimously in 1870.

William S. Plumer

Walnut St. Church

The Civil War divided not only the nation and families, but also individual churches, the most celebrated case being that of the Walnut Street Church of Louisville, KY. Pastor Stuart Robinson of the Second Church in Louisville led three-fourths of the Kentucky churches into the Southern Church (PCUS) in 1868. A minority of the Walnut Street Church, however, sued successfully for the property, a case which went to the U.S. Supreme Court. Robinson was elected moderator of the PCUS in 1869. He was followed by William Swan Plumer who, having been moderator of the 1838 Old School Assembly, became the only man to serve as moderator of both the Old School and southern churches.

Stuart Robinson

1873 The Evangelical Alliance was founded in 1846 as an ecumenical body for the promotion of evangelical Christianity among the churches in America and Europe. A strong supporter of the Alliance, Philip Schaff assisted Samuel I. Prime in the publication of the papers from the New York City conference in 1873.

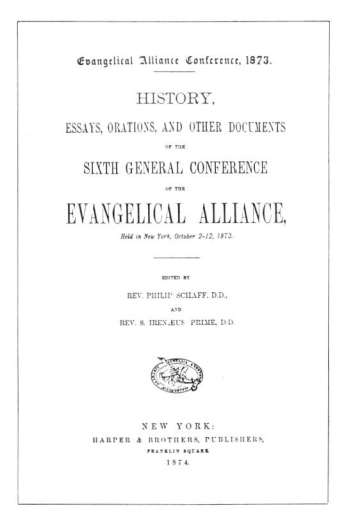

Fourth Presbyterian Church

E. P. Roe

Great fires burned in St. Louis in 1849 and in Chicago in 1871. The Fourth Presbyterian Church in Chicago was heavily damaged in the conflagration. Presbyterian minister E. P. Roe (1838-1888) visited Chicago while it was still smoldering. After returning home to Highland Falls, NY, he wrote *Barriers Burned Away* (1872), a conversion novel typical of the nineteenth century. Roe wrote seventeen other novels combining moral purpose and entertainment. Below, the First Presbyterian Church of St. Louis stands out against the background of the mighty Mississippi in this painting of the city.

View of St. Louis from Lucas Place

Charles Hodge

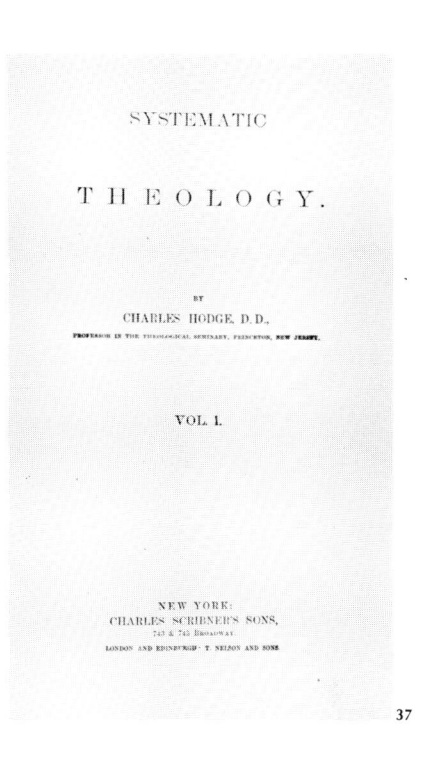

An "autumn harvest" of Presbyterian theologies appeared in the second half of the nineteenth century. Charles Hodge, who taught over 3000 students during his fifty years at Princeton Seminary, produced his three volume *Systematic Theology* (1871-72), while Robert Lewis Dabney of Union Theological Seminary, VA, published his in 1870. Cumberland theologian, Richard Beard turned out his *Lectures on Theology* in three volumes between 1864-1870. At Union Theological Seminary, NY, W. G. T. Shedd (1820-1894) began his teaching career as theologian in 1874, and published his *Dogmatic Theology* between 1888-94, another three volume set. Seeds had already been planted for theological unrest which accompanied and followed the appearance of these weighty tomes, representing much learning but not the last words on Reformed theology.

William G. T. Shedd   **Robert L. Dabney**   **Richard Beard**

Francis Landey Patton, professor of the Presbyterian seminary in Chicago, exchanged heated words over new theological currents with David Swing, pastor of the Fourth Presbyterian Church. Patton brought Swing to trial for heresy before Chicago Presbytery. A gifted speaker, Swing won acquittal, although the experience moved him to leave the Presbyterian ministry. Patton left Chicago to teach at Princeton Seminary.

David Swing 41

Francis L. Patton 42

Elizabeth P. Prentiss (1818-78) wrote religious and juvenile fiction, exalting filial piety in young ladies. Her *Stepping Heavenward* (1869) sold over 100,000 copies in America and was popular in Europe. Cornelia Spencer (1825-1908) gained recognition statewide in North Carolina as an author, columnist, and educational crusader. Writing for the *North Carolina Presbyterian*, she gave advice to young women on many subjects from politics to proper church behavior. *Harper's Weekly* underscored the need for promptness in church attendance, but also indicated that many worshipers often slept in church when listening to a "composing sermon."

Elizabeth Prentiss 43

Cornelia Spencer 44

Country Congregation—Disturbed by a Latecomer. 45

A Composing Sermon 46

118

The period 1866-83 witnessed the founding of many colleges by Presbyterians including Wooster (1866, pictured right), King (1867), Lewis and Clark (1867), Bloomfield (1868), Trinity (1869), Wilson (1869), Westminster in Utah (1875), Grove City (1876), Sheldon Jackson (1878), Hastings (1882), and Huron, Rocky Mountain, and Tarkio all in 1883. Pictured below is a prayer meeting for temperance being held in an ale shop by the women of the Xenia, Ohio, Presbyterian church.

Old Main, College of Wooster

Jane Stuart Woolsey

New York's Presbyterian Hospital opened its doors in 1872 to persons for health care regardless of race, color, or creed. Jane Stuart Woolsey, who with her mother and sisters helped to organize the Church of the Covenant, New York City, became resident directress. She set up various departments and coordinated the nursing program of a new city hospital.

Presbyterian Hospital, New York

William H. McGuffey

Presbyterian minister, William Holmes McGuffey was the most celebrated educator of the nineteenth century. His *Readers* made America literate and spun together Protestant virtues and national ideals which shaped the mind of the nation. A professor of ancient language, he taught at Miami University, OH, and at the University of Virginia. He also made a sizeable contribution to higher education. Presbyterians in the South published *The Children's Friend* as a part of their Christian education program.

Jane L. Clemens

Attending Sunday-School in *Tom Sawyer*

Mrs. Samuel Clemens, according to some critics, served as the model for Mark Twain's Aunt Polly. Converted by Ezra Stiles Ely, Mrs. Clemens was a member of the Presbyterian Church in Hannibal, MO. Although there is no evidence that her illustrious son ever became a communing member of the congregation, congregational life left an imprint on him, and apparently on *Tom Sawyer*, which Twain published in 1875.

Sam Clemens, teenager

Walter Lowrie 57   John C. Lowrie 58

Woman's Board of Foreign Missions, Saratoga, 1879   59

Sarah F. Hanna 60

Presbyterian churches played a leading role in the spread of the Gospel to the four corners of the globe. The Honorable Walter Lowrie, a United States Senator from Pennsylvania, served as a secretary of the Board of Foreign Missions, 1837-1868, while his son the Reverend John C. Lowrie held that post from 1850-1891. Mrs. Sarah F. Hanna helped form the General Women's Missionary Society for foreign missions in 1875 for the UPCNA. The Woman's Board of Foreign Missions of the PCUSA met at Saratoga, NY, in 1879 just after its formation in 1878.

John L. and Jane E. Wilson

Foreign missions owed its high place among southern Presbyterians mainly to the tireless work of John Leighton Wilson (1809-86). From South Carolina, Wilson labored for twenty years in Africa before serving the Board of Foreign Missions in New York (1853-61). He then served as secretary for foreign and home missions of the southern church until his death. His influence for missions was enormous. One of his publications contributed to the abolition of slave trade on the coast of Africa. Other prominent missionaries to West Africa include several generations of the Nassau family (below) which served as missionaries to West Africa.

The George and Mary Chamberlain Family

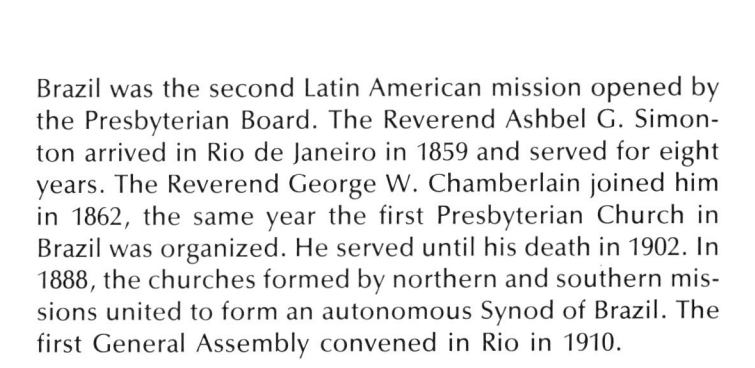

Ashbel G. Simonton

Brazil was the second Latin American mission opened by the Presbyterian Board. The Reverend Ashbel G. Simonton arrived in Rio de Janeiro in 1859 and served for eight years. The Reverend George W. Chamberlain joined him in 1862, the same year the first Presbyterian Church in Brazil was organized. He served until his death in 1902. In 1888, the churches formed by northern and southern missions united to form an autonomous Synod of Brazil. The first General Assembly convened in Rio in 1910.

David Trumbull

Melinda Rankin

David Trumbull (left) went to Chile in 1845 to serve the English-speaking people of Valparaiso where he founded a union church in which he labored for forty-four years. Upon his death, he was mourned by the Chilean people for his work in education, for religious liberty, and his general statesmanship. Miss Melinda Rankin began work among the Mexicans in Brownsville, TX, in 1852. In 1864, she crossed the Rio Grande to work in Matamoros. She founded a girls' school in Monterey in 1866, which was later taken under the Board. A woman of strong will and concentration, she labored for twenty years in Mexico.

Mary Pierson Eddy

Samuel and Henry H. Jessup

American Mission, Beirut

Presbyterian missions organized the first girls school in the Turkish Empire in 1835. That became the Beirut Female Seminary in 1866 and then the American School for Girls. Dr. Mary Pierson Eddy was the first woman ever permitted to practice medicine in the land. Based in Beirut, she itinerated on horseback, slept in a tent, and visited the most rugged parts of the country, bringing medicine and the Gospel to many women and children. Longtime missionaries, Rev. Samuel Jessup (served 1863-1912) and Dr. Henry H. Jessup (1856-1910) also contributed greatly to the Syrian mission.

The "Ibis"

Associate Reformed (later UPCNA) missions to Egypt was initiated when Rev. and Mrs. Thomas McCague arrived in Cairo in 1853. Mrs. McCague founded the first girls' school in Egypt which was a means of evangelism. The purchase in 1860 of a river sailboat, the *Ibis,* was used for evangelism along the Nile River. Sailing by night, tying up at a village by day, the missionaries conducted services, sold tracts, held discussions, and answered questions, all of which created interest in the Gospel.

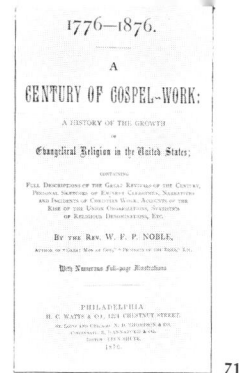

Moody-Sankey Revival, Philadelphia

1876 The country's centennial was marked in various ways by Presbyterians. The Reverend W. F. P. Noble wrote a history of the growth of evangelical religion in the United States. Back from a three-year campaign in Britain, evangelists D. L. Moody and Ira Sankey conducted a two-month campaign in a Pennsylvania Railroad freight warehouse in Philadelphia, made fit by John Wanamaker for the revival. In Charlotte, North Carolina, the community celebrated the centennial of the Mecklenburg Declaration of Independence.

Mecklenburg Declaration Celebration

Lincoln University

Lincoln University, Oxford, PA, was one of the few institutions of higher learning for blacks after the Civil War. Founded in 1854 as Ashmun Institute by John Miller Dickey, a minister, it trained missionaries for African colonization efforts. It later broadened its programs to meet the needs of freedmen for liberal arts and also theological education. For many years it was under the control of New Castle Presbytery. Francis J. Grimke (1850-1937) (seated left) and his brother Archibald, studied at Lincoln and graduated first and second in their class of 1870. Sons of a prominent Charleston, SC, white citizen and a Negro slave girl, Archibald entered law and Francis graduated from Princeton Seminary. He was ordained to the Presbyterian ministry, and served the 15th Street Church in Washington, DC.

Knoxville College in Knoxville, TN, was established in 1875 by the United Presbyterian Church of North America as part of a mission to Freedmen. First operated as a normal school, in 1877 it became a liberal arts college and the center of the denomination's effort to provide teachers and pastors for the southern states. At right, the college's YMCA cabinet poses for the camera.

Knoxville College YMCA Cabinet

Financed by a gift of Mary D. Biddle of Philadelphia, two ministers attached to the U.S.A. Synod of Baltimore, Samuel C. Alexander and Willis L. Miller, began theological instruction for Negroes in 1867 at Charlotte, NC. It became the Henry J. Biddle Memorial Institute, renamed Johnson C. Smith University in 1923. The Johnson C. Smith Seminary was established in 1931.

Henry J. Biddle

C. A. Stillman

In 1876 the PCUS established the Institute for the Training of Colored Ministers under the auspices of C. A. Stillman, minister of the First Presbyterian Church, Tuscaloosa, AL. The Institute gradually provided for a four years liberal arts program and changed its name to Stillman College to honor the founder. He is shown on the porch of this building, and William Sheppard (fourth from left), studying for mission work in Africa, poses for this portrait with hat in hand.

Theological Institute, Tuscaloosa

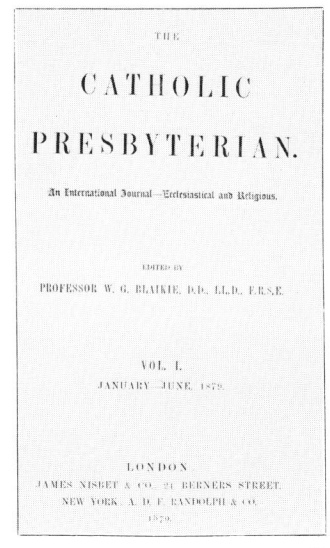

James McCosh

1876 An "Alliance of the Reformed Churches throughout the World holding the Presbyterian System" was founded largely through the efforts of Dr. James McCosh, Princeton College president, and Dr. Philip Schaff of Union Seminary, NY. The first conference met in London in 1876 with twenty-two churches represented. Dr. W. G. Blaikie of the Free Church of Scotland started the Alliance's publication, *The Catholic Presbyterian*, in 1879.

Moses Drury Hoge

Gen. Stonewall Jackson

Dr. Moses Drury Hoge of Second Church, Richmond, VA, successfully persuaded the Presbyterian Church in the United States to join the World Presbyterian Alliance in 1876. In this same period, Hoge delivered the dedicatory speech for the statue in Richmond of Confederate general and fellow Virginia Presbyterian "Stonewall" Jackson.

Stage, 1880 Presbyterian World Alliance Meeting

The Second General Council of the Presbyterian World Alliance convened in Philadelphia in September 1880. The Governor of Pennsylvania and the Mayor of Philadelphia held a reception for the conference. In his opening sermon, Rev. William Paxton of New York said: "We are not Catholics, but Catholic. We are not *the* Catholic Church, but a part of the great Universal Church of Jesus Christ."

Members, 1880 Presbyterian World Alliance Meeting

In Pittsburgh, members of the First Reformed Presbyterian Church settled their differences over their minister with the hurling of fists, hymnbooks, and a heavy cuspidor. It was not only amusing to the street crowd but to the editor of *The Police Gazette*, a tabloid which the clergy condemned as immoral. The editor, a Mr. Fox, reported such clerical incidents with relish and entitled this one, "Muscular Christianity." The illustration from his paper depicts "the liveliest prayer meeting ever held."

"Muscular Christianity"

DESIGN No. 2.

— FRONT ELEVATION —

— SIDE ELEVATION —

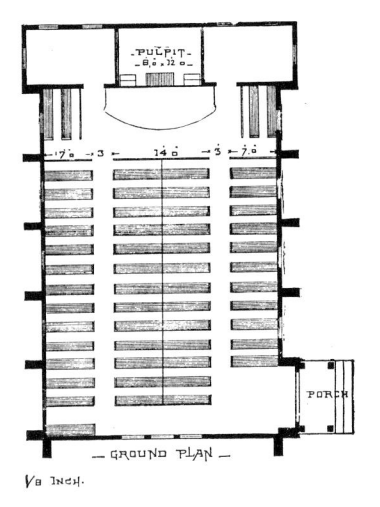

— GROUND PLAN —
⅛ INCH.

The Church Erection Board was established by the Old School Assembly in 1855 and was located in St. Louis. The New School Committee on Church Extension was located in Philadelphia. With reunion, the Board was moved to New York City where money for church buildings was collected and allocated. The Board listed contributions from the churches and also recommended architects and building designs.

Some churches went up, some came down. Pictured here is the Pine Ridge Presbyterian Church of Natchez, Mississippi, before and after it was struck by a tornado in 1880.

The Rocky Mountain Presbyterian

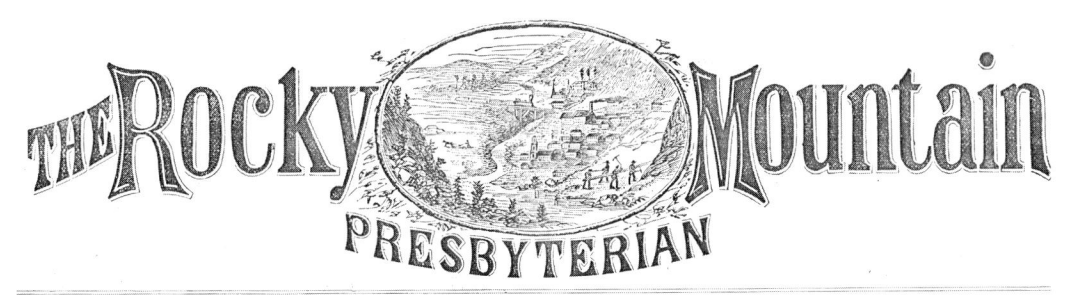

Sheldon Jackson, Editor.   DENVER, COLORADO, AUGUST, 1872.   VOL. 1, NO. 6.

Missions to the far West brought forth the brilliant and colorful, improvising and pioneering Sheldon Jackson (1834-1909). Known as "The Little Giant," he travelled over 26,000 miles a year between 1869 and 1881! After working in Wyoming, Montana, Idaho, Utah, and Arizona, he went to Alaska and founded the Alaska mission. One hundred churches owe their existence to his work and he helped organize eight northwest synods. Mrs. Mary E. James helped organize support for home missions.

Sheldon Jackson

Sheldon Jackson Chapel, Fairplay, CO

Mary E. James

The Brush Church, Phoenix, AZ

In Phoenix, AZ, Presbyterians worshipped in the "brush church" as early as 1878-79, when the church was organized. The first Presbyterian churches among the Indians of the Dakotas were organized in 1868, although the Synods of South and North Dakota were not constituted until 1884 and 1885, respectively. The Indian encampment (below) stood near Good Will Indian Mission, SD. Some Indians gather with the home missionary outside the manse near Porcupine.

Manse, Porcupine, SD

William Anderson Scott

Calvary Presbyterian Church

The Synod of the Pacific established San Francisco Theological Seminary in 1871 at the urging of the Reverend William Anderson Scott (1813-85). The Calvary Presbyterian Church founded by Scott provided the Seminary's first building and Scott served as Professor of Biblical and Ecclesiastical History there from 1870 to 1885. The first building of the Seminary served as the Japanese Presbyterian Church and the Young Men's Christian Association Building in 1896.

San Francisco Theological Seminary

133

1883 Members of the Third Presbyterian Church, Louisville, KY, enjoy a picnic in the 1880s. Relations between the PCUSA and the PCUS had not been a picnic during the days of Reconstruction. The wounds of the Civil War were deep, and aggravated by actions and attitudes of both denominations. Finally, after considerable negotiations and a recognition of mutuality, the General Assemblies approved fraternal relations and the exchange of official delegates in 1883. The long road to reconciliation was begun.

The evolution controversy triggered by Charles Darwin's studies, was just one of the problems which Presbyterians faced in the latter part of the century and made for turmoil, despite fraternal feelings between northerners and southerners. James Woodrow, an uncle of Woodrow Wilson, was Perkins Professor of Natural Science at Columbia Seminary. He cautiously supported an aspect of evolution, while at the same time affirming the authority of the Bible. He argued there was no contradiction between science and the Scriptures. During the 1880s Woodrow was constantly pressured to change his views. He refused and would not resign from the seminary staff. The PCUS Assembly finally forced Woodrow's removal. He went to teach at the University of South Carolina and became president there in 1894. Woodrow was just one who attempted to enter the dialogue between science and religion in these years.

James Woodrow

134

VII
THE AGE OF PRESBYTERIAN ENTERPRISE

1883-1906 During the "Gilded Age," Presbyterians were highly visible and played important parts in the birth of America's industrial society, supplying religious and political leadership and sanctions. Presidents, justices, and politicians, such as Grover Cleveland, Benjamin Harrison, William Strong, John Harlan, John Wanamaker, William Jennings Bryan moved naturally back and forth from life in government to that of the denomination. Presbyterians helped to shape and manage the growth of America's industrial empire at home and abroad, and supported Christian education and home and foreign missions, the growth of which is symbolized in the great new offices built at 157 Fifth Avenue in New York and the Witherspoon Building in Philadelphia. They did not always agree with one another about reform policies and practices during the "great barbecue" of America's natural and human resources.

Presbyterians produced their share of "robber barons" as well as "industrial statesmen." Justice Harlan's claim that the Constitution is color blind did not stop the rise of "Jim Crow" in South, North, East and West. Despite the great systematic theologies produced by Presbyterians after the Civil War, giving the impression of great assurance, the church engaged in heated discussions of the problem of biblical authority. The church amended the *Westminster Confession of Faith* in 1903 to clarify and to explain to the world that the denomination's constituents believed in God's love, the work of God's Spirit, and the importance of missions to a needy world.

The heralding angel (above) of the Second Presbyterian Church, Chicago, trumpets the good news of the Gospel and also the age of American enterprise, one center of which was Chicago. Decorator Frederic Clay Bartlett, designed the angel, while craftsmen in Florence, Italy hand-carved the baptismal font (left).

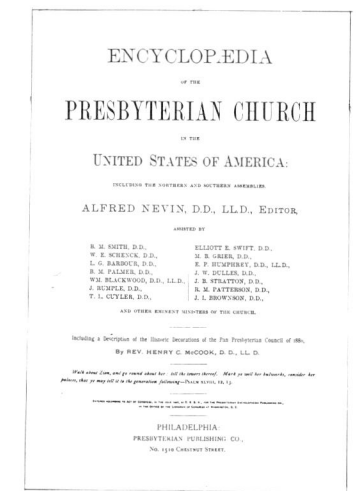

1884 Alfred Nevin published the massive *Encyclopedia of the Presbyterian Church in the United States of America* (1884). The editor, a pastor and religious journalist brought together an illustrated record of laity, clergy, missionaries, and various other aspects of Presbyterian history, north, south, east, and west, with considerable self-consciousness about that past and the Presbyterian place in the order of things.

The Reverend Samuel Burchard of the Murray Hill Presbyterian Church, New York City, was the "best abused" man in the United States in the 1884 election. Supporter of Republican James Blaine, Burchard maintained that the election had to do with "Rum Romanism, and Rebellion." The words incensed the Irish Catholic population and they may have voted for Burchard's fellow Presbyterian Grover Cleveland, a Democrat. The cartoon in *Judge* shows Burchard nursing his political bruises, condemned to a life of "Remorse, Repentance, and Ridicule."

Grover Cleveland (1837-1908), son of Richard Cleveland, a Presbyterian minister, was born in a parsonage at Caldwell, NJ. He served as a reforming mayor and governor of Buffalo and New York state, before running for President in 1884. Cleveland was charged with having an illicit relationship with Maria Halpin while mayor of New York.

Democrats were embarrassed by the ditty "Ma, Ma, where's my Pa? Gone to the White House, ha, ha, ha!" Cleveland was elected and was later married in the White House to Frances Folson by Byron Sunderland, pastor of the First Presbyterian Church, Washington, DC. The cartoon appeared in *Judge* in 1884.

"Ma, Ma, where's my Pa?"

President Cleveland at his desk

Bethany Presbyterian Church

Bethany Church Session

Philadelphia merchant and philanthropist, John Wanamaker (1838-1922) built one of the largest Sunday schools in the nation at the Bethany Presbyterian Church, Philadelphia, On Sundays over 2,000 teachers and scholars gathered to study. Elder Wanamaker was also an active supporter of the YMCA and the evangelistic campaigns of Dwight L. Moody. He served as a political adviser to Benjamin Harrison and was Postmaster General during the Harrison administration. He regularly returned to Philadelphia from Washington to superintend the Bethany Sunday School.

Bethany Church Sunday School Hall

Andrew Carnegie (1837-1919), an immigrant from Scotland, was proud of his rise from poverty to the position of one of the richest men in the world. He wrote in "Wealth" for the *North American Review* (1889) about the laws of individualism, competition, and accumulation. He also held it was disgraceful when a rich man died still possessing his riches. He and Mrs. Carnegie were leading philanthropists. While Mrs. Carnegie was a member of the Presbyterian Church, her husband was not. He acknowledged that the minister of Brick Presbyterian Church in New York was his pastor.

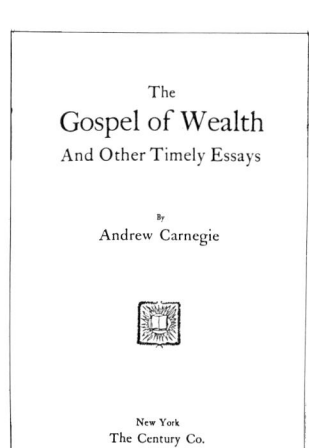

Andrew Carnegie

The
Gospel of Wealth
And Other Timely Essays

By
Andrew Carnegie

New York
The Century Co.
1900

George Westinghouse (1846-1914) and his wife are shown near the power plant of the Westinghouse Electric Company at Niagara Falls from which power was transmitted, marking the beginning of the Age of Electricity. The inventor and his wife, Marguerite Walker, made substantial contributions to the Presbyterian Church in the Pittsburgh area.

Judge Thomas Mellon (1813-1908) immigrated from Ireland in the middle of the nineteenth century and settled in Pittsburgh where he became a leader in public affairs and founded the Mellon fortune. The Mellons were leaders in the Presbyterian Church in the western part of Pennsylvania.

**Mellon Homestead
Castletown, No. Ireland**

Thomas Mellon

Louis H. Severance

Frederick Weyerhaeuser

Louis Henry Severance (1838-1913), Cleveland, OH, was a principal stockholder in the Standard Oil of Ohio. He made a fortune in chemicals and banking. He took a special interest in Presbyterian missions and supported hospitals in Japan, Korea, and India. He also helped in the rebuilding of the College of Wooster after a fire in 1901.

Contemporary Frederick Weyerhaeuser (1834-1914) was the German-born lumber-king of the northwestern United States, reportedly one of the wealthiest men in the world. Weyerhaeuser led a secluded life. A Lutheran turned Presbyterian, he and members of his family were active in the House of Hope congregation, St. Paul, MN, and gave support to Macalester College.

A steamship owner whose vessels plied the Pacific, Robert Dollar (1844-1932) contributed to the education of ministers by endowing professorships at San Francisco Theological Seminary where he was a trustee.

Robert Dollar

Henry & Lily Flagler

Memorial Church

Henry M. Flagler (1830-1913), son of a Presbyterian minister and partner of John D. Rockefeller, developed Florida as his province with the East Coast Railway Line. A Presbyterian elder, he built numerous churches including the Memorial Presbyterian Church of St. Augustine in Italian Renaissance architecture.

THE WORLD'S FIRST REAPER
Public Test of
Cyrus Hall McCormick's Invention
Steele's Tavern, Virginia, July 1831.

22

Haymarket Sq. Riot   24

Cyrus McCormick   23

Cyrus Hall McCormick (1809-1884), inventor and manufacturer, revolutionized farming with the McCormick reaper which he developed and tested in Steele's Tavern, VA, in 1831. McCormick, his wife, Nettie, and their family represented a strong Presbyterian influence in the windy city. The Haymarket Square riot, demonstrating labor unrest, took place outside of McCormick's plant. Presbyterians were so influential in Chicago affairs that one commentator called it a Presbyterian city.

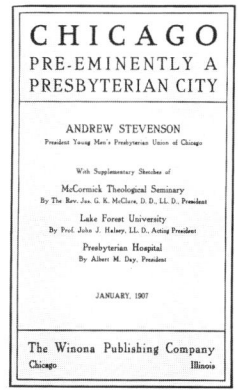

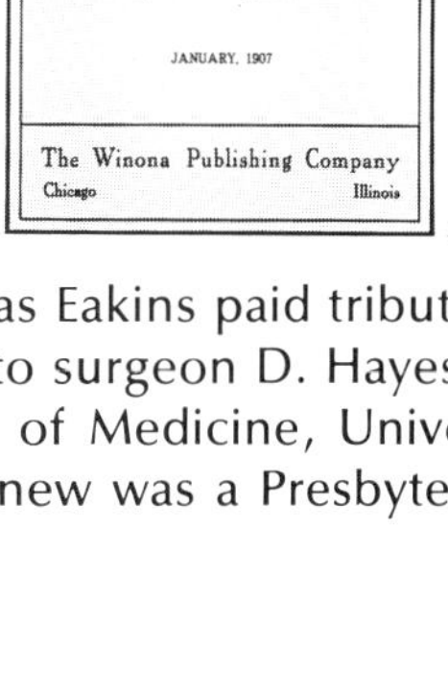

CHICAGO
PRE-EMINENTLY A
PRESBYTERIAN CITY

ANDREW STEVENSON
President Young Men's Presbyterian Union of Chicago

With Supplementary Sketches of

McCormick Theological Seminary
By The Rev. Jas. G. K. McClure, D. D., LL. D., President

Lake Forest University
By Prof. John J. Halsey, LL. D., Acting President

Presbyterian Hospital
By Albert M. Day, President

JANUARY, 1907

The Winona Publishing Company
Chicago   Illinois

25

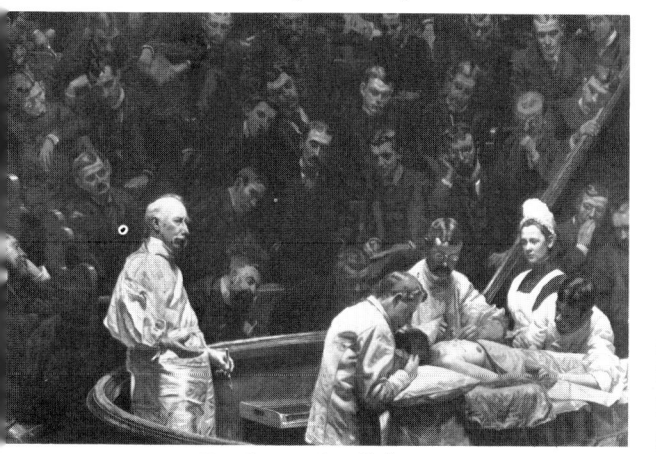

Dr. Agnew in clinique   26

Artist Thomas Eakins paid tribute in this painting of 1889 to surgeon D. Hayes Agnew of the Department of Medicine, University of Pennsylvania. Agnew was a Presbyterian layman.

1886 Cartoonists enjoyed poking fun at flamboyant Thomas DeWitt Talmage (1832-1902), pastor of the Central Presbyterian Church, Brooklyn. So numerous were his hearers that his congregation built large tabernacles to accommodate them. In *Puck* (1886), the cartoonist comments on Talmage's advice with regard to marriage in the age of enterprise. He warned men and women about being unequally yoked together.

T. DeWitt Talmage

"There is no worse predicament on earth than to be unequally yoked together."

"Sometimes you will find a man who so spreads himself over the sidewalk of life that there is no room for any one else."

"A woman had better live a lonely life a thousand years than be annexed to one of the many vultures with which our modern society is infested. These women, in their single blessedness, are angels."

"Don't marry a perfect man; I had two financial transactions with two perfect men, and they wofully cheated me."

Men are swindled; they make a bargain from a sample—

"And when the goods are delivered, they find they are not equal to the sample."

"Avoid an alliance with a man who despises the Christian religion. Marry him, and you will probably both go to hell together."

President Harrison speaking in New York, 1889

Grandson of President William H. Harrison, Benjamin Harrison (1833-1901), observed the bicentennial of the Constitution of the United States in 1889 by going to New York to speak where George Washington had taken the oath of office one hundred years before. From Indiana, a Republican, Harrison did not impress the cartoonist of *Puck*. Just as his grandfather's hat was too big for his head, so the artist thought that Harrison was too little for the presidential chair.

Harrison took an active part in the life of the religious community. He taught Sunday school at the First Presbyterian Church of Indianapolis. When he died the congregation installed a Tiffany window as a memorial to a favorite son.

Centennial General Assembly Medallion 1888

Harrison Memorial Window

Forward

VOL. I.   JANUARY, 1882.   No. 1.

Presbyterians gave considerable attention to youth work. The PCUSA attempted to keep in touch with its youth through *Forward*, a periodical devoted to youth concerns. Lucy Craft Laney (1854-1933) was a black educator, daughter of slaves, whose father was a Presbyterian minister. Laney developed a school for black children in Augusta, GA, which she named after Frances E. H. Haines, a PCUSA church leader. From small beginnings in 1886 the Haines Normal Institute grew into an educational enterprise of more than a thousand students. John McCullough (1805-1870) and Benjamin W. Chidlaw (1811-1892) travelled the country as Sunday school missionaries planting Sunday schools across the Midwest and the South.

Lucy C. Laney

John McCullough

Benjamin W. Chidlaw

Sue McBeth's School

Sue L. McBeth

Susan Law McBeth (1830-1893) was born in Scotland, grew up in Ohio, and spent her life in Indian territory among the Nez Perces in Lapwai, Idaho. She devoted herself to raising the religious, moral, and educational level of the people. She gave much time to the development of a Nez Perces dictionary. Through her theological school she trained native ministers. James Hayes, one of her graduates, preached for years to western tribes. She also organized church life. The photograph taken by McBeth shows the first women's missionary society in Idaho.

James Hayes

First Women's Missionary Society in Idaho, 1891

Sheldon Jackson, "The St. Paul of America," a planter of churches in the West, was General Agent of Education in Alaska by 1885. Jackson's concern for Alaska began in 1877, but it was not until 1884 that the Presbyterian Church took note of the area. In 1877 Jackson had left his friend, Amanda McFarland, in Fort Wrangell to found a school, later moved to Sitka. For the rest of his life Jackson was "The Bishop of all Beyond" in Alaska. He was responsible for the introduction of reindeer into the area in 1891 to provide a source of food and clothing. He also introduced the public schools. In 1897 Jackson was elected Moderator of the General Assembly. The picture below shows the First Presbyterian Church, Juneau, and is a part of the extensive photographic collection which Jackson left as a record of life in the North.

Sheldon Jackson 41

Jackson landing reindeer, Pt. Clarence, 1892 42

Amanda McFarland 43

Presbyterian Church, Juneau, AK 44

1889 Cumberland Presbyterian Nolin Presbytery ordained Mrs. Louisa M. Woosley, the first woman to become a Presbyterian minister. For two decades the Cumberland General Assembly refused to recognize her ordination. Woosley argued her case in a book, *Shall Women Preach?* (1891). George P. Hays, one-time Moderator of the PCUSA General Assembly, demonstrated changing attitudes in his *May Women Speak?* (1889), and answered affirmatively.

Nettie McCormick, wife of Cyrus, active in her husband's business after the Chicago fire, carried on philanthropic interests. She supported McCormick Theological Seminary. McCormick Seminary, founded in 1829 in Hanover, IN, moved to Chicago in 1859 and expanded its campus and influence in the Chicago environment. Fowler Hall bears the name of Mrs. McCormick's family.

Nettie McCormick

Fowler Hall, McCormick Theological Seminary

Union Theological Seminary also benefited from McCormick generosity. It moved from rural Virginia to Richmond in 1896. Under the leadership of W. W. Moore it became a leader in theological education in the South.

Union Theological Seminary, VA

Austin Presbyterian Seminary was founded in 1902.

Austin Presbyterian Seminary

147

B. B. Warfield 50    A. A. Hodge 51

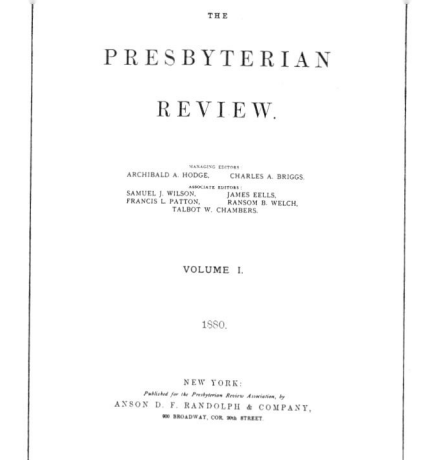

52

1892 In the era of good feelings after the Old School-New School reunion of 1869, Princeton Theological Seminary and Union Theological Seminary, NY, cooperated in publishing the *Presbyterian Review*. A. A. Hodge of Princeton and Charles Briggs of Union edited the journal. In a series of articles on "higher criticism" of the Bible, Hodge, and his colleague, theologian B. B. Warfield, argued that the Bible in its original autographs was without error, a position which Briggs could not support. He accused his colleagues of an "orthodoxism" which was not truly Presbyterian. His own biblical views led to a heresy trial in which he was acquitted by New York Presbytery. He was then suspended by the General Assembly. Union withdrew from the jurisdiction of the PCUSA, and Briggs went into the Episcopal ministry. The General Assembly meeting in Portland, adopted the Princeton position of biblical inerrancy as that of the denomination. The portrait of the Union Theological Seminary, NY, faculty was taken in 1888. Briggs is in the center, standing, while Philip Schaff is seated, second from the left. Briggs wanted the church to go in his direction, but James McCosh was not sure what that meant.

Union Theological Seminary, NY, Faculty, 1888

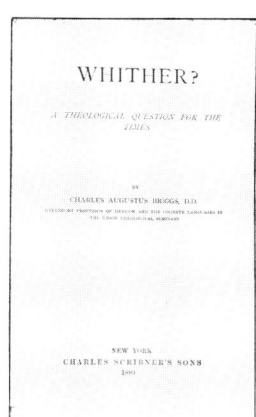

54

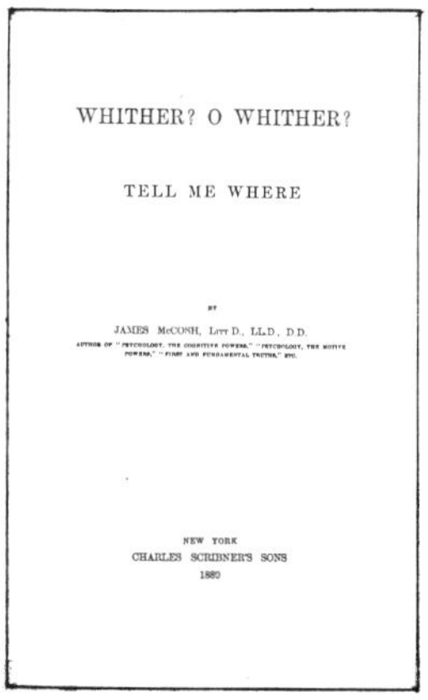

53

55

J. H. Barrows

1893 Because of interests in missions and other religions, John Henry Barrows, pastor of the First Presbyterian Church, Chicago, helped to organize the World Parliament of Religions in connection with the World's Columbian Exposition. This gathering brought to the country representatives of the major world religions. Charles Briggs and Philip Schaff offered addresses at the meeting. The latter who could not deliver his presentation because of illness, made an appeal for the "Reunion of Christendom." He suggested that the Pope might call an ecumenical council in Jerusalem for such a purpose. As for Barrows, he invited Buddhists to his church and preached about "Christ the Wonderful."

World Parliament of Religions

Architect Henry H. Richardson made Romanesque architecture popular in the latter part of the century. The congregation of the First Presbyterian Church of Detroit followed this trend and built their new church in 1889 in the form of a Greek Cross with a central pulpit with choir stalls behind it. The architects were George Mason and Zachariah Rice, imitators of the Richardson style.

First Presbyterian Church Detroit

F. F. Ellinwood

1895 Foreign missions became a larger enterprise after the Civil War. In 1895 Presbyterians completed a modern office building in New York City long known as 156 Fifth Avenue and as the headquarters of the Board. The Rev. Frank F. Ellinwood served as secretary of the agency from 1871-1907. In 1883 the Women's General Missionary Society organized and gave the mission work of the UPCNA a great impulse.

156 5th Ave. NYC

Board of Directors, Women's General Missionary Society

Charles William Forman (1821-1894), a minister from Kentucky, went to India in 1847, and worked among Bengali Christians establishing a college in 1886 which afterward became the Forman Christian College. Forman was the first of a large family to serve under the Board in India.

Emma Dean Anderson sailed for the Punjab in India in 1881. A member of the UPCNA, she served in India for fifty-six years. Because of her mission to homeless women her fame spread widely, and her name became a household word among Presbyterians of her denomination.

C. W. Forman

Emma Anderson & Children

Forman Christian College

John H. Converse, Philadelphia, and the Bryn Mawr Presbyterian Church supported the work of William J. Wanless, MD, in Miraj, India. A Canadian by birth, knighted by King George V, Wanless went out under the PCUSA Board of Foreign Missions in 1889 and developed medical care for many Indians.

Wanless Hospital, Miraj, India

William J. Wanless

151

Calvin & Julia Mateer

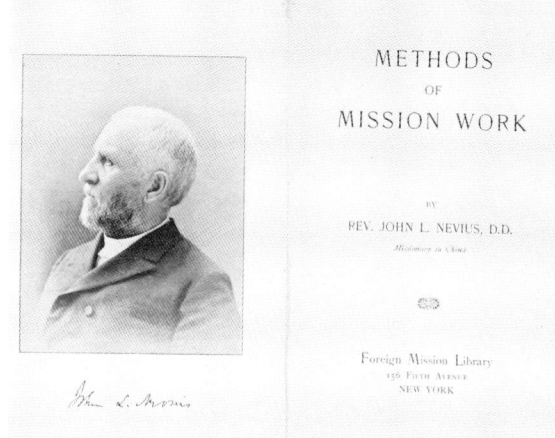

Anna Safford

American Presbyterians committed mission resources to the conversion of China. John L. Nevius (1829-1893) served in China from 1854-1893, and held that missionaries ought to concentrate on Bible study and the development of self-governing, self-supporting, and self-propagating Chinese churches as soon as possible. Calvin Wilson Mateer (1836-1908) and his wife engaged in education and founded a school which became Shantung Christian University. They were concerned that missionaries and Chinese ministers set high standards of competence for themselves.

An artist painted a picture of Anna Safford, a PCUS missionary to China being transported by Chinese carriers. Hampton C. DuBose, another PCUS missionary, carried on a fight against the drug traffic, organizing the National Anti-Opium League in 1896. Absalom and Carrie Sydenstricker, from West Virginia, spent their lives as evangelists in China. Pearl is shown in the picture below to the left of her father, and as she instructs Chinese girls in English, and a warning about black rats.

Sydenstrickers & Aurah

H. C. DuBose

Pearl Sydenskricker with class

Horace Grant Underwood and his wife, Lillias, helped to establish the Presbyterian mission in Korea beginning in 1884-1885. Ecumenical in spirit, the Underwoods promoted the Nevius plan for a self-propagating, self-governing, and self-supporting, Korean Church. In addition they encouraged education, especially of physicians and nurses. Lillias Underwood, a doctor, pioneered in medical work.

Horace Underwood

Lillas Underwood

L. H. Severance donated funds for the Korean hospital which bore his name.

James Curtis Hepburn (1815-1911) was one of the earliest missionaries to Japan. Although a physician, he also engaged in writing tracts and in translating the Scriptures into Japanese, a copy of which he presented to the emperor in 1872. For his thirty-three years of work for the Japanese people the emperor decorated him on his nintieth birthday. Robert Eugenius McAlpine of Alabama pioneered in missions for the PCUS in Japan.

James C. Hepburn

McAlpine Family

Stephen and Mary Mattoon started their work as missionaries in Thailand where they served in the middle of the nineteenth century. Upon return to the United States following the Civil War, the Mattoons served at Biddle Institute in North Carolina in educating blacks for service in the churches.

Stephen and Mary Mattoon

1898 Missionary Conference

As the foreign mission work of the church grew so did the attempt to orient missionaries to the fields in which they were to serve. The first outgoing missionary conference of the PCUSA took place in 1898. The participants posed for their pictures. A young Robert E. Speer sits on the floor in front of the group. Speer was appointed secretary of the board in 1891 after study at Princeton University and Theological Seminary. A layman, he had a decisive impact upon the board which he guided. The PCUS board located in Nashville, TN, began publication of a monthly to stimulated interest in foreign missions among children.

154

To meet the challenge of the new industrial order, Robert E. Thompson (1844-1924), Presbyterian minister and professor of political economy at the University of Pennsylvania, published *De Civitate Dei. The Divine Order of Human Society* (1891). He sounded a social note against the individualism of the times, and argued that Christianity provided an integrating principle for the age of enterprise.

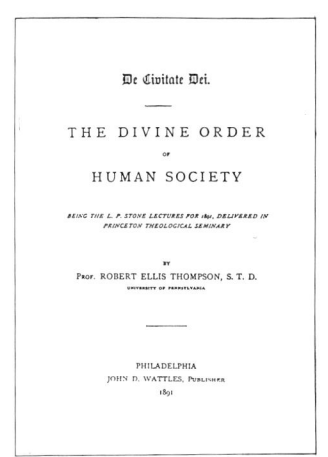

Robert E. Thompson

Parkhurst bests Tammany

Charles Parkhurst

Charles Parkhurst (1842-1933), pastor of the Madison Square Presbyterian Church in New York City and a contemporary of Thompson, crusaded for better government. So successful was he and his companions in New York in challenging the corruption of Tammany Hall that the voters elected a reform administration in the 1890s. Parkhurst preached a sermon in 1892 about collusion of police with crime, a charge which gained him national notoriety. The cartoonist in *Puck* shows him triumphant after chopping off the Tammany Tiger tail.

Madison Sq. Church

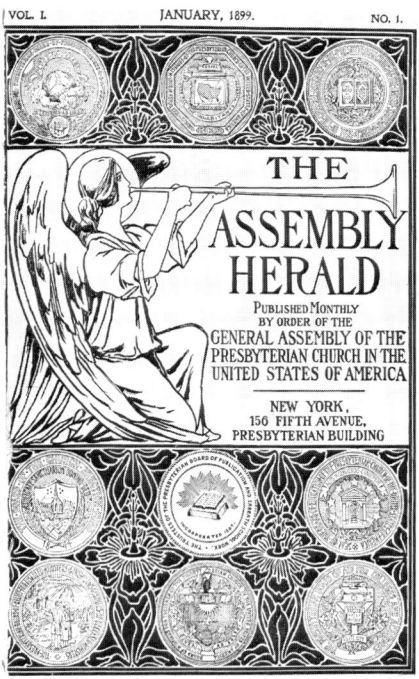

1897 The Witherspoon Building of Philadelphia with its statues of John Witherspoon, James Caldwell, and Samuel Davies, Francis Makemie, John McMillan, and Marcus Whitman demonstrated the growth of American life as well as of American Presbyterianism. The statues now are at the Presbyterian Historical Society. The building became the headquarters of the Stated Clerk of the General Assembly, the board for Christian education, and the Board of Pensions. The *Assembly Herald* kept the constituency of the denomination aware of what the various agencies were doing. Year by year General Assemblies, called to order with the moderator's gavel, gave direction to enlarged ecclesiastical enterprises.

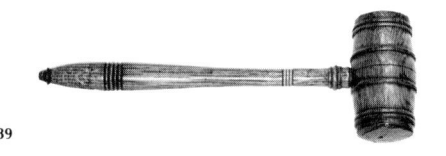

The quest for order in an increasingly industrial society, made its impact upon the churches. Among Presbyterians the office of the Stated Clerk took on more importance. In the PCUS, Joseph Ruggles Wilson held this position from 1865 to 1898. A pastor and professor he exercised considerable power in the affairs of the denomination. He is shown here with members of his family and household. Woodrow Wilson is seated at the left. William Henry Roberts (1844-1920) exercised his responsibilities as Stated Clerk of the PCUSA from 1884 to 1920, and laid the foundation for the influence of that office not only in denominational business, but also in the ecumenical church.

William H. Roberts

The Wilson Family

Louis F. Benson

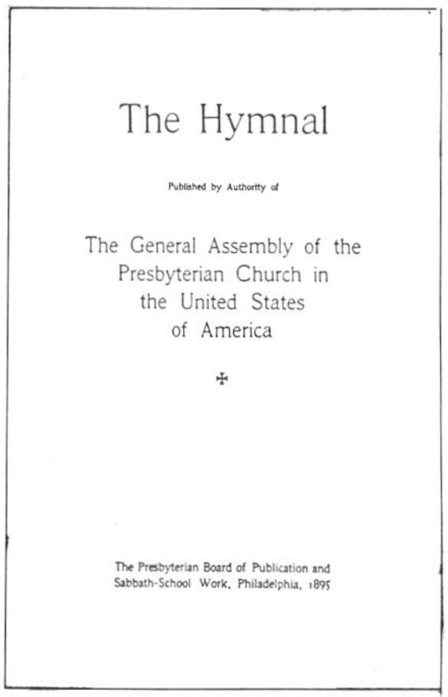

The Hymnal

Published by Authority of

The General Assembly of the
Presbyterian Church in
the United States
of America

✢

The Presbyterian Board of Publication and
Sabbath-School Work, Philadelphia, 1895

Louis Fitzgerald Benson (1855-1930), a PCUSA minister of Philadelphia, took an interest in improving worship. Benson edited an official hymnal for the denomination in 1895, a book which became the model for succeeding volumes. Along with Henry Van Dyke of New York City, he formed the Church Service Society in 1897 to give direction to new liturgical interests following the concerns of Robert Baird in the 1850s.

William E. Dodge

The Dodge family played a prominent role in the life of America and the religious community for generations. William E. Dodge (1805-1883) built his family fortune in tin and copper, and participated in numerous reform movements. Son of David Low Dodge, one of the founders of the peace movement in America, such concerns came naturally to him, and also to his daughter Grace Hoadley Dodge (1856-1914). Influenced by Dwight L. Moody, she devoted her time and her considerable fortune to the YWCA and educational causes. She, too, was a Presbyterian. Cleveland Hoadley Dodge, son of William E. and brother of Grace, expanded the family fortune in the Phelps Dodge Corporation. He expressed his interest in Presbyterian missions, among other things, especially in the Middle East.

Grace Dodge (center)

Cleveland Dodge

William Strong

William Strong (1808-1895), Associate Justice of the Supreme Court, was one of the most active laymen of his day. He lectured on religion and law at Union Theological Seminary, NY, and participated in the process which led to the amendment of the *Westminster Confession of Faith* in 1903.

1895-1896 For American blacks these years were fraught with important events. Frederick Douglass died in 1895 and a great company of people crowded into the Central Presbyterian Church, Rochester, NY, to mourn the passing of a great American advocate of justice. George Washington Cable (1844-1925), a deacon at the Prytania Street Presbyterian Church, New Orleans, LA, a novelist who wrote of Cajuns and Creoles, protested the treatment of blacks in the convict lease system which virtually reduced them to slavery. He complained of the "silent south" in face of the "negro question" and obvious mistreatment of the race.

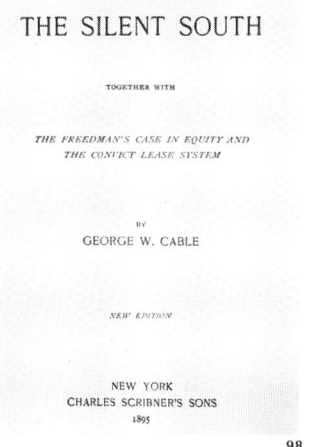

George Cable

Frederick Douglass' Funeral

John M. Harlan

Associate Justice of the Supreme Court, John M. Harlan (1833-1911), an elder in the New York Avenue Presbyterian Church, teacher of the Harlan Bible Class, argued in a dissent to *Plessy v. Ferguson* (1896) that the Constitution of the United States was color blind. He protested the majority opinion of the court that blacks could be separate, but equal in the life of the nation.

William J. Bryan

THE SACRILEGIOUS CANDIDATE

1896 William Jennings Bryan electrified the Democratic National Convention of 1896 with his famous "Cross of Gold" speech and won the nomination of the party for the presidency. He was dubbed "The Sacrilegious Candidate" by the cartoonist in *Judge*, although he was a Presbyterian layman. Bryan was a "populist" in leanings who campaigned against the gold standard. He carried his message to the people. The whistle stop is in Montgomery, WV during the political debate.

Women's Executive Committee of Home Missions

Charles L. Thompson

Frances E. H. Haines

Charles Lemuel Thompson (1839-1924), received his first commission from the Board of Domestic Missions in 1862, and later served as General Secretary of the Board of Home Missions from 1898 to 1914. He was an ecumenist and helped to found the Home Mission Council to coordinate the work of the American Protestant community. Frances E. H. Haines was the first secretary of the Woman's Executive Committee of Home Missions, and introduced business methods into the work. The staff of the executive committee sits for its portrait sometime toward the end of the century.

William H. Schureman (1853-1941), with camping outfit and organ, brought the bread of life to the people of Wyoming and Colorado during the last years of the nineteenth century. He was a Sunday School Missionary under the Presbyterian Board of Publication and Sabbath School Work.

1899 Waldensians settled in Valdese, NC, in 1893. Charles Albert Tron was the first pastor of the Italian immigrant congregation which dedicated its church building on July 4th, 1899. The person who put up the flag over the entrance to the church was so excited on the occasion that the stars are flown upside down. The Waldensians have been closely associated with Presbyterians of the state.

Charles A. Tron

Members of the First Armenian Presbyterian Church of Fresno, CA, built this house of worship in 1901, shortly after they had organized as a congregation and been received into the Presbytery of Stockton. Author William Saroyan, son of a Presbyterian pastor, attended this congregation during his early days in the state.

Presbyterian work among Hispanics in the American Southwest grew with the planting of churches and schools. Miss Rebecca Meeker, a teacher, stands on the top of an adobe building which doubled as a church and a school, while her father and sister and friends pose in front of the bell tower, Truchas, NM. Matilda Allison was superintendent of a boarding and industrial school for girls, 1881-1903, in Santa Fe, a school later named Allison-James in her honor.

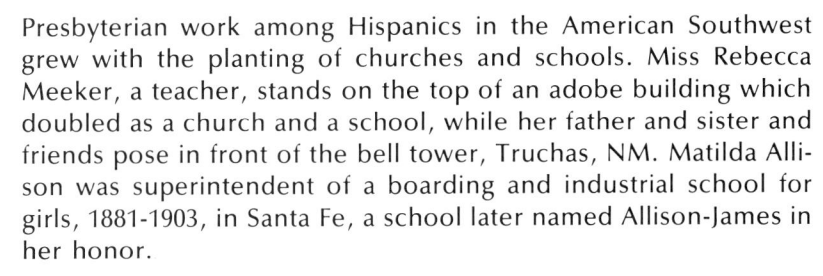

Matilda Allison

The Presbytery of Puerto Rico (below) was organized in September, 1902, indicating Presbyterian presence in the American territory.

1900 A great ecumenical missionary conference was held in New York City to assess the past and plan for the future. Christian and American interests were sometimes thought of as the same. Benjamin Harrison was the honorary chairman and is pictured here in an opening session. Presbyterian James Dennis (1842-1914), author of the three volume analysis, *Christian Mission and Social Progress* (1887, 1899, 1906), was one of the planners of the meeting. So was Arthur Judson Brown (1856-1963) who was a secretary of the Board of Foreign Missions (PCUSA) from 1895-1929.

The Ecumenical Conference
New York, 1900

William M. Paden (1854-1931) carried on his missionary activities among the Mormons of the Rocky Mountain district. From 1897 to 1912 he was the pastor of the First Presbyterian Church, Salt Lake City. Protest against polygamy led to a prohibition of its practice. The *Home Mission Monthly* pictured the Utah Gospel Mission Wagons.

Committee for Revision of the Creed

1903 For many years a number of Presbyterians tried to revise the *Westminster Confession of Faith* to deal with some of the fresh insights which they believed God had given into the Scriptures since the Confession was written in the seventeenth century. Under the leadership of a Committee of Twenty-One, including both Benjamin Harrison and John M. Harlan, the PCUSA finally adopted chapters "Of the Holy Spirit," "Of the Gospel of the Love of God and Missions," and deleted references in the Confession to the pope at Rome as the "antichrist." The PCUS adopted these same amendments in 1943.

Abraham Kuyper

W. A. Brown & Sons

The theological divisions within American Presbyterians may be gauged by European visitors to America during these years. Abraham Kuyper, famous Dutch theologian and statesman, delivered the Stone Lectures at Princeton Theological Seminary in 1898, while Adolf Harnack, German historian, visited Union Theological Seminary, NY. William Adams Brown was Harnack's host on the occasion. Brown (1865-1943), a Presbyterian minister and professor at the seminary, thought of himself as a mediating thinker, as indicated in his *Christian Theology in Outline* (1906).

C. E. San Francisco Rally 121

Monmouth College Baseball Team 122

The future belonged to the young. The UPCNA helped to organize its young people as the Young People's Christian Union which met on the campus of Monmouth College in 1889. A number of Monmouth College students were enthusiastic about baseball on the campus as this picture of the team of the 1880s illustrates. Many Presbyterian churches were caught up in the activities of the Christian Endeavor, founded as an interdenominational movement. It held a large rally in San Francisco at the end of the century. PCUS youth met at Lookout Mountain, TN, and posed precariously for a picture. At the beginning of the new century, Presbyterians assessed their callings and responsibilities in the work of the body of Christ.

123

PCUSA Youth, Lookout Mtn.

Students from Trinity College, San Antonio, huddle for football. A coed was ready to cheer them on.

124

125

166

VIII
THE CHURCH'S WORK AND THEOLOGICAL CONFLICT

Maria Peel

1906-1930 Earthquakes shook San Francisco in 1906–and earthquakes shook Presbyterian institutions. Presbyterians opened the twentieth century by adopting a *Book of Common Worship,* and by observing a reunion between a portion of the Cumberland Presbyterian Church and the Presbyterian Church in the United States of America. World War I, another kind of earthquake, shocked western society. For a moment it hid some of the theological tensions known as the "Fundamentalist-Modernist" controversy among Presbyterians. By affirming the Reformed tradition found in the *Westminster Confession of Faith,* and allowing liberty of interpretation of some controverted points, Presbyterian leaders kept the PCUSA from a major division in the 1920s and 1930s. During the "roaring twenties" Presbyterians expended considerable efforts to do the church's work in new urban settings, in rural areas, and among various portions of the populations, and to do so in cooperation with other Protestant denominations through the newly organized Federal Council of Churches. Presbyterian laity made notable contributions in the spheres of politics, journalism, and music. Women finally won the right to be ordained as elders, and attended the General Assembly as commissioners for the first time in 1931. An economic earthquake shook the nation and the world in 1929, and Presbyterians had to face the deepening Depression during the years that followed.

1906 In 1892 San Francisco Theological Seminary dedicated buildings in its new location in Marin County's Ross Valley. In 1906 the earthquake which devastated San Francisco shook the seminary. The library, Scott Hall (left), had to be repaired.

Mrs. Maria Peel (above), member of the Bardstown Road Presbyterian Church, Louisville, KY, started attending Sunday School in the first decade of the twentieth century. She collected seventy-two bars as awards for her perfect attendance record to the year 1981 when this picture was taken as a senior citizen.

1906 In 1810 a major division occurred among American Presbyterians when some organized into a separate denomination called the Cumberland Presbyterian Church. In the first decade of the twentieth century this breach was healed, in part, when the Cumberlands and the Presbyterian Church in the United States of America came together in Columbus, OH, in 1907. From the perspective of many this reunion was possible because of amendments to the *Westminster Confession* in 1903. Ira Landrith (left), a native of Texas and editor of the *Cumberland Presbyterian,* was moderator of the Cumberlands in 1906, while the noted missionary from China, Hunter Corbett (center), was the moderator of the PCUSA for that year. William Henry Roberts (right), Stated Clerk of the General Assembly of the PCUSA, was elected moderator to preside over the 1907 meeting of the reunited church. When the vote was taken in 1906, about one third of the Cumberland Presbyterians declined to enter the new ecumenical adventure.

1907 General Assembly, Columbus, OH

Ira Landrith ³    Hunter Corbett ⁴    William H. Roberts ⁵

Henry Van Dyke

1906 Concerned for liturgical renewal, Henry Van Dyke (1852-1933) led the movement for *The Book of Common Worship* which the General Assembly (PCUSA) adopted "For Voluntary Use" in 1906. This book contained orders for regular and special services, a Treasury of Prayers, Psalter, and collection of ancient hymns and canticles. Van Dyke, pastor of Brick Presbyterian Church, NY, and professor at Princeton University, wrote the words of the hymn "Joyful, joyful, we adore thee."

Emily Bissell initiated the anti-tuberculosis Christmas Seal program in America. A charter member of the Westminster Presbyterian Church, Wilmington, Delaware, and social worker, Mrs. Bissell bought the first seal from the American Red Cross in 1907.

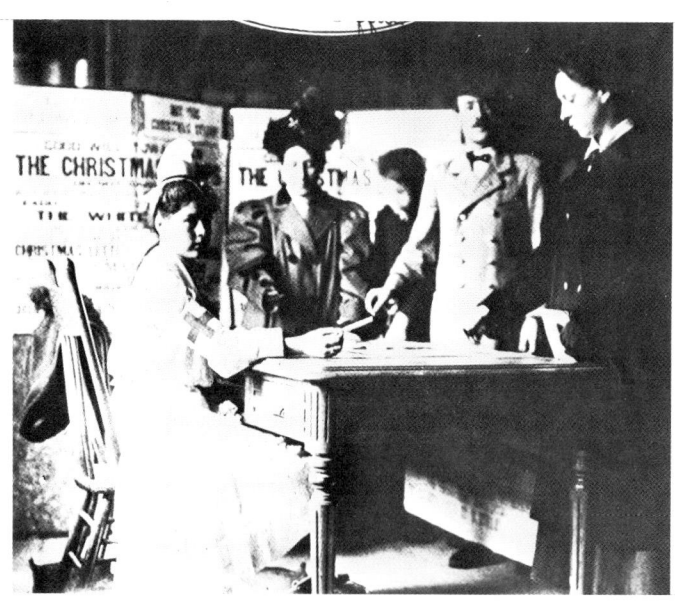

Federal Council of Churches
Organizational Meeting
Philadelphia, PA, 1908

Samuel J. Niccolls

1908 Presbyterians joined with delegates from thirty-three other denominations to organize the Federal Council of Churches of Christ in Philadelphia. The members joined "to manifest the essential oneness of the Christian Churches in America in Jesus Christ as their divine Lord and Savior, and to promote the spirit of fellowship, services and cooperation among them for the prosecution of work that can be better done in unison." Samuel J. Niccolls, pastor of the Second Presbyterian Church in St. Louis, was a Presbyterian delegate to the meeting and introduced the word "divine" into the simple confessional commitment of all member denominations. William Henry Roberts, moderator of the General Assembly (PCUSA) in 1907, was Acting Chairman of the Council in 1908. Following the pattern of the Council's "Social Creed," in 1910 the denomination adopted a pronouncement which acknowledged wealth to be a trust, for a more equitable distribution of riches, abatement of poverty, and other modifications of the industrial order to make it more just. The *Amethyst*, official organ of the church, carried a prayer for temperance by Walter Rauschenbusch, prophet of the "Kingdom of God," on its May, 1912 cover.

The Reverend Samuel Lapsley (1886-1892) of Selma, Al, and William H. Sheppard (1865-1927), son of Waynesboro, VA, slaves, helped establish the American Presbyterian Congo Mission in 1889. Lapsley was stricken with fever and died a few years after his arrival in Africa. As a memorial to his pioneering work, the PCUS raised money for a mission boat for use in the Congo. It was named the Lapsley. Children's Bands—one shown here from Asheville, NC, 1904—contributed pennies which were used to purchase the boat.

"The Lapsley"

William H. Sheppard & Family

Sheppard, a graduate of Stillman College and pictured with his family, worked in the Congo for twenty years. Because of his writings and observations, the Royal Geographic Society of London elected him a fellow. Sheppard was popular with the Congolese among whom he worked to evangelize.

1909 William McCutchan Morrison (1867-1918), from Lexington, VA, a graduate of Washington and Lee University and the Presbyterian Theological Seminary in Louisville, KY, joined Sheppard in the Congo. A linguist of considerable skill, he composed a grammar and dictionary of African dialects and translated parts of the Bible. He and Sheppard made public and called world attention to cruel oppression and the destruction of the country's resources carried on by the agents of King Leopold of Belgium who controlled the Congo. The Kasai Company which exploited Africans in the production of rubber brought Morrison and Sheppard to trial in 1909 for libel, a suit the missionaries won. The missionaries' cause gained support in the British Parliament and the United States Senate. Even Mark Twain had a good word to say for the missionaries, champions of Africans against economic exploitation.

William M. Morrison

Charles Stelzle (1869-1941) told of his struggle with poverty in his book, *A Son of the Bowery*. Mechanic turned minister, he organized the Workingman's Department of the PCUSA in 1903 and also Labor Temple in New York City. There he carried on a mission among the laborers and their families. The Temple carried on a full program for people, many immigrants, lost in the urban environment. Stelzle also supported the temperance movement against the saloon as part of his plan for a better social order. In 1912 he wrote a volume on behalf of workers which he entitled *The Gospel of Labor*, a response to Carnegie's views on the "gospel of wealth."

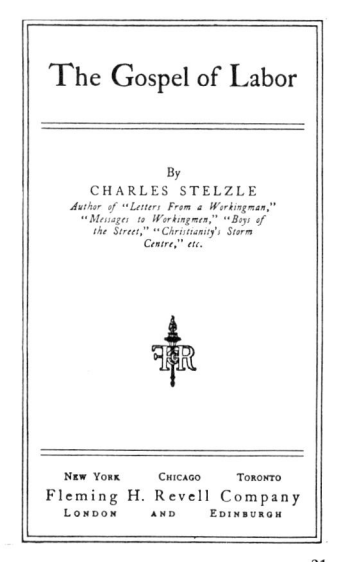

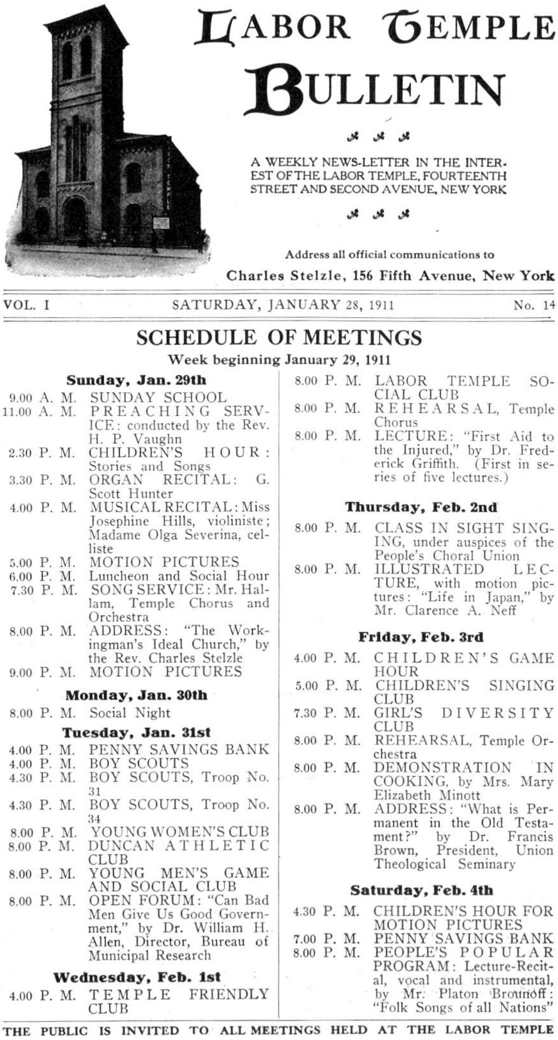

174

John J. Eagan

Sociologist Edward Alsworth Ross grew up in a Presbyterian household and on the *Westminster Shorter Catechism*. From it he learned a definition of sin. He attempted to adapt the doctrine of sin to the industrial age and the corporate practices of business in his book *Sin and Society* (1907).

John J. Eagan (1870-1923) served as elder of Central Presbyterian Church, Atlanta, and superintendent of the Sunday School. He was also president of American Caste Iron Pipe Company, Birmingham, AL. He tried to conduct business enterprises as a responsible Christian after the goals set forth by the Federal Council of Churches in 1908. He also headed the first biracial councils which attempted to build bridges between the races in the South and across the country after World War I. ACIPCO employees erected a statue in tribute of him in Birmingham.

Alexander McKelway

Alexander Jeffrey McKelway, III, was a minister of the PCUS and an editor of the *Presbyterian Standard*. In 1906 he became secretary of the National Child Labor Committee to push for legislation to protect children from the harsh practices of industry.

175

Warren Wilson College 28

Warren Wilson (1867-1937), a minister of the PCUSA, guided the churches in their effort to meet the needs of people in rural America at a time of rapid industrial growth. He headed the Department of Rural Church of the Board of National Missions and established the school later named Warren Wilson College outside of Asheville, NC, to offer higher education to the young people of Appalachia.

Warren H. Wilson 27

Henry A., Henry C., & Henry Wallace

29

Henry Wallace (1836-1916, seated right), his son, Henry Cantwell Wallace (standing), and his grandson, Henry Agard Wallace, were Iowa farmers. The senior Wallace was a UPCNA minister, and Henry Cantwell was an active member of the denomination. They edited *Wallaces' Farmer*, a weekly journal which promoted "Good farming, clear thinking, and right living." For years Henry Wallace contributed Sabbath school lessons for his readers. Henry Cantwell and Henry Agard became Secretary of Agriculture.

30

E. O. Guerrant

E. O. Guerrant (1838-1916), a Kentuckian and minister of the PCUS, was a pioneer missionary in the Appalachian Mountains. He spent his life as an evangelist-at-large and leader of the Society of Soul Winners until his death in the second decade of the century. His work was carried on by Sunday school missionaries shown praying with a family on the porch of their home.

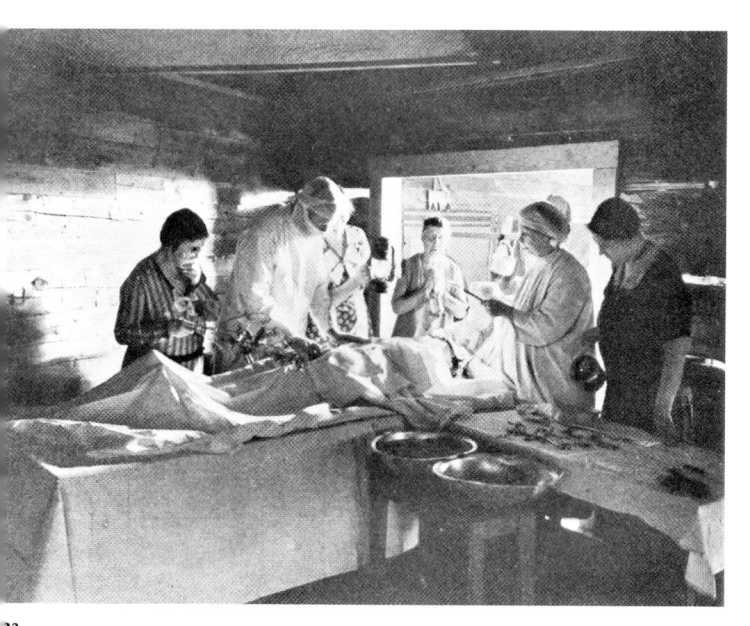

In the Blue Ridge Mountains of North Carolina Dr. Eustace Sloop and his wife, Dr. Mary T. M. Sloop, offered medical care for mountain people. They settled in Crossnore, NC, in 1911. They are shown operating in a cabin under difficult conditions.

Presbyterians gather in the 1920s near Colcord, WV, for a baptism by immersion.

The Fundamentals

A Testimony

Volume I

Compliments of
Two Christian Laymen

Lyman Stewart

Milton Stewart

1910 In the attempt to define the faith in light of the contemporary intellectual ferment, Lyman and Milton Stewart, Presbyterians, and owners of the Union Oil Company of Los Angeles, CA, financed the publication of *The Fundamentals* in 1910. They distributed three million copies to pastor, professor, missionary student, and other church leaders in the English-speaking world. American Presbyterians B. B. Warfield, Robert E. Speer, Charles R. Erdman, professor, Princeton Theological Seminary and John Timothy Stone, pastor of the Fourth Presbyterian Church, Chicago, contributed to the interdenominational venture.

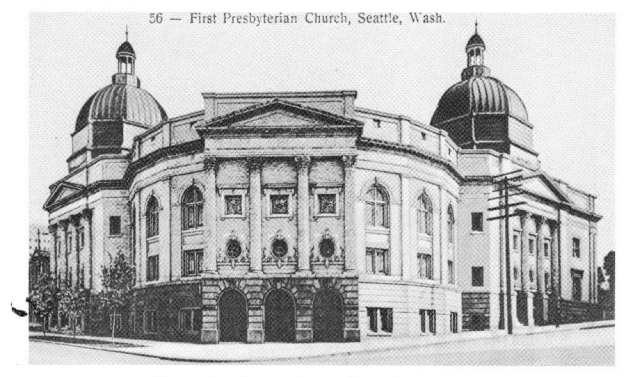

First Presbyterian Church, Seattle

Mark Allison Matthews (1867-1940), born in Georgia, built the First Presbyterian Church, Seattle, Washington, into the largest Presbyterian Church in the nation in 1912 with an average attendance at Sunday School of 4,000 pupils weekly. Matthews ran a radio station and tried to serve the needs of the community. A theological conservative, he tried to hold back the tides of liberalism within the church, and dismissed women who sought ordination as a "freak class."

Mark Matthews

Louise Carnegie [40]   William P. Merrill [41]

William P. Merrill (1867-1954) pastor of the Brick Presbyterian Church, NY, presided over the founding of the Church Peace Union in 1914. Supported by Andrew Carnegie and Louise Carnegie, who was a member of the congregation, Merrill promoted the study of peace among the churches in cooperation with other organizations.

Margaret O. Sage [42]

Margaret Olivia Sage, wife of Russell Sage and philanthropist, distributed over $40,000,000 of her husband's money to charitable causes including $1,500,000 to the PCUSA Woman's Board of Home Missions.

Louisville Theological Seminary, joined by Danville Theological Seminary in [43] 1901, opened its Gothic campus in 1910 under the presidency of Charles W. Hemphill. Hemphill is shown here in front of the new campus in downtown Louisville with the Class of 1915.

Woodrow Wilson & Family, 1912

45

44

President Wilson & Cabinet, 1913

1913 Woodrow Wilson (1856-1924) was inaugurated President of the United States of America. Former president of Princeton University and governor of New Jersey, he ran on the platform of a "New Freedom" and as a progressive Democrat. Wilson was a Presbyterian elder. He is shown here with his wife and daughters (from left to right, Margaret, Mrs. Wilson, Eleanor, and Jessie), and members of his cabinet, a number of whom were also Presbyterian elders, including William Jennings Bryan who was a Secretary of State. Wilson finally came out in support of women's suffrage, and cartoonist William H. Walker pictures him dancing with "Freedom."

46

47

1917 Woodrow Wilson tried to keep the United States out of World War I. When the nation finally entered the conflict to make the world safe for democracy, as Wilson put it, Presbyterians supported the war effort as just. Robert E. Speer was chairman of the Federal Council of Churches war time commission to coordinate the activities of member denominations. Presbyterians sent supplies of food and clothing to Allies and carried on work of support for men and women in the Army and Navy through the National Service Commission. Lafayette College organized an ambulance unit (below).

After William Jennings Bryan resigned from Wilson's cabinet, the President made Robert Lansing (1864-1928) his Secretary of State. Lansing (standing) is shown here with John Watson Foster, an Indiana Republican and Secretary of State under Benjamin Harrison, and the young John Foster Dulles and his sister, Eleanor. Lansing was Foster's son-in-law, and the uncle of John and Eleanor Dulles.

Wilson defined America's war aims in his Fourteen Points which included the organization of the League of Nations. Wilson thought the League would help the countries of the world work out those problems which would remain after the peace treaty was signed. That the President's trip to Europe was a triumph this picture (below) of him with the children of England amply demonstrates. He was unable to persuade the Senate of the United States to enter the Covenant of the League of Nations. Presbyterians in general supported the League.

John W. Chapman

Billy Sunday

J. Wilbur Chapman (1859-1918), for many years pastor of the Bethany Presbyterian Church in Philadelphia, was a revivalist of national and international fame. He organized the first Committee on Evangelism of the PCUSA to increase the membership of the churches. This became a Permanent Committee in 1913.

William Ashley Sunday (1863-1935) was better known as "Billy." An Iowan, he gained some early notoriety as an outfielder for the Chicago White Sox. After his conversion, he worked with J. Wilbur Chapman for a while and then struck out on his own. He preached vigorously for fighting men of God, and he led many to "hit the saw-dust trail," to shake his hand as a sign of their conversion. Artist George Bellows gives a vivid picture at one of Sunday's meetings.

Charles & Alice Bierkemper & Navajo boy

Charles Harry Bierkemper and his wife, Alice, established a mission station at Ganado in northwestern Arizona, among the Navajo Indians in 1901. The mission included a church, school, and the Sage Memorial Hospital, built in 1930, at which young women from different tribes and nations trained to be nurses (above).

Meanwhile, the church gave attention to work among immigrants. A conference on Italian evangelization (below) took place in Albany, NY, in 1920.

Francis Grimke   Charlotte Grimke

59   60

Francis Grimke (1850-1938) served as pastor of the Fifteenth Street Presbyterian Church, Washington, D.C. He gained national recognition as preacher and opponent of discrimination in the church and in the government of the United States. Because of injustices toward blacks in America, he attacked the World War I aims of the nation as a lie. His wife, Charlotte L. Forten Grimke was an educator and writer.

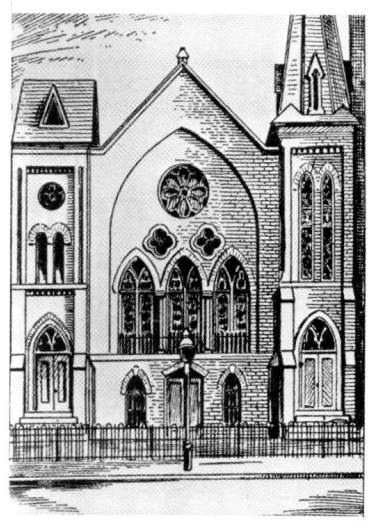

Fifteenth St. Church   61

Africo-American Presbyterian

62

The Afro-American Presbyterian Council took shape in 1893. Blacks felt that the presbyteries of which they were members did not offer them the fellowship which they wanted and needed. At the same time the Council was holding this meeting in 1929 the *Afro-American Presbyterian* announced the death of Mrs. Johnson C. Smith who had supported the work of Johnson C. Smith University through the years.

Mrs. Katherine Jones Bennett (1864-1950) of Englewood, NJ, served as president of the Woman's Board of Home Missions (PCUSA) from 1909-1923, and then as vice-president of the Presbyterian Board of National Missions. In 1927 Mrs. Bennett and Miss Margaret Hodge issued a report finding unrest among women dissatisfied with their status and role, and the "benevolent paternalism" of men who granted some voice, but no vote in ecclesiastical matters. Mrs. Bennett and Miss Hodge went with members of the General Council of the PCUSA to visit the White House and Calvin Coolidge during a Council Meeting, 18 March 1925 (above).

Hallie P. Winsborough

A southerner who lived most of her life in Kansas City, MO, Mrs. W. C. Winsborough's interests involved home and foreign missions, and interdenominational and racial relations. The first church-wide meeting of women in the PCUS took place in Atlanta in 1912 (right). The work of auxiliaries involved prayer, study and giving for all the causes of the church.

The first conference for "Colored Women" in the PCUS took place in 1916 at Stillman Institute, Tuscaloosa, AL.

Trained for Christian Service

The Group of Nineteen Twenty

The demand for trained Christian leaders far exceeds the supply. Never was the need of trained, efficient Pastors' Secretaries, Church Helpers, Deaconesses, Missionary and Social Service Workers as great as now. And the church is prepared to pay adequate salaries for efficient workers.

Our school offers a thorough and practical training for the needs of the field. During the school year students are given actual practice work in the city. The entrance requirements and recommendation for positions are Christian character, refinement and a good preparatory education. Students registering now will have the benefit of the present low rates for their entire term. Rates will be advanced in the fall.

For Full Information Address REV. WALTER H. WAYGOOD, Supt.

Philadelphia School for Christian Workers of the Presbyterian and Reformed Churches
1122 SPRUCE STREET   PHILADELPHIA, PA.

In search of larger service, women enrolled in schools to prepare for professional service in the churches. The Philadelphia School for Christian Workers of the Presbyterian and Reformed Churches offered to train women as secretaries, missionaries and social service workers, among other things.

Donaldina Cameron (1869-1968), left, waged a forty-two year fight from 1895 to 1937 against vice in San Francisco's Chinatown. Chinese girls rescued from prostitution called her mother, or "Lo Mo" in Chinese.

Donaldina Cameron

J. Gresham Machen

1923 In 1923, J. Gresham Machen (1881-1937) published *Christianity and Liberalism* in which he argued that Liberalism abroad in the churches was un-Christian and unscientific. Machen was a professor at Princeton Theological Seminary and noted biblical scholar. His powerful statement lent support to those who made a particular interpretation of the authority of the Scriptures, Christ's virgin birth, miracles, sacrifice and resurrection as measures of Christian faithfulness.

69

Shall the
Fundamentalists Win?

BY
HARRY EMERSON FOSDICK, D.D.

A SERMON PREACHED AT THE
FIRST PRESBYTERIAN CHURCH, NEW YORK
MAY 21, 1922

(Stenographically Reported by Margaret Renton)

70

FOR THE FAITH
NO. 1

Shall Unbelief Win?

A REPLY TO DR. FOSDICK
by
CLARENCE EDWARD MACARTNEY

"To sin by silence when we should protest
Makes cowards out of men. The human race
Has climbed on protest. Had no voice been raised
Against injustice, ignorance and lust,
The Inquisition yet would serve the law,
And guillotines decide our least disputes.
The few who dare must speak, and speak again,"
To right the wrongs of many.

15 CENTS THE COPY

WILBER HANF
1724 Arch Street
Philadelphia, Pa.

71

AN AFFIRMATION
designed to safeguard the unity and liberty of the
Presbyterian Church in the United States of America

with all signatures and
the Note Supplementary

May 5, 1924

The Jacobs Press
Auburn, N. Y.

72

Controversy among American Presbyterians involved Harry Emerson Fosdick. Fosdick was a Baptist preacher who held the pulpit of the First Presbyterian Church in New York City for a time. He held liberal views and rubbed conservatives wrong by preaching a widely-distributed sermon entitled "Shall the Fundamentalists Win?" Fosdick was supported by the New York Presbytery, as the *New York Times* reported, but forced out of the pulpit by the General Assembly. Clarence Macartney, pastor of the First Presbyterian Church, Pittsburgh, PA, responded with a sermon entitled: "Shall Unbelief Win?" In 1924 numerous Presbyterians signed "An Affirmation" arguing that they were both Christian and Presbyterian, even though they differed with others in the denomination about the way in which the *Westminster Confession* should be interpreted.

188

1925-1927

Charles R. Erdman (1866-1960), a professor at Princeton Theological Seminary and a conservative himself, was elected moderator in 1925. A pastor at heart, he wished to save the denomination from another division. He appointed a Special Commission to study the spiritual condition of the church and the causes of the turmoil. The Commission (below) made its report in 1927. It held that over the years the denomination had worked out ways by which to maintain the essential confessional position of the church and yet allow for some flexibility in interpreting the faith. The Commission judged the five points which the General Assembly had adopted in 1910 and reaffirmed thereafter were unconstitutional tests of orthodoxy and a usurpation of the authority of the presbyteries.

Charles R. Erdman

Special Commission of 1925

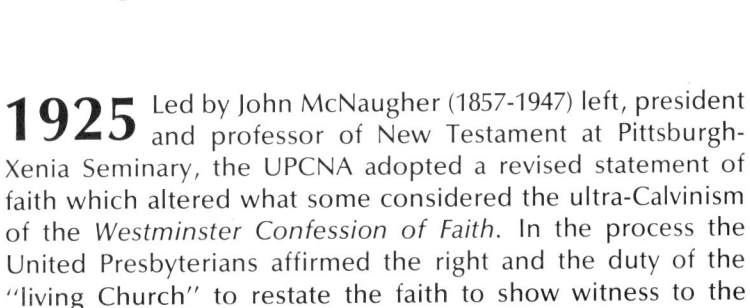

John McNaugher

1925

Led by John McNaugher (1857-1947) left, president and professor of New Testament at Pittsburgh-Xenia Seminary, the UPCNA adopted a revised statement of faith which altered what some considered the ultra-Calvinism of the *Westminster Confession of Faith*. In the process the United Presbyterians affirmed the right and the duty of the "living Church" to restate the faith to show witness to the continual guidance of the Holy Spirit.

1925 William Jennings Bryan, now a member of the First Presbyterian Church, Miami, FL, drew large crowds (above) for popular "Bryan Bible Talks." Bryan, almost President of the United States, was almost elected moderator of the General Assembly (PCUSA) during the theological controversies of the "roaring twenties." He delivered the Sprunt Lectures at Union Theological Seminary in Richmond, published as *In His Image* (1922), and went on to take part against Scopes in the evolution trial in Tennessee. Bryan was dubbed "boobus Americanus," and in this cartoon, monkeys seem to have descended from him. Known as the "Commoner," he was one of America's greatest orators.

The Committee of Publication of the PCUS carried on its work from its base in Richmond, VA, and offered to deliver materials to church workers from Richmond to Texarkana.

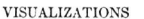

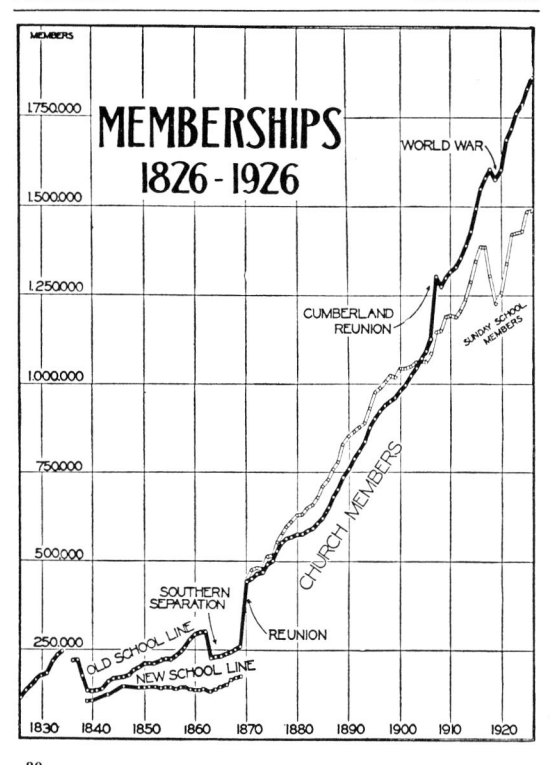

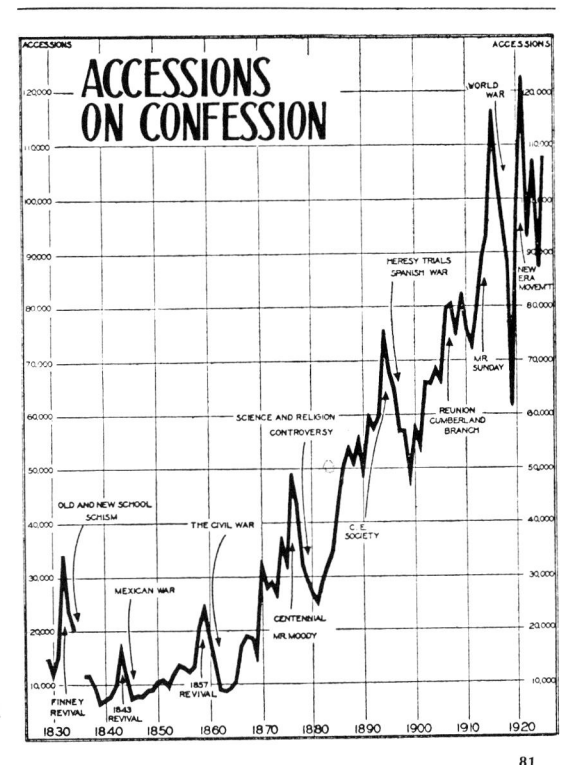

1926 In his study of *Presbyterian Statistics* (1927), Herman C. Weber portrays the history of American Presbyterians in these visual representations of membership growth and accessions on confession of faith from 1826-1926. He charted the growth and decline of the churches of the various Presbyterian denominations in connection with some of the important events of American history, including theological ferment, revivals, divisions, reunions, and wars.

When Sinclair Lewis wrote about *Babbitt* (1922), an American businessman, he made him and his pastor, Presbyterian.

Presbyterians of the PCUS built the Church of the Pilgrims in Washington, DC, dedicated in 1929, to make a witness in the nation's capitol.

Geographer and explorer, Gilbert Hovey Grosvenor (1875-1966, right) edited the *National Geographic Magazine* from 1903-54, when he was succeeded in that same position by his son, Melville Bell Grosvenor (left). Shown with his father, Gilbert Grosvenor married the daughter of Alexander Graham Bell. Grosvenor and his son belonged to the National Presbyterian Church in Washington, DC.

Cofounder, editor and publisher of *Time*, in 1923, Henry R. Luce (1898-1967, above) grew up in Shantung Province, China. His father, Henry Winter Luce (1868-1941) was a Presbyterian missionary and educator. The weekly news magazine flourished as an opinion maker. Luce also founded *Fortune* in 1930 and *Life* in 1936.

Henry W. Luce & Children

James Wallace

DeWitt Wallace (1889-1982) founded the *Reader's Digest* in 1922, an American publishing enterprise which grew to be the most widely circulated magazine in the world. Wallace was the son of James Wallace, a Presbyterian minister and president of Macalester College, St. Paul, MN, to which DeWitt and his wife, Lila Bell, contributed.

DeWitt & Lila Bell Wallace

1926 John Finley Williamson (1888-1964), along with his wife, Rhea, offered choral training for church musicians at the Westminster Presbyterian Church, Dayton, OH, in 1926. Through international tours and performances, Williamson won acclaim and the support he needed to organize the Westminster Choir College in Princeton, NJ, 1934. He and his wife revolutionalized choral music in the churches.

Clarence Dickinson (1873-1969) directed the School of Sacred Music, Union Theological Seminary, New York from 1928 to 1945. A virtuoso and composer of renown, he played the organ at the Brick Presbyterian Church, New York, and was founding member of the American Guild of Organists.

The Compton Family

Arthur Holly Compton (1892-1962, standing, left) won the Nobel Prize for Physics in 1927. He lived in Wooster, OH, and attended the College of Wooster, where his father, Elias Compton (standing, right) taught science. Wilson and Karl Compton were noted educators, and Mary was a missionary to India. During the 1930s Arthur Holly Compton (below, left) served with Presbyterian minister Everett R. Clinchy (second from left) as Protestant representatives on the board of the National Conference of Christians and Jews, when it was founded in 1927. It attempted to deal with religious prejudice in America. Clinchy was first president of the NCCJ.

1930 In 1930 the Presbyterian Church (PCUSA) voted to ordain women to the eldership after a long debate over their status in the church, while at the same time denying them the right to be ordained as clergy. Five women elders attended the 143d General Assembly in 1931 as commissioners. From left to right, they are B. J. Silliman, UT; Lena L. Jennings, OH; O. G. Roberts, PA; Helen B. Logsdon, CA; Mary A. Yielding, OK.

IX
FROM DEPRESSION TO GLOBAL RESPONSIBILITIES

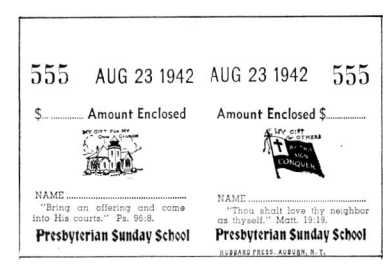

1930-1958 Depression, World War II, Cold War, the Atomic Age—these great events challenged Presbyterians as they did other Christians around the globe. Presbyterians in all parts of the country attempted to alleviate the pain of the Depression, and the PCUSA and the PCUS called for a fairer economic system. Presbyterians also supported the quest for a just and durable peace during World War II, calling for a postwar world without hate and revenge. Moreover, in the spirit of Woodrow Wilson they gave their backing to the United Nations Organization and to the organization of the World Council of Churches in 1948, global experiments which might help the peoples of the world deal with the problems left over from the war, and new ones of the atomic age. Presbyterian preachers, evangelists, educators, scholars, and pastoral counselors attempted to meet some of the religious concerns of these years, and cooperated with other Protestants through participation in the National Council of Churches, organized in 1950. Moreover, Presbyterians sought a healing of the divisions among themselves in efforts to reunite and unite the PCUSA, the PCUS, and the UPCNA. They committed themselves to a desegregated society, and to sharing power with women as well as blacks in ecclesiastical affairs. Unhappy over a sterile and dangerous anti-communist mentality, they made efforts to deescalate the ideological conflicts, East-West, and North-South, as fraternal workers with other Christian churches around the world.

In *Look Homeward, Angel* (1929), Thomas Wolfe wrote about members of the First Presbyterian Church, Ashville, NC, where he and his family attended. He took the title from an angel which his father kept standing in his monument shop in the town. Wolfe also wrote about tensions at home in *You Can't Go Home Again* (1934).

1929 The stock market crash of October, 1929, plunged the nation into a deep and long-lasting depression, and shook the people's confidence in the promise of American life. American Presbyterians ministered to the needs of the people who were out of work, out of food, out of clothes, out of shelter—out of hope. In the "Labor Day Message" for 1932, Presbyterians expressed concern for the continuing crisis.

When Franklin Delano Roosevelt ran for the presidency in that year, he was opposed by Norman Mattoon Thomas (1884-1968), standard bearer of the Socialist Party. Thomas was the grandson of Stephen and Mary Lourie Mattoon, missionaries to Thailand, and the son of Emma and Welling Thomas, a Presbyterian minister. Norman, born in Ohio, graduated from Union Theological Seminary, New York, and served churches in the city. Neither a Marxist nor a New Dealer, he preferred Socialist change and as his ideas became better known, two major parties often adopted planks from his platform.

LABOR DAY MESSAGE for 1932

The Challenge of the Present Economic Crisis to the Church

Board of National Missions of the Presbyterian Church in the U. S. A.

Committee on Social and Industrial Relations,
John McDowell, Secretary, 156 Fifth Avenue,
New York, N. Y.

Emma & Welling Thomas & Family
Norman is second from right

Henry Sloane Coffin

Reinhold Niebuhr

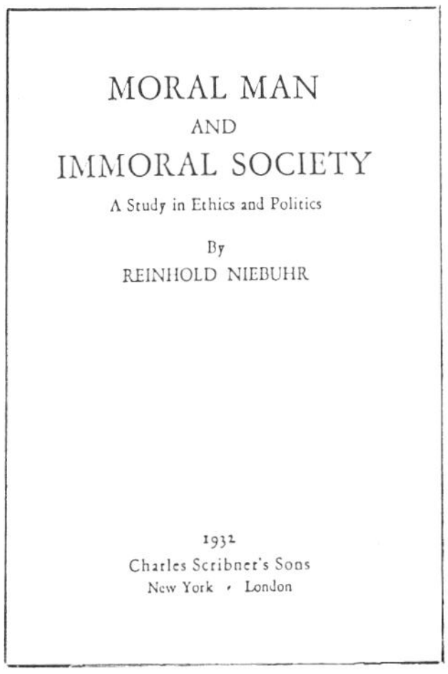

MORAL MAN
AND
IMMORAL SOCIETY
A Study in Ethics and Politics
By
REINHOLD NIEBUHR

1932
Charles Scribner's Sons
New York · London

1932 After a pastorate in Detroit where Henry Ford carried on his mass-production revolution, Reinhold Niebuhr (1892-1971) moved to New York City's Union Theological Seminary where he taught ethics. Henry Sloane Coffin, a Presbyterian pastor and educator, was president of the institution, and John C. Bennett, another Christian ethicist, taught with him there. In his *Moral Man and Immoral Society* (1932) Niebuhr took sin in human relations and organizations seriously. He tried to meet the Depression with Christian realism. His *Nature and Destiny of Man* (1941-43), theological in its focus, also viewed problems of the international order from this perspective. Niebuhr was raised in Missouri in the German Evangelical Synod, a denomination which blended Lutheran and Reformed traditions.

"Brother Bryan"

Ernest Trice Thompson

In the South, Ernest Trice Thompson (1893-1985), professor at Union Theological Seminary, Richmond, VA, challenged the concept of the "spirituality" of the PCUS. He helped southerners map a more responsible approach to social change. The Committee on Moral and Social Welfare, the result of the concern of Thompson and others, carried on this work after having been founded in 1934.

James Alexander Bryan served Birmingham's Third Presbyterian Church. In 1934 the city erected a statue of "Brother Bryan" who prayed with people in the city's hospitals, shops, factories, offices, and prisons as their official chaplain.

East Liberty Presbyterian Church

Andrew W. Mellon

The Mellon family played a prominent role in Pittsburgh Presbyterian life. Andrew W. Mellon was Secretary of Treasury during the presidency of Warren G. Harding. He and his brother, Richard, gave the land for the East Liberty Presbyterian Church, Pittsburgh, PA. Richard and his wife put up the funds for the imposing Gothic structure. Pastor Stuart Nye Hutchison presided over the dedication of the building in 1935 designed by Ralph Adams Cram. In the carving of the Last Supper, sculptor John Engel focused on the moment Christ gave thanks.

Thomas J. Watson (1874-1956), founder of International Business Machines, was an active elder in the Brick Presbyterian Church, New York City, and a large contributor to its educational program and building.

Thomas J. Watson

The First Presbyterian Church of Kilgore, TX, found itself at the center of the East Texas oil field and boom during the height of the Depression of the 1930s.

Pearl Sydenstricker (1892-1973), daughter of missionaries to China, married John L. Buck, an agricultural missionary to the same country. Pearl Buck wrote stories about the land of her birth beginning in 1923 and reached wide acclaim for *The Good Earth* in 1931. She remembered her father, Abraham Sydenstricker, in *Fighting Angel,* and her mother, in *The Exile*. For her writing she won the Nobel Prize for literature in 1938.

Pearl Buck

Marianne Moore (1887-1972) wrote poetry. Raised in the home of her grandfather, John R. Warner, pastor of the First Presbyterian Church, Kirkwood, MO; brother of navy chaplain, John Warner Moore, Marianne began her career as an author in the 1920s. In 1935 T. S. Eliot contributed a foreword to her *Selected Poems,* and called her one of the few durable poets of the time. She was a faithful member of the Lafayette Presbyterian Church in Brooklyn, NY.

Marianne Moore

James Stewart, a member of the Beverly Hills Presbyterian Church, Beverly Hills, CA, played the idealistic country boy who traveled to Washington, DC, as a senator and in a short time learned the harshness of American politics. "Mr. Smith Goes to Washington" was a hit in 1939 when it was released.

199

Robert E. Speer

1932 Robert E. Speer (1867-1947) embodied in his life and work the dedication of Presbyterians to world-wide mission from 1891-1937 when he was secretary of the Board of Foreign Missions, PCUSA. Traveler, lecturer, writer, administrator, Speer opposed some of the findings of *Re-Thinking Missions: A Layman's Inquiry* (1932) which did not stress the "finality of Jesus Christ" and the need for the evangelization of the world. A layman himself, he was a Christian statesman.

Umeko Momii, a minister of the PC(USA), sits with her family in Japan in the 1930s when she was a young girl. Her father, Toyohiko Kagawa (1888-1960) was converted to Christianity by Presbyterian missionaries, studied at Princeton Theological Seminary for two years, and spent his life as a champion and evangelist of the Japanese poor.

Some Presbyterians thought that agricultural missions were not part of the Christian obligation. Sam and Jane Higginbottom took the "gospel of the plow" to Allahabad, India, in order to deal with hunger so prevalent in that land. In the name of Christ, they taught princes and untouchables, alike. The General Assembly of the PCUSA elected him moderator in 1939.

Toyohiko Kagawa & Family

Sam Higginbottom

1941 In 1941 the United States entered World War II, a shattering event. Henry Stimson, Secretary of War (1911-13), Secretary of State (1929-33), and again Secretary of War (1940-45), drew the first numbers in the draft lottery. Stimson was a life-long Presbyterian and a trustee of the National Presbyterian Church. Presbyterians discussed questions of "a just and righteous cause" and a "just and durable peace," and tried to support service men and women. The Warren Memorial Presbyterian Church, Louisville, KY, served soldiers free meals and encouraged singing, as did the First Presbyterian Church, Stillwater, OK. Stated Clerk of the PCUSA General Assembly, William Barrow Pugh, visited troops in England in 1943.

201

PCUS Chaplain Julian Spitzer conducts worship on the U.S.S. Baltimore while at Pearl Harbor in 1946 after the "tumult and the shouting" died and the peace restored.

Lieutenant Colonel Mary-Agnes Brown, served as Theater Director of the Women's Army Corps at the headquarters of General Douglas MacArthur in the South Pacific. General Omar Bradley awarded her the Legion of Merit medal for her involvement in the campaigns of New Guinea, Philippines and Luzon. She took an active part in the life of the Bethesda Presbyterian Church in Maryland.

After the war Presbyterians mounted "The Restoration Fund" to help revitalize its "spiritual agencies" around the world. They also took part in relief and reconstruction programs of ecumenical agencies.

Arthur Holly Compton

> Atomic
> Quest
>
> A PERSONAL NARRATIVE
>
> By ARTHUR HOLLY COMPTON
>
> NEW YORK · OXFORD UNIVERSITY PRESS · 1956

1945 Arthur Holly Compton taught physics at the University of Chicago where he was also director of the Metallurgical Atomic Project. This project paved the way for controlled release of nuclear energy, the first atomic bombs, and the opening of the Atomic Age. Shortly after the war Washington University, St. Louis, MO, inaugurated him Chancellor. He served as elder of the Second Presbyterian Church in that city.

John Foster Dulles

A son and grandson of Presbyterian ministers, John Foster Dulles (1888-1959) was a prominent New York lawyer and an active Presbyterian layman. During World War II he served as chairman of the Commission on a Just and Durable Peace of the Federal Council of Churches which prepared a "statement of Guiding Principles" and "Six Pillars of Peace" which were studied widely during the war years. Dulles is pictured in the pulpit of the Brick Presbyterian Church of which he was a member. American Presbyterians followed Dulles in his support of the United Nations. He addressed the opening session of the World Council of Churches (1948) in Amsterdam.

1946 Westminster College, Fulton, MO, and the world heard Sir Winston Churchill in 1946. He warned of the "iron curtain" which separated East and West, and of the "Cold War" of the post-World War II era. President Harry Truman and President Franc McCluer of the college accompanied Churchill on the occasion. The Presbyterian institution erected the Memorial and Library on the campus to honor the wartime leader. The chapel, designed by Christopher Wren, was moved from England to the Mid-West.

President Truman & Winston Churchill

Churchill Memorial & Library Westminster College, MO

1949 John Leighton Stuart (1876-1962), an educational missionary of the PCUS and President of Yenching University, Beijing, served as ambassador to China during difficult years between 1946-1949 when Mao De-Tung came to power in that country. Although he gave his life to the Chinese people, and was imprisoned by the Japanese, Mao wrote an essay "Farewell, Leighton Stuart," in which Stuart appears as an example of the "running dogs of imperialism."

Madame Chiang Kai-shek & John Leighton Stuart

Clarence Macartney

Americans displayed considerable interest in religion as a response to World War II and in meeting the challenge of the "atheistic Communism" and "Cold War." Clarence E. Macartney, pastor of the First Presbyterian Church of Pittsburgh and known as the "St. Paul of Pittsburgh," had a wide impact. He preached from an oudoor pulpit. His noon-day luncheons, one for men and one for women, drew a full church in the 1950s.

**First Presbyterian Church, Pittsburgh
Tuesday Noon Club**

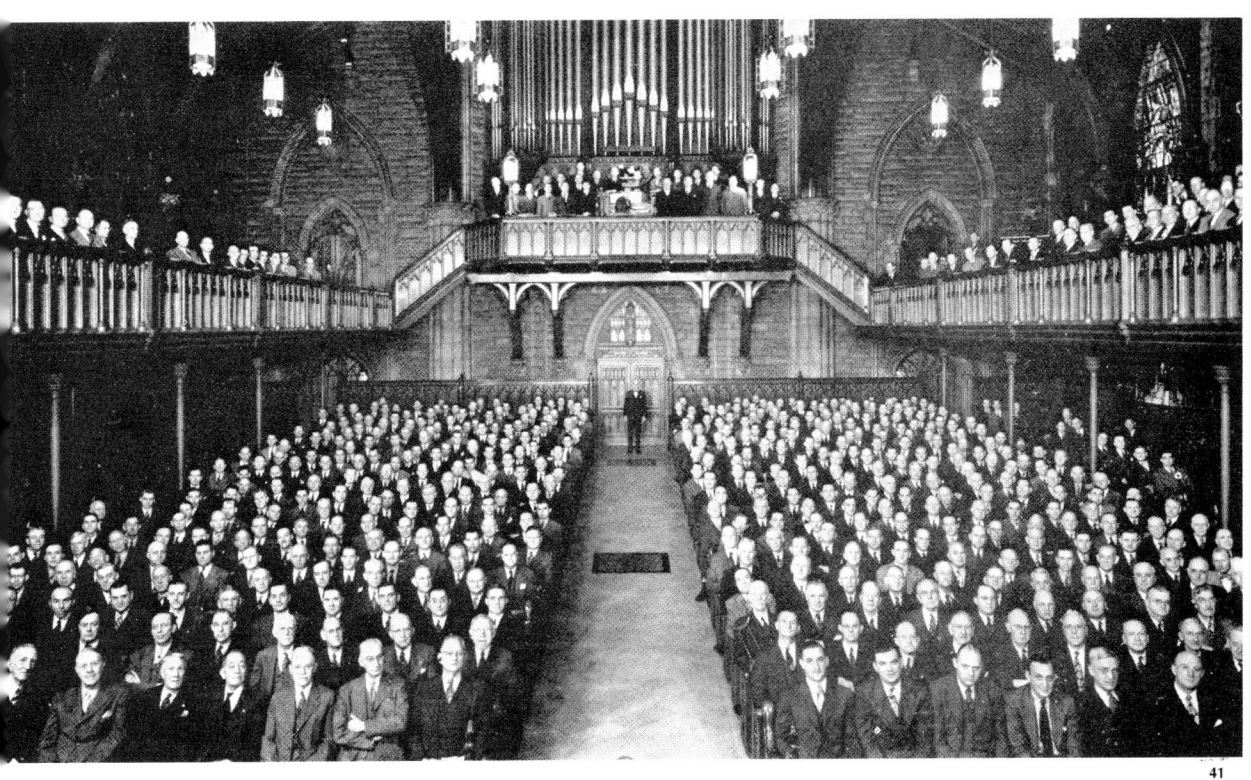

I Carry a Union Card
John G. Ramsay

During these years John G. Ramsay gained recognition for his work as a churchman and labor leader. Growing up in the Fourth Presbyterian Church, Knoxville, TN, he learned during the Depression that poverty in the midst of abundance is sinful. He was a steel worker for seventeen years before he was elected to the presidency of the United Steelworkers of America, CIO. He gave leadership to the Religion and Labor Fellowship.

Donald G. Barnhouse George Buttrick

Presbyterian preachers exercised strong leadership from the pulpit. George Buttrick, pastor of the Madison Avenue Presbyterian Church, New York, was a "preacher's preacher," author of *Prayer*, and editor-in-chief of *The Interpreter's Bible* and the *Interpreter's Dictionary of the Bible*. Dispensationalist Donald Grey Barnhouse pioneered in radio preaching as pastor of Philadelphia's Tenth Presbyterian Church. He edited *Eternity Magazine*. Peter Marshall made his impact upon the nation as popular preacher of the New York Avenue Presbyterian Church in Washington and as chaplain of the United States Senate, a post to which he was elected in 1947. His widow, Catherine, widened his popularity with a bestselling biography *A Man Called Peter* (1951). John A. Redhead reached a wide audience by his ability to interpret the faith in simple and supportive terms at the First Presbyterian Church, Greensboro, NC.

John A. Redhead, Jr. Peter Marshall

Louis H. Evans

Louis H. Evans delivered inspirational addresses at the Bible Conference, Montreat, NC, in 1953, as minister-at-large for the PCUSA. Evans gained his reputation as pastor of the First Presbyterian Church, Hollywood, one of the largest congregations of the denomination during these years. The choirs, children as well as adults, numbered three hundred and fifty.

First Presbyterian Church Hollywood, CA, Choir

Albert B. McCoy 49

Roy Ahmaogak 50

Richard C. Smith 51

Other Presbyterians witnessed in special ministries "From Frontier to Frontier." Roy Ahmaogak, born in a house of whalebone and sod, traveled to preach to Alaskans under the midnight sun, while Richard C. Smith served miners in West Virginia, the land of coal, organizing the Mountaineer Mountain Mission in 1946. Albert B. McCoy, worked as a Sunday school missionary in the south, until he became the first black field secretary of the Department of Work with Colored People, a position he held until 1951. Warren Ost began a Christian Ministry in the National Parks in 1952. He planted the cross in Death Valley as a witness to the Gospel.

Warren Ost 52

New Life Movement Committee

Effective Evangelism:

The Greatest Work in the World

by GEORGE E. SWEAZEY

HARPER & BROTHERS   PUBLISHERS   NEW YORK

The General Assembly (PCUSA) mounted the New Life Movement in 1947, with George E. Sweazey as chairman of the Department of Evangelism. Sweazey shown with his colleagues summarized the purpose and method of the work in *Effective Evangelism* (1953). In addition to the New Life Movement the denomination joined other churches in reconstruction work in war-torn Europe and Asia and collected twenty-three million dollars in the Restoration Fund by 1952.

Ralph Hall

Presbyterians in the West and South also supported evangelistic efforts. Pastor Ralph Hall preached to ranchers in New Mexico. The Covenant Presbyterian Church, Charlotte, NC, equipped the Presbyterian Chapel on wheels, which provided for church services, Sunday school, day school and for a Mother's Club. Warner Hall, pastor of the congregation, stands in the door of the trailer.

Paul Calvin Payne

1948 In 1948 the PCUSA launched one of its most ambitious Christian education programs. After years of study, the denomination concluded that the church "must teach... or die" and came up with the Faith and Life Curriculum to be used in the home as well as the church for the education of the whole family. Paul Calvin Payne, secretary of the Board of Christian Education, directed the curriculum and his staff produced graded lessons, attractively illustrated books and magazines, which covered in three year cycles the themes of Christ, the Bible, and the life in the Christian Church. Children were helped in *Growing*, the aid for teachers and parents of kindergarten children, while adults were challenged by the *Crossroads*, the magazine edited by George L. Hunt.

Henrietta Mears

Henrietta Mears, educator at the First Presbyterian Church, Hollywood, produced her own curriculum called Gospel Light which was widely used.

Gayraud Wilmore and student

Presbyterians turned their attention to the colleges and universities to develop campus ministries and student centers for Christian fellowship and reflection. Gayraud Wilmore, a graduate of Lincoln Theological Seminary, worked with students, deans, and local Presbyterian pastors, as a representative of the Student Christian Movement to develop campus programs. Donald Moomaw, football player for the University of California, Los Angeles, led a church service with his fiancee, Marilyn Amends, after his conversion to Christ. Moomaw joined Campus Crusade, founded by William Bright, a Presbyterian.

Marilyn Amends & Donald Moomaw

Presbyterian Student Center Foundation, University of Wisconsin

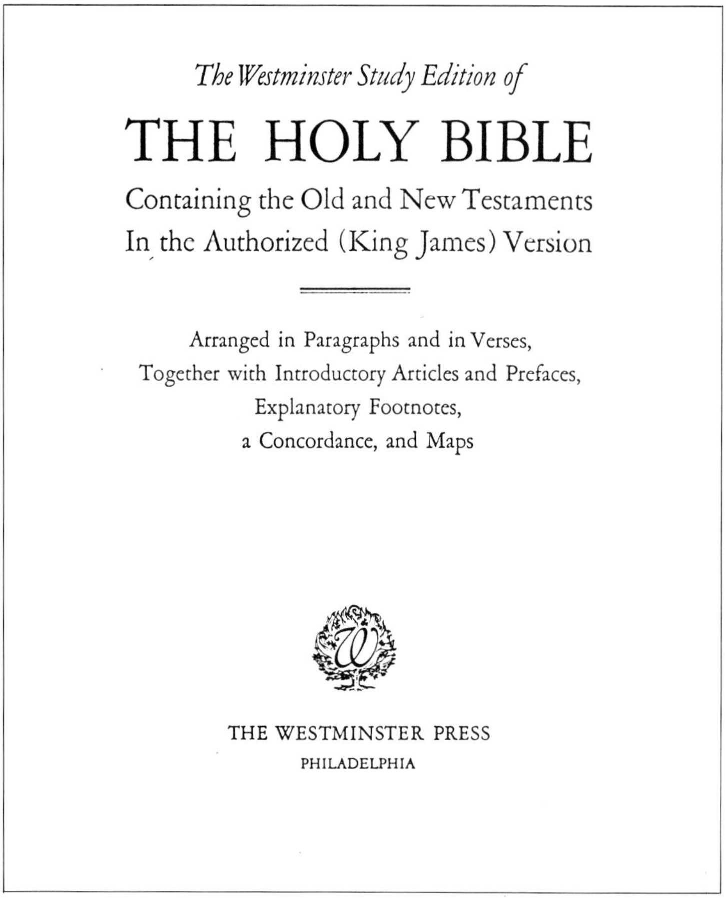

The Westminster Study Edition of

THE HOLY BIBLE

Containing the Old and New Testaments
In the Authorized (King James) Version

Arranged in Paragraphs and in Verses,
Together with Introductory Articles and Prefaces,
Explanatory Footnotes,
a Concordance, and Maps

THE WESTMINSTER PRESS
PHILADELPHIA

George Ernest Wright

Floyd V. Filson

John Bright

George Ernest Wright, professor of Old Testament at McCormick Theological Seminary, Chicago, before going to Harvard, was an archaeologist and theologian who was, with his colleague in New Testament, Floyd V. Filson, part of the biblical theology movement of the period. This movement helped Presbyterians deal with some of the problems of the "Fundamentalist-Modernist" controversy. John Bright, Cyrus McCormick, Professor of Old Testament at Union Theological Seminary, Richmond, produced the *History of Israel* (1959), widely used text on the subject. Wright and Filson collaborated on the publication of the *Westminster Atlas of the Bible* (1945-1956).

In the 1950s the Westminster Press published a number of distinguished volumes in the biblical, theological, historical fields, such as the Library of Christian Classics The John Knox Press published the *Layman's Bible Commentary*. John Knox Press drew smiles with the religious best seller *The Gospel According to Peanuts* (1965).

Sensing the need for scholarly quarterlies oriented toward the work of leaders in the churches, Princeton Theological Seminary and Union Theological Seminary, Richmond, published *Theology Today* and *Interpretation*. John A. Mackay and Hugh Thomson Kerr gave vigorous editorial direction to the former, founded in 1944, while Donald Miller and Balmer Kelly edited the latter, founded in 1947.

Presbyterian Life became one of the most widely circulated religious journals in the country.

In the meantime, life went on in the church. Indian women in Oklahoma found an outlet for their service and creativity by gathering together to quilt blankets for those who needed them.

213

John S. Bonnell & Korean War Veterans

Seward Hiltner

Karl Menninger

Presbyterians took part in the pastoral care movement. John Sutherland Bonnell, pastor of the Fifth Avenue Presbyterian Church and author of *Psychology for Pastor and People* (1948) spoke to the Korean War casualties. Seward Hiltner, professor at Chicago Divinity School and Princeton Theological Seminary,—counselor, editor, and author of many books, including *Pastoral Counseling* (1949),—made an indelible impact upon the field. William B. Oglesby, Jr., professor of pastoral counseling at Union Theological Seminary, Richmond, and a student of Hiltner, spent his energies in training ministers to be faithful shepherds and acquainting lay people with the issues of pastoral care in the Christian context. These minister-teachers were in close contact with Karl Menninger, one of the founders of the Menninger Foundation, Topeka, Kansas, a leading psychiatric research center. Menninger, elder in the First Presbyterian Church and Sunday school teacher, wrote *Whatever Became of Sin* (1973) to remind an age adrift of moral responsibility.

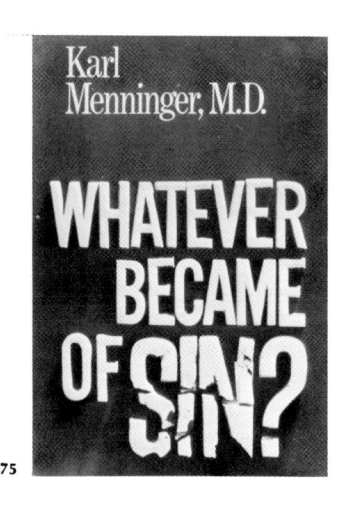

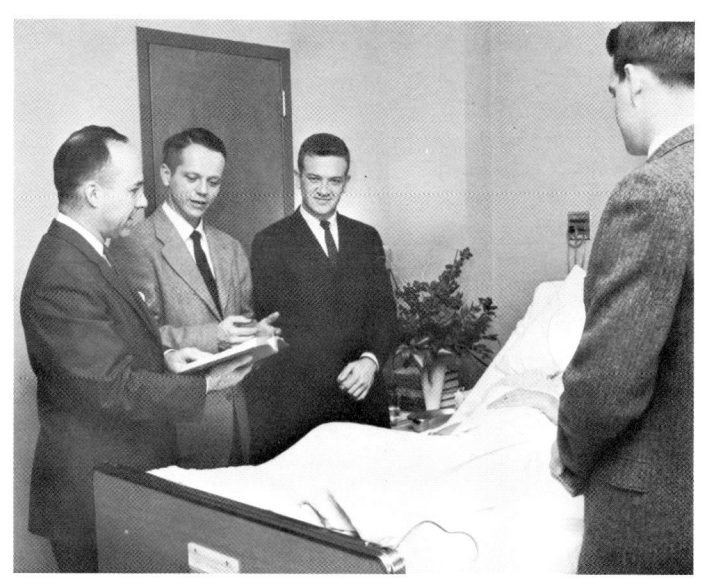

William B. Oglesby & students

National Council of Churches, Officers (1950)

1950 Twelve national interdenominational agencies, some of which took shape in the nineteenth century, joined in 1950 to form the National Council of Churches of Christ in the United States. Successor to the Federal Council of Churches, its purpose was to express a common faith, and build programs mutually helpful to the churches and the nation. Officers of the new Council included a number of Presbyterians. From the left to right they are (seated) Samuel McCrae Cavert (second), Mildred McAfee Horton (fifth); (standing), Hermann Morse (first), Paul C. Payne (third), Charles T. Leber (fifth).

RSV Bible printing (1952)

NCC Dept. of Church & Economic Life

Samuel Cavert participated in ceremonies which inaugurated the printing of the Revised Standard Version of the Bible. Cavert, General Secretary of the NCC, was a Presbyterian minister deeply immersed in ecumenical affairs all his ministry. One of the first studies which the Council completed under the Department of the Church and Economic Life was of ethics in a business society. Among Presbyterians at a meeting of the Department were Roswell Barnes (front, left), Cameron P. Hall (fourth, left), and Dean Rusk (third, right).

1952 Dwight David Eisenhower and his wife, Mamie joined and attended the National Presbyterian Church when they lived in the White House. The pastor, Edward L. Elson, and Willem Adolf Visser 't Hooft, Dutch Reformed churchman and General Secretary of the World Council of Churches, greet the Eisenhowers after the Sunday morning services.

Eisenhower named John Foster Dulles as his Secretary of State. Dulles, grandson of John Foster, Secretary of State under Benjamin Harrison, and nephew of Robert Lansing, Secretary of State under Woodrow Wilson, assisted the President in making foreign policy and in steering the ship of state through troubled waters. Cartoonist Herblock of the *Washington Post,* expressed some anxiety about the possibilities.

216

"You Sure Everything's All Right, Foster?"

... from *Herblock's Here and Now* (Simon & Shuster, 1955)

1953 During the early 1950s the spirit of distrust known as "McCarthyism" spread across the land. American clergy were accused of disloyalty to the nation and of being either communist or communist sympathizers. John A. Mackay (1889-1981), seen here with his wife, Jane, was President of Princeton Theological Seminary and Moderator of the PCUSA in 1953. He wrote "A Letter to Presbyterians Concerning the Present Situation in Our Country and in the World," later adopted by the General Assembly of the PCUSA. He attacked the sterile anti-communism of the years and challenged the churches to continue the search for truth, justice, and prophetic ministry.

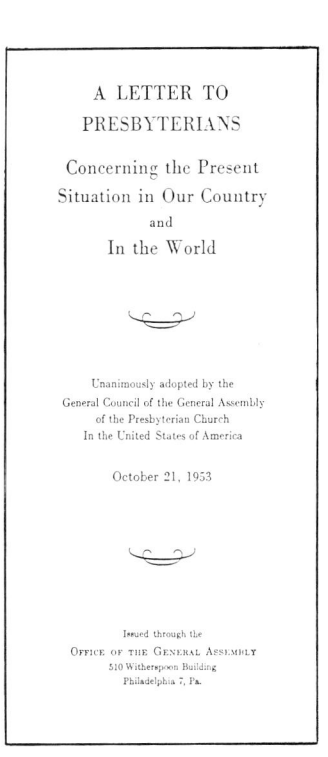

1954 The World Council of Churches held its Second Assembly in Evanston, IL, in 1954. The theme of the conference was "Christ, the Hope of the World." That same year *Time* featured Henry Pitney Van Dusen on the cover as ecumenist. Van Dusen, professor of theology, President of Union Theological Seminary, New York, and close friend to Henry Luce, was deeply involved in shaping the message of the World Council on hope.

First Presbyterian Church
Stamford, CT

LOCATION OF CHURCHES BY STATE
Look on the Map for the Combined Totals

	United	U.S.	U.S.A.
New England			
Maine			1
New Hampshire			8
Vermont	7		5
Massachusetts	10		26
Rhode Island	3		7
Connecticut	1		10
Middle Atlantic States			
New York	75		755
New Jersey	10		381
Pennsylvania	294	1	1108
Delaware	1		31
District of Columbia	2	4	25
Maryland	3	18	94
West Virginia	6	174	77
Virginia	3	470	38
East Central States			
Michigan	15		248
Wisconsin	6		194
Illinois	49		524
Indiana	20		305
Ohio	119		584
Kentucky	2	160	122
West Central States			
Minnesota			249
Iowa	54		337
Missouri	9	116	291
North Dakota			106
South Dakota			135
Nebraska	12		169
Kansas	50		224
East Southern States			
North Carolina	2	687	151
South Carolina		315	73
Tennessee	7	233	171
Georgia		271	24
Alabama	4	202	48
Florida		166	64
Mississippi		250	37
West Southern States			
Arkansas		137	64
Louisiana		127	11
Oklahoma	5	45	142
Texas		367	250
Southwestern States			
Colorado	11		121
New Mexico		5	63
Utah			17
Arizona			70
Nevada			10
California	31		426
Northwestern States			
Montana			64
Wyoming	1		28
Idaho	4		50
Washington	18		189
Oregon	11		126
Territories			
Alaska			18
Puerto Rico			45
TOTAL	829	3733	8336

The external design and floor plan of the First Presbyterian Church, Stamford, CT, dedicated in 1958, is in the shape of a fish, an early Christian symbol. The first letters of the words Jesus Christ, God's Son, Savior, form the word *Ichthus*, the Greek word for "fish." The sounding board above the pulpit is shaped like an open Bible, signifying the congregation's submission to the authority and judgment of the Word.

"One in Love"

"All One Body We..."
A Preview of the Proposed Presbyterian Church of the United States

Evangelism
Net Increase
United . . 7,422
U. S. . . . 26,131
U.S.A. . . 43,924
Total . . 77,477

Combined Presbyterian Church Related Colleges

	United	U.S.	U.S.A.	Total
Church-related Colleges	6	23	41	67
Enrollment	1,361	8,000	26,000	35,361

Seminaries

	United	U.S.	U.S.A.	Total
Seminaries	1	4	9	13
Students enrolled	188	807	1,442	2,437

LEGEND
Combined Churches in each state

Colleges ★   Seminaries ●

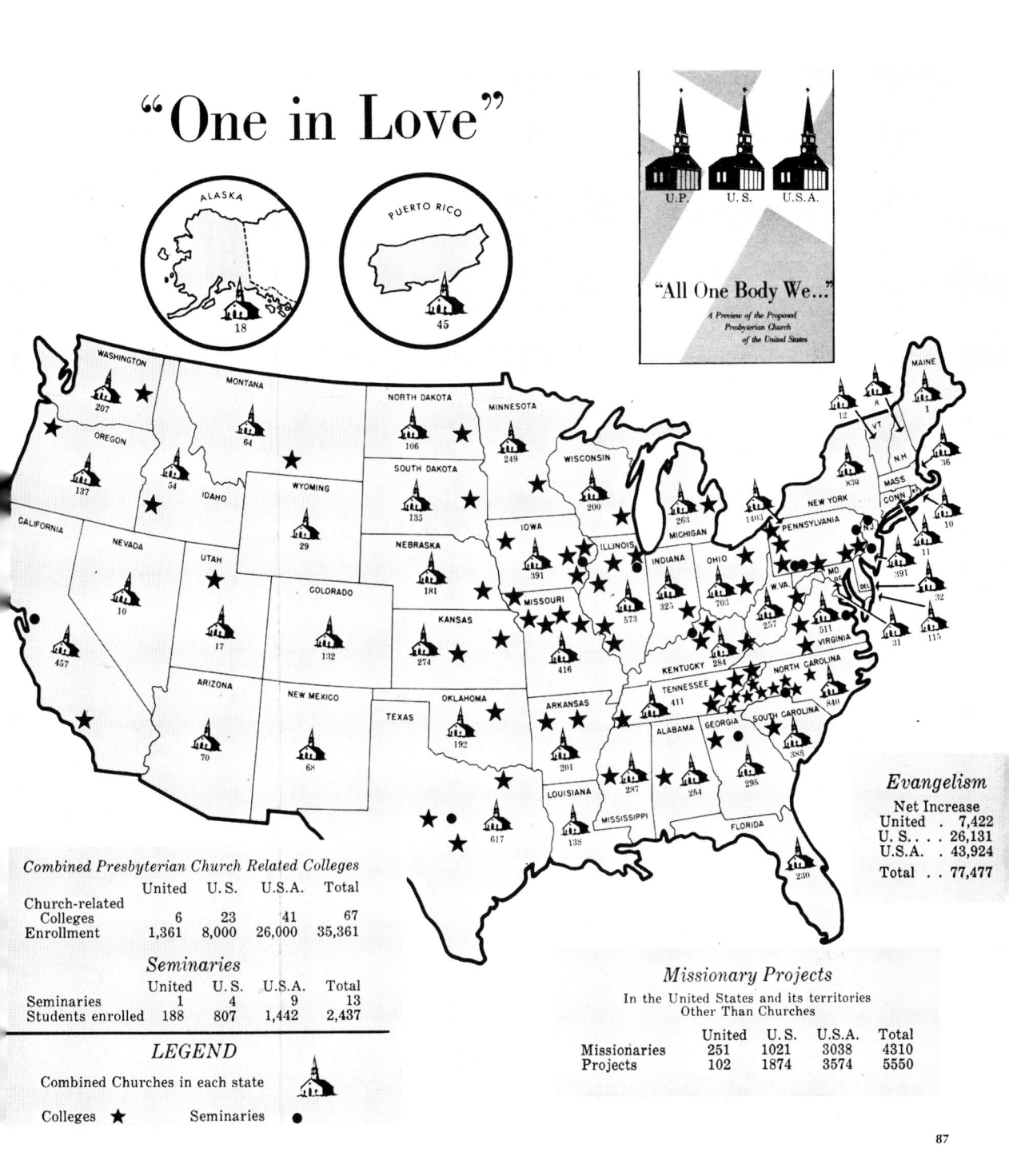

Missionary Projects
In the United States and its territories Other Than Churches

	United	U.S.	U.S.A.	Total
Missionaries	251	1021	3038	4310
Projects	102	1874	3574	5550

During the early years of the 1950s the PCUSA, the PCUS, and the UPCNA engaged in conversations about the organic union of the three largest Presbyterian denominations. To see the shape of the new denomination, those interested in the union prepared a map of statistics showing where Presbyterian churches were located. There were 8336 PCUSA, 3733 PCUS, and 829 UPCNA congregations with a total of more than 3,500,000 communicant members. The map also showed the location of colleges and seminaries affiliated with the Presbyterian Church.

Francis P.
Miller
Family

1954 The Supreme Court of the United States decided for the desegregation of the nation's school system. Presbyterians joined the general demand for the end of segregation and racism in the United States. The PCUS had made a statement on this subject in the same year the Supreme Court made its judgment. Southerners were not silent, as the title to Donald Shriver's book of Presbyterian sermons suggests, and laity often took the lead in the struggle. Francis Pickens Miller, a twentieth century Virginian made his home in Charlottesville. He traveled many years for the World's Student Christian Federation and was well acquainted with the ecumenical church. In 1952, he ran for Governor of Virginia on a desegregation platform. He lost but the state moved in his direction. In the meantime, the debate went on among Presbyterian men marching in Nashville.

In 1954 the new home of Pittsburgh-Xenia Theological Seminary of the UPCNA was dedicated in Pittsburgh, PA.

220

Princeton Seminary Touring Choir (1948)

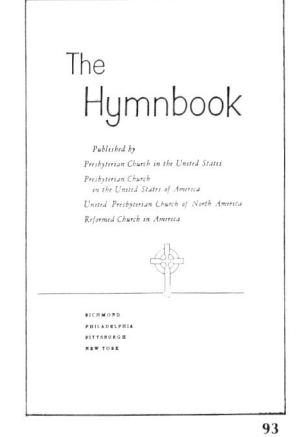

1955 For years David Hugh Jones taught music at Princeton Theological Seminary and directed the touring choir. He conducted worship services across the nation, recruiting young men and women for the ministry. Jones was also the general editor of the *Hymnbook* in 1955, which was the result of the cooperation of the PCUSA, PCUS, UPCNA, the Associate Reformed Presbyterian Church, and the Reformed Church in America. The *Hymnbook* with its worship aids was widely used among American Presbyterians.

1956 In an attempt to deescalate the ideological conflict between West and East, American Christians related to the National Council of Churches visited Orthodox leaders in Russia. Eugene Carson Blake, (front, left) Stated Clerk of the PCUSA and president of the National Council at the time, was a prominent member of the group. Blake had been the pastor of the First Presbyterian Church, Pasadena, CA, before becoming the denomination's chief executive officer.

Embudo Presbyterian Hospital, owned and operated by the Board of National Missions, served Spanish-speaking New Mexicans in a valley of the Sangre de Cristo Range of the Rocky Mountains. Pioneering in the church's medical work in the Southwest in the early decades of the century, Embudo expanded its services in the 1950s.

Embudo Presbyterian Hospital, NM

National Presbyterian Church

In 1947, after attempts which began as early as 1830, the PCUSA established the National Presbyterian Church in Washington, D.C., on the foundation of the former Church of the Covenant and the First Presbyterian Church. The latter traced its origins to the carpenter shop on what is now the White House grounds. Harold Wagoner, a Presbyterian elder and architect, designed the new building, which was completed in 1969, to serve as a focus of Presbyterian presence in the capital and as a conference center under the leadership of Edward L. R. Elson.

Arthur Judson Brown's Birthday Party

1956 Arthur Judson Brown directed the work of the Board of Foreign Missions of the PCUSA for many decades. In 1956 he celebrated his 100th birthday at a party at which he was greeted by Christians from around the world. He lived long enough to experience the emergence of a world Christian community and a rethinking of the church's one mission.

Younger leaders such as PCUSA missionary Richard Shaull of Brazil, and PCUS missionary William H. Crane, born in the Belgium Congo of missionary parents, brought to mission thinking the urgency of Third World problems which influenced mission policy and practices after World War II. Crane was a prisoner of war in Germany. Afterward he served as Africa Secretary of the World Student Christian Federation before becoming a staff member of the Division of World Mission and Evangelism of the World Council of Churches before his death in 1970.

William H. Crane

In 1956 the PCUSA held a mission conference at Lake Mohonk, NY, with representatives of various national churches and discussed the "New Day Dawning" in mission and the need for Presbyterians to be partners in obedience and fraternal workers with Christians throughout the world. The PCUS went through a similar reconsideration of its mission work.

Lake Mohonk Conference

Rachel Henderlite

Margaret E. Towner

1956 The PCUSA finally voted to admit women to the ministry. In 1956 the Cayuga-Syracuse Presbytery ordained Margaret E. Towner at a service conducted in the First Presbyterian Church, Syracuse, NY. Hanover Presbytery ordained Rachel Henderlite at All Souls Presbyterian Church, Richmond, VA, in 1965 making her the first ordained clergywoman of the PCUS. The All Souls Church was the first racially integrated congregation of the Presbytery.

1958 James Robinson, pastor of the Church of the Master, New York City, founded and directed "Operation Crossroads Africa" a private, non-government, voluntary work-camp program to help Africans and educate Americans about the world.

X
CONFRONTATION, RECONCILIATION AND THE FUTURE

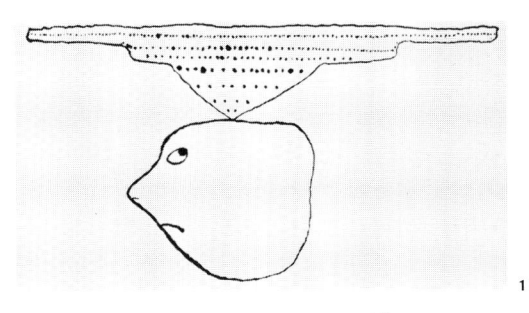

The Presbyterian Pyramid
Drawing by St. Clair McKelway; © 1952, 1980 *The New Yorker Magazine, Inc.*

1958 Presbyterians celebrated the union of the United Presbyterian Church of North America and the Presbyterian Church in the United States of America in 1958 at the beginning of this period of history. The new United Presbyterian Church in the United States of America was dedicated to a larger ecumenical vision and mission in the nation and world. Twenty-five years later in 1983, the Presbyterian Church in the United States and the United Presbyterian Church ended the schism caused by the Civil War, in the celebration of reunion and the organization of the Presbyterian Church (U.S.A.). A quest for identity, confrontation, and change marked the intervening years. Men and women, clergy and laity, Native Americans, blacks, Hispanics, Asian-Americans and other minorities, conservatives, charismatics, liberals, young and old sought roles and to make a contribution in the church. Issues such as human rights and civil rights, world and national poverty in the midst of plenty, responsible marriage and homosexuality, ecumenical relations, church growth and decline, ecclesiastical restructuring, war and peacemaking marked Presbyterian life and discussions among the faithful. Confessing anew that "God was in Christ reconciling the world to himself" (II Cor. 5:19), Presbyterians faced problems and promises, joining with other Christians, Orthodox and Roman Catholics, in a ministry of reconciliation, and with all human beings in a quest for a safer and more humane world community in the nuclear age and on spaceship earth.

St. Clair McKelway, writer for the New Yorker, poked fun at his ancestry. Relatives extended back into colonial America, from the Smiths of Hampden-Sydney to Alexander McKelway, a champion of child labor legislation. This heritage McKelway envisioned as pressing on his skull (above) as a weighty Presbyterian pyramid. Meanwhile Robert McAfee Brown, with deep roots in American Presbyterianism, was writing the *Spirit of Protestantism* (1961). A popular author, Brown taught at Macalester College, Stanford University, Union Theological Seminary (NY), and the Pacific School of Religion. Many Presbyterians shared Brown's catholic and ethical spirit, and his view that we are a pilgrim people.

Robert McAfee Brown

1960 The ecumenical spirit among Presbyterians in the 1950s culminated in the formation of the United Presbyterian Church in the United States of America (UPCUSA) when the Presbyterian Church in the United States of America and the United Presbyterian Church of North America voted to merge. Harrison Ray Anderson (right), descendant of Gardiner Spring and pastor of the Fourth Presbyterian Church of Chicago, was a long-time proponent of ecumenism and chairman of the union committee. The General Assemblies of the denominations processed through the streets of Pittsburgh in the rain on May 27, 1958 to celebrate the occasion.

Theophilus Mills Taylor (left), a minister of the UPCNA and professor of New Testament studies at Pittsburgh-Xenia Theological Seminary, was elected the first moderator of the new denomination. As moderator he accepted Celtic crosses from the past moderators of the two churches. He expressed the desire that the Presbyterian Church in the United States might soon become a part of the body.

1960 Herbert Meza (right), pastor of the St. Stephens Presbyterian Church, Houston, TX, helped to organize and preside over the meeting of the Houston Ministerial Association, at which John F. Kennedy spoke. As a presidential hopeful he delivered a response to those Americans who were suspicious of his candidacy because of Roman Catholic thought on "church-state" relations.

Organic unity among American Protestants was urged by Eugene Carson Blake, Stated Clerk of the UPCUSA, in a sermon delivered at Grace Cathedral of the Protestant Episcopal Church in San Francisco, at the invitation of Bishop James A. Pike with whom Blake is pictured. A Consultation on Church Union was convened in 1962 to discuss plans to deal with Protestant divisions running back to the Reformation, and to formulate plans for a communion which would be catholic, reformed and evangelical.

James Hastings Nichols, professor of church history at Princeton Theological Seminary and author of *History of Christianity, 1650-1950* (1956), attended sessions of Vatican Council II (1963-65) as a Protestant observer. He stands here in front of St. Peter's in Rome.

The UPCUSA elected C. Willard Heckel, professor of law at Rutgers University, Moderator of the General Assembly in 1972. He won a rare first ballot victory, showing the confidence the commissioners had in his leadership. Heckel was a lifelong member of the Bloomfield Presbyterian Church, NJ.

Willard Heckel

During these decades the National Council of Presbyterian Men played an active role in church affairs. They met at the Palmer House in Chicago in 1958 to celebrate a tenth anniversary of organized men's work.

William O. Douglas

J. Howard Pew

William O. Douglas (1898-1980) spent his earliest years in the manse of his father and mother, William and Julia Douglas, home missionaries to the West. Appointed Associate Justice of the Supreme Court by Franklin Delano Roosevelt, he served with distinction, yet to the consternation of some. An author, in *An Almanac of Liberty* (1954), he cited the "Presbyterian Letter" of 1953 as a landmark statement against repression. He was also a leading environmentalist.

J. Howard Pew (1882-1971), president of the Sun Oil Company, headed the Presbyterian Foundation and the National Lay Committee, formed to gain support for the new National Council of Churches in 1950. Pew was deeply troubled about what he thought was a dangerous mixing of religion and politics in the period.

Edward D. Grant, a native of Scotland and chemical industrialist of Baton Rouge, LA, made a distinguished record as head of the Board of Christian Education, PCUS, in Richmond. He was moderator of the General Assembly in 1962.

Lamar Williamson, elder and lawyer, kept minutes for forty-one years as clerk of the session of the First Presbyterian Church, Monticello, Arkansas. As he added humor to his minutes, so he spiced his official duties with memorable acts. When deacons failed to repair the roofs of the church, he walked down the aisle one Sunday with umbrella at full mast until they got the point.... *And a Time to Laugh* (1966) carries excerpts from Williamson's years of observing the way Presbyterians behave in their solemn meetings.

Edward D. Grant

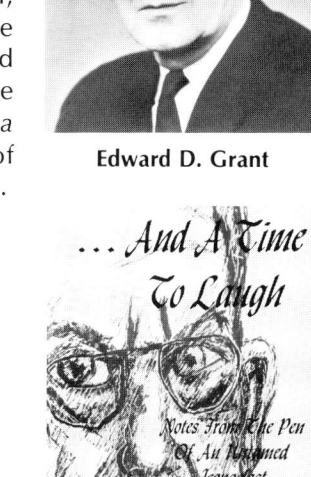

Lamar Williamson

Frank P. Graham & Jawaharlal Nehru

John Glenn

Ruling elder, Frank Porter Graham (1886-1972), President of the University of North Carolina, Chapel Hill, supported desegregation in his local congregation, his state, and the South. Graham's skill as a diplomat was tested as a representative of the United Nations in the 1950s and 1960s. Graham is shown here with Prime Minister Nehru dealing with the Kashmir problem.

John Glenn crawls into space capsule, Friendship, for his 1962 flight into space. From New Concord, Ohio, a graduate of Muskingum College, and an active Presbyterian, Glenn entered politics after his career with the armed services and NASA. Ohio thought he had the "Right Stuff," and elected him senator.

United Presbyterian Women, formed in 1958, met in assembly to worship and to discuss the work of the church.

Letty Russell

Lois Stair

Sara Moseley

In the PCUS and the UPCUSA, churches elected women as elders and commissioners to judicatories. Finally, in 1972, the UPCUSA elected Lois Stair from Michigan moderator of the General Assembly. The PCUS followed suit by electing Sarah B. Moseley of Sherman, TX, moderator in 1978. Presbyterian women found voice and a champion in Yale professor of theology and women's studies, Letty M. Russell who wrote on *Human Liberation in a Feminist Perspective* (1974).

1963 Presbyterians joined blacks and other Americans in a protest for civil rights in the 1960s. J. Randolph Taylor, pastor of the Church of the Pilgrims, Washington, D.C., and head of the Fellowship of Concern, PCUS, participated with others in the "March on Washington," 1963. Over 200,000 gathered at the Lincoln Memorial and heard Martin Luther King witness: "I Have a Dream." Eugene Carson Blake, stated clerk of the UPCUSA, entered a police wagon after his arrest in Baltimore, MD. On 4 July 1963, he and a distinguished group of black and white leaders attempted to integrate an amusement park.

Edler G. Hawkins

Lawrence Bottoms

Eugene C. Blake

Presbyterian J. Oscar McCloud, shown with his wife, Robbie, and Mary Jane Patterson, exercised power in the church as head of the Program Agency of the UPCUSA. Edler Hawkins served as the first black moderator of the denomination in 1964, while Lawrence Bottoms was elected to that office in the PCUS in 1974.

Mary Jane Patterson, Oscar & Robbie McCloud

Minorities within the Presbyterian denominations organized to make their concerns known in the church. Jorge Larabraud, Mexican-American, spoke for that community as he worked both for the National Council of Churches and the PCUS as secretary of the Council on Theology and Culture. Cecil Corbett gave leadership to Native American causes. Various oriental groups organized the National Asian Presbyterian Council in 1972.

Jorge Larabraud

Cecil Corbett

1982 National Asian Presbyterian Council Assembly

Presbyterian School of Christian Education

Accent was on youth in the 1960s and 1970s. The Presbyterian School of Christian Education, Richmond, VA, provided a rich variety of approaches to education. On public television, Fred Rogers, Presbyterian minister, Pittsburgh, PA, conversed with children in "Mister Rogers' Neighborhood." Youth stimulated innovations in public worship with guitars and in dance, and Rev. Pat McGeachy, Nashville, TN, gave leadership to this movement. Children of the Church of the Divine Redeemer, San Antonio, TX, studied Mexican dancing.

Mister Rogers' Neighborhood

Pat McGeachy

Students demonstrated their political interests in this mock political convention in Westminster College, New Wilmington, PA, in 1960.

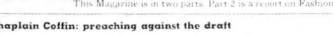

Presbyterians divided in the debate over the war in Southeast Asia during the 1960s and 1970s. William Sloane Coffin, Jr., Presbyterian and Yale University Chaplain, gave active leadership to the civil rights movement and antiwar protest.

Two PCUS ministers of Little Rock, AR, F. Wellford Hobbie and Guy Delaney, gave voice to the generation gap with this billboard which they paid to have displayed in their city. The pastors were attacked for their opposition to the war effort.

Dean Rusk (1909-) dropped a fifteen-foot shot through a basketball net when he returned to Davidson College, where he played center as a student in 1929. Son of a Presbyterian minister, Robert Hugh Rusk, Dean Rusk was Secretary of State, 1960-1968.

St. Andrews College, Laurinburg, NC, was built in the 1960s to accommodate the handicapped.

St. Andrews College Students

Maggie Kuhn, founder of the Gray Panthers, saw to it that the church and the nation remembered those in the winter of their years. Kuhn, long with the Presbyterian Board of Christian Education, became an active champion of the elderly. Thomas B. Robb, a Presbyterian minister, celebrated retirement in his book entitled, *The Bonus Years* (1968). Westminster Towers, sponsored by the First Presbyterian Church, Orlando, FL, is home for many of the retired, and is among numerous Presbyterian facilities located across the nation.

Westminster Towers

Eugene Smathers

Kiowa, CO, Camp Meeting

Big Lick, TN, rural minister, Eugene Smathers, was elected moderator of the UPCUSA General Assembly in 1967. John M. Walker pastor in North Carolina helped mountain people understand the Gospel with his wood carvings. In this one (above) Walker shows Jesus with the disciples in Emmaus breaking bread, wearing the overalls of Appalachians. *Foxfire* focused attention on the Rabun-Gap Napoochee school where Presbyterians helped to train young men and women of the region.

The First Presbyterian Church, Santa Fe NM (below), represented the growing importance of the Sunbelt, while in Kiowa CO, the ranchers held a camp meeting. William Everhart was the preacher.

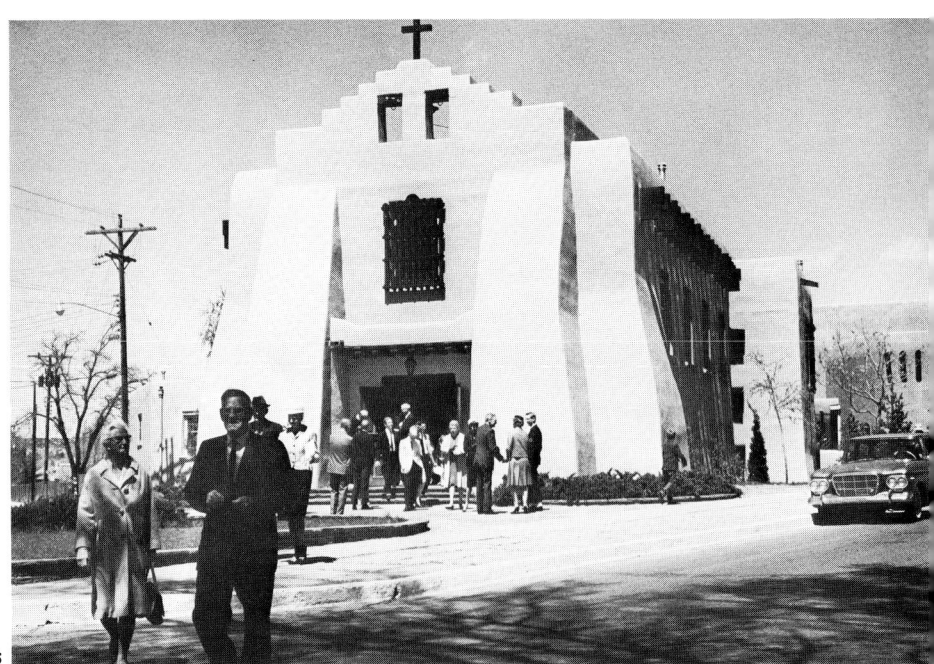

Theologians of the 1950s and 1960s returned to the Bible and the Reformation for guidance in dealing with the problems of the age. For these Neo-Reformation or Neo-Orthodox theologians, Martin Luther, John Calvin, and John Knox provided inspiration and insight. Houston's Central Presbyterian Church built a Chapel of the Reformation with statues of the key Reformers. Knox stands life-size with the frisbie in his hand—put there by some playful church members.

1962 American Presbyterians were influenced by Swiss theologian Karl Barth (1886-1968). He visited the United States in 1962 to deliver lectures at Princeton Theological Seminary. James I. McCord, president, and George S. Hendry, professor of theology, were his hosts. Barth visited the Civil War battle fields around Richmond, VA, where he fired a Confederate rifle. He asked for a copy of Robert L. Dabney's *Systematic and Polemic Theology* (1871), and informed one inquirer during his stay that his faith could be summarized in the words: "Jesus loves me, this I know, For the Bible tells me so."

1967 Reflecting theological ferment, United Presbyterians adopted a *Book of Confessions* in 1967 at the General Assembly held in Portland, OR. This included the *Nicene Creed, Apostles' Creed,* the *Scots Confession,* the *Heidelberg Catechism,* the *Second Helvetic Confession,* the *Westminster Confession of Faith* and *Shorter Catechism,* the *Theological Declaration of Barmen,* and the *Confession of 1967,* all represented in the symbols of the banners. Edward A. Dowey of Princeton Theological Seminary was chairman of the committee which brought in the proposal.

Edward A. Dowey

Carl McIntire, of the Bible Presbyterian Church, hired a coffin and a hearse to observe what he believed to be the death of American Presbyterianism.

238

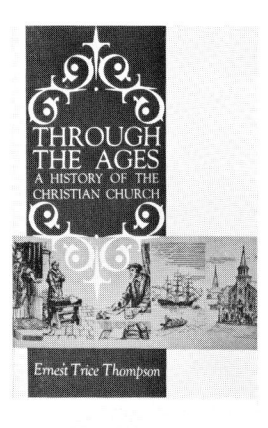

Under the direction of Marshall C. Dendy, secretary of the Board of Christian Education, Richmond, VA, the PCUS began to use the Covenant Life Curriculum, a major educational program of graded books and aids. It allowed Christians to study the Bible, theology, history, and ethics. William Bean Kennedy, minister and professor of the PCUS, introduced the curriculum with his study, *Into Covenant Life* (1963).

Theologian, seminary president, pastor, Albert C. Winn presided over the writing and discussion of "A Declaration of Faith," a new confessional proposal for the PCUS with a Book of Confessions. Although the proposal did not receive the approval of the necessary three-fourths of the presbyteries in 1976, the General Assembly adopted the Declaration as a contemporary statement of Christian faith and life and encouraged its use in the churches.

Albert C. Winn

Presbyterians persisted through earthquake, wind, and fire, although natural disasters still took a toll on churches. The First Presbyterian Church, Monroe, LA, was surrounded by water in a flash flood of 1978, and a hurricane tossed the concrete Celtic cross of the Central Presbyterian Church, Mobile, AL, across the street in 1979.

According to some Presbyterians the Holy Spirit gave spiritual gifts and stirred what was known as the Charismatic Movement within the churches. Leaders George C. "Brick" Bradford (left), Oklahoma City, and James A. Brown (right and above), pastor of the Upper Octorara Presbyterian Church, Parkesburg, PA, examine a new book by J. Rodman Williams, professor of Austin Theological Seminary (center). Williams described the present renewal as *The Era of the Spirit* (1967). Brown leads his congregation in prayer and praise.

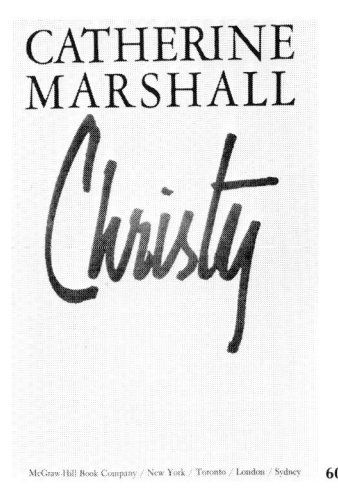

Author Catherine Marshall wrote widely read books of spiritual guidance, such as *Beyond Our Selves* (1961), and contributed to *Guideposts* magazine. She remembered her own Presbyterian childhood in the novel *Christy* (1967).

Camp Hanover

Robert Lee, professor at San Francisco Theological Seminary, explored an aspect of the period in his book, *Religion and Leisure in America* (1964). At retreat and conference centers, such as Camp Hanover (VA), Ghost Ranch (AZ) and Montreat (NC), Presbyterians learned to play and to use their time more creatively.

Ghost Ranch

Assembly Inn, Montreat

241

Tom Clark

Always concerned to preserve the American Presbyterian heritage since its founding in 1852, the Presbyterian Historical Society moved into a new building in 1967, in Philadelphia. Supreme Court Associate Justice Tom Clark, a member of the National Presbyterian Church, Washington, spoke at the dedication. To house the rapidly expanding archival collections of the United Presbyterian Church, the National Council of Churches, and many other organizations, the Society added new space in 1977. Statues of Francis Makemie, John Witherspoon, John McMillan, Samuel Davies, James Caldwell and Marcus Whitman in front of the building recall the past. William B. Miller has directed the Society since 1960.

Francis Makemie

John Witherspoon

Texas Presbyterians originally organized what was to become the PCUS Historical Foundation, now located in Montreat, NC. The Foundation expanded its facility in 1982.

242

WARC, Nairobi, 1970

1970 The World Alliance of Reformed Churches (founded as the World Presbyterian Alliance in 1875) met in Nairobi, Kenya, in 1970. At that meeting the Alliance received into membership the International Congregational Council. Now known as the World Alliance of Reformed Churches (Presbyterian and Congregational), the ecumenical body of Christians publishes the *Reformed World*.

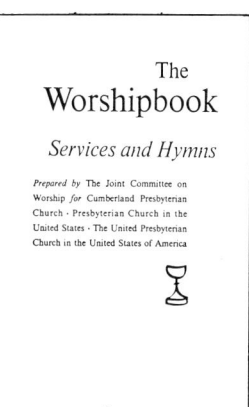

To upgrade and update worship and singing, the Joint Committee on Worship for the Cumberland Presbyterian Church, the PCUS, and the UPCUSA, produced *The Worshipbook* (1970).

At a time some Presbyterians were expanding their ecumenical ties, in the South the Presbyterian Church in America organized. Made up of congregations troubled by what they perceived to be liberal theological tendencies and unbiblical practices, for example the ordination of women, the church held its first General Assembly in the Briarwood Presbyterian Church, Birmingham, AL.

First General Assembly, Presbyterian Church in America

243

THE PRESBYTERIAN Layman

A monthly publication of the Presbyterian Lay Committee, Inc., an organization of Presbyterian laymen dedicated to the adherence of our Church to its primary mission—the teaching and preaching of the Gospel of Jesus Christ.

Roger Hull

Paul Cupp

Troubled by trends in the UPCUSA, a number of members headed by Roger Hull, elder and president of New York Life Insurance Co., and Paul Cupp, Mutual Life Insurance, among others established the Presbyterian Lay Committee, Inc., and published *The Presbyterian Layman* in order that conservative concerns might be more forcefully represented throughout the churches.

Former medical missionary to China, elected moderator of the PCUS in 1972, L. Nelson Bell championed conservative causes in the denomination. He helped to found the *Southern Presbyterian Journal* in 1940 and *Christianity Today* in 1956. This family portrait includes Dr. and Mrs. Bell with their children and grandchildren, John N. Somerville (standing, left) and his wife (seated, left), missionaries of the PCUS in Korea, Billy and Ruth Graham (standing, fourth and fifth, left), and B. Clayton Bell (standing, right). Leighton Ford, son-in-law, Presbyterian minister, and evangelist, was not available for this picture.

Interchurch
Center, NYC

During the 1970s Presbyterians, UPCUSA and PCUS, went through a process of restructuring ecclesiastical organization. The UPCUSA organized its work under the General Assembly with a General Assembly Mission Council, and moved most of its national operations to 475 Riverside Drive, New York City. The PCUS developed its Assembly programs under the General Assembly Mission Board, and moved its operations to the Presbyterian Center, Ponce de Leon Ave., Atlanta, GA. The denominations also tried to shift more responsibilities to the synods, presbyteries and sessions.

Presbyterian Center, Atlanta

For years editors Aubrey N. Brown (left), Ernest Trice Thompson (center), and George Laird Hunt (right), championed progressive causes such as civil rights, economic justice, and ecumenism through the *Presbyterian Outlook*, an independent weekly published in Richmond, VA.

245

Eugene Carson Blake, General Secretary of the World Council of Churches, expressed the Council's ecumenical spirit as well as that of his own denomination in welcoming His Holiness Athenagoras, Ecumenical Patriarch (Constantinople) to the organization's headquarters in 1967. He also welcomed Pope Paul VI to the Ecumenical Centre in Geneva in 1969. These visits symbolized closer contacts between Protestants, Orthodox and Roman Catholics in an ecumenical age.

Claire Randall, General Secretary of the National Council of Churches and a Presbyterian, stands in the Forbidden City, Peking, in 1981 during the first official visit of United States Christians with Chinese Christians in the People's Republic of China in three decades.

246

John Templeton, member of the Englewood Presbyterian Church, NJ, investment counselor, and resident of the Bahamas, awarded the Templeton Prize for progress in religion to Mother Teresa, Calcutta, for her work among India's poor. The presentation took place in 1973.

1980 In 1980 the UPCUSA adopted a report entitled "Peacemaking: The Believers' Calling," a paper later adopted and adapted by the PCUS. Motivated by pastoral concern, the denominations invited constituents to consider the call of the Bible to all Christians to be peacemakers in their homes, communities and the world. Filled with an urgency about the arm's race, Presbyterians joined hundreds of thousands of marchers in New York in 1982 to express this concern. Donald Shriver, minister of the PCUS and President of Union Theological Seminary, NY, joined the demonstrators, while Stated Clerk, William P. Thompson addressed the United Nations Disarmament Conference expressing concern about the threat of nuclear war.

247

1983 The two General Assemblies met in Atlanta to take final action, and brought into existence the Presbyterian Church (U.S.A.), ending the major division of American Presbyterians. Moderators John Anderson (PCUS) and James Costen (UPCUSA) celebrated the Lord's Supper with commissioners of the reunited church. They used communion ware belonging to the Upper Octorara Presbyterian Church, PA, representing the church's colonial heritage. James E. Andrews (second, left) became Stated Clerk of the new denomination.

J. Randolph Taylor, pastor of the Myers Park Presbyterian Church and co-chairman with Robert C. Lamar, Albany, NY, of the reunion committee, was elected the first moderator of the PC(U.S.A.) General Assembly.

J. Randolph Taylor

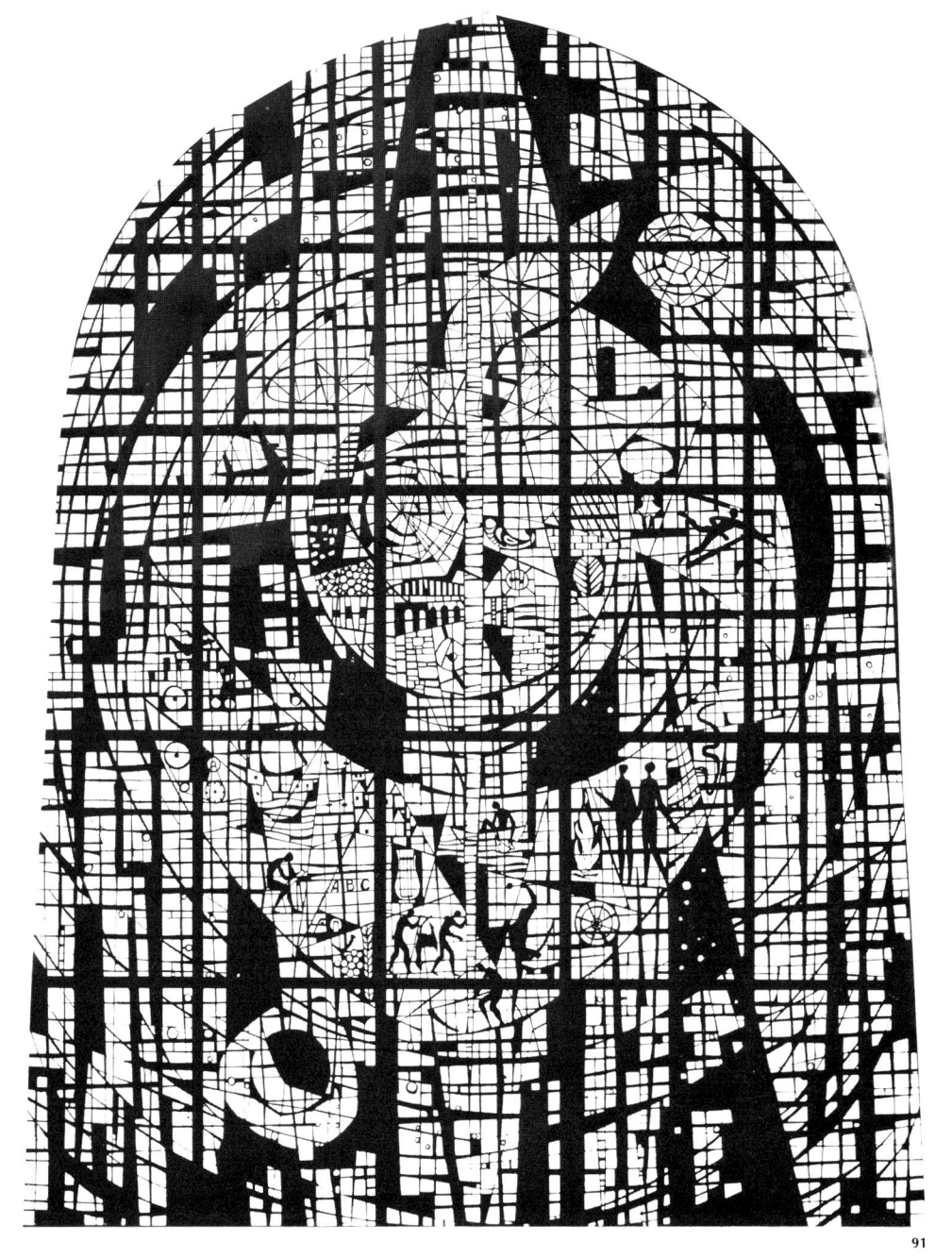

The Great Foyer Window of the Harvey Browne Memorial Presbyterian Church, Louisville, KY, represents the providential eye of God, and reminds Presbyterians of God's whole creation, the history of the whole human family, and of the drama of salvation through Jesus Christ. The Willet Stained Class Studio, Philadelphia, PA, depicts this larger view of the human drama in the context of which Presbyterians have been witnesses.

Using the biblical text, Galatians 5:1: "Stand fast therefore in the liberty wherewith Christ hath made us free, and be not entangled again with the yoke of bondage," the Westminster Presbyterian Church, Minneapolis, MN, erected a bronze sculpture showing the four states of being free as a Christian testimony. The eighteen foot high sculpture by Paul T. Granlund stands in the center of the city and beckons toward God's future.

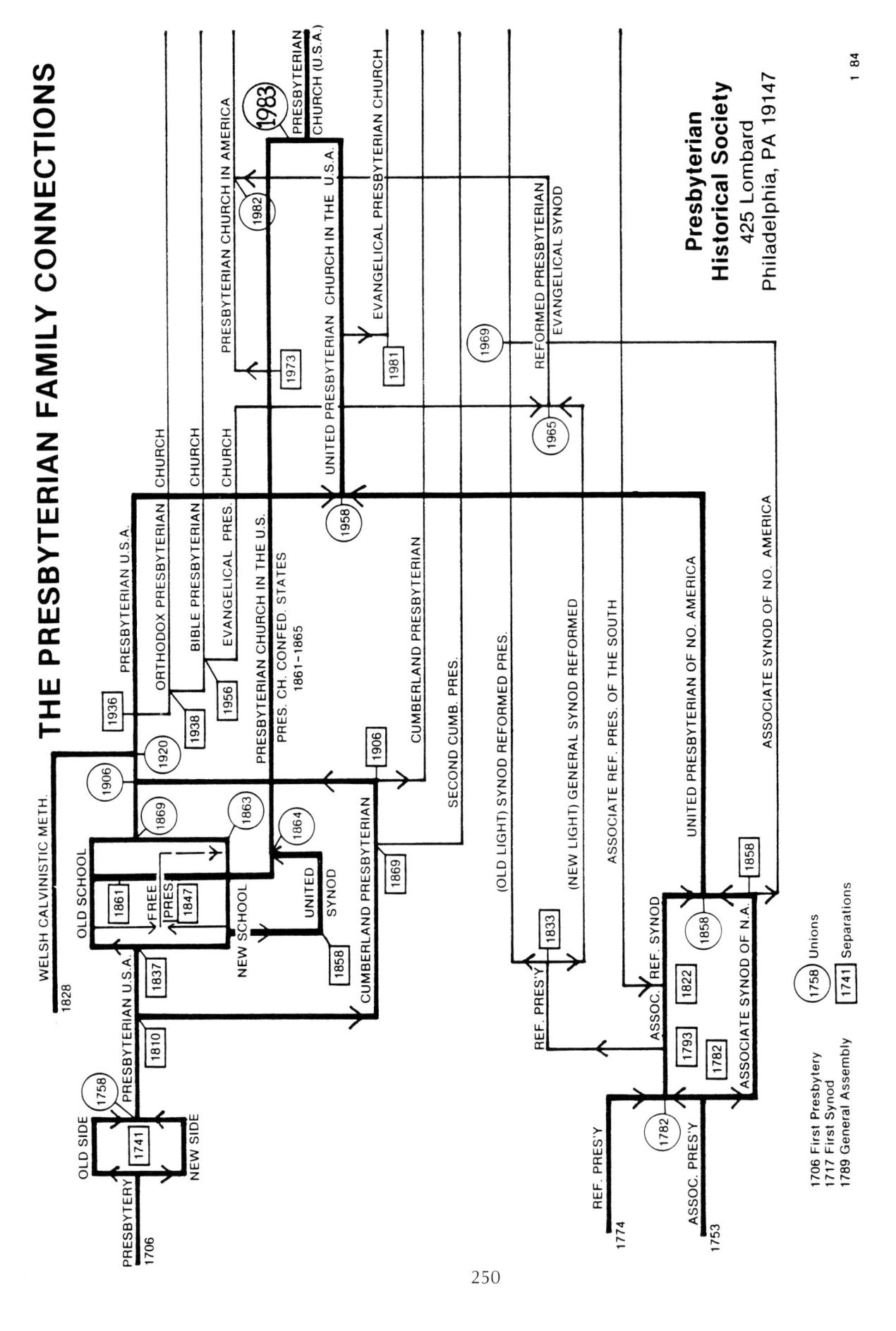

THE PRESBYTERIAN FAMILY CONNECTIONS

Presbyterian Historical Society
425 Lombard
Philadelphia, PA 19147

1706 First Presbytery
1717 First Synod
1789 General Assembly

(1758) Unions
[1741] Separations

Acknowledgments

The author and publisher have made every effort to trace the ownership of all printed materials, and to the best of their knowledge have secured all necessary permissions. Should there be any correction regarding the use of any print, the author, upon notification, will be pleased to make proper acknowledgment in future editions.

Sincere thanks are due to the following individuals, publishers, institutions and agents for their cooperation in allowing the use of their materials.

Prints not listed below are from the collections of the Presbyterian Historical Society.

Abbreviations: HF = The Historical Foundation, Montreat, NC
LC = From the Collections of the Library of Congress
RNS = Religious News Service Collection
PL = *Presbyterian Life*
UTS, VA = Union Theological Seminary, VA, Library
VASL = Virginia State Library

Chapter I

Print no.:
1. The Willet Stained Glass Studios, Inc.
3, 4. Iona Community.
5. Waldensian Museum, Waldensian Presbyterian Church, Valdese, NC 28690.
6. Giorgio Tourn, *The Waldensians, The First 800 Years* (Claudiana, 1980), picture 12. Used with permission of The American Waldensian Society, NY.
7. *Ibid*, picture 15.
8. PL, "Photo by R.J.C."
9. Solomon Modell, *A History of the Western World*, v.2, ©1974. Adapted by permission of Prentice-Hall, Inc., Englewood Cliffs, NJ in *Europe in the Reformation*, by Peter J. Klassen, ©1979, p. 282.
10. E. Doumergue, *Iconographie Calvinienne* (Lausanne, Georges Bridel, 1909), pl. XIII.
11. Musee historique de al Reformation, Geneve.
14. E. Doumergue, *Geneva Past and Present*... (Geneva, Atar, [n.d.]) opp. p. 44.
15. Bibliotheque publique et universitaire, Geneva.
16. Pierre-Ch. George.
17. W. Sibley Towner.
21. HF.
23. UTS, VA.
24. Joseph H. Dubbs, *Historic Manual of the Reformed Church* (Lancaster, PA, 1888).
25, 26, 27. The Evangelical and Reformed Historical Society.
30. Painting by Stanley Meltzoff, © National Geographic Society.
31. UTS, VA.
34. By permission of the Folger Shakespeare Library.
41. The Trustees of the British Museum.
43. LC.
45. Ulster Museum.
46. Picture Collection, Branch Libraries, The New York Public Library.

Chapter II

Print no.:
1. PL, Carl G. Karsch photograph.
8. UTS, VA.
12. George W. Winans, *First Presbyterian Church of Jamaica, New York*... (Jamaica, NY, The Church, 1943), op. p. 21.
13. John Speer photograph.
14. The Session of the First Presbyterian Church, Southampton, NY.
18, 19. Ralph R. Johnson photograph.
21. By permission of the Houghton Library, Harvard University.
23. HF.
24. PL, Carl G. Karsch photograph.
29. John Wollaston painting. LC.
35. By permission of the Houghton Library, Harvard University.
37. Joseph Badger, *Mrs. Jonathan Edwards (Sarah Pierpont)*. Bequest of Eugene Phelps Edwards. Yale University Art Gallery.
39. Jonathan Edwards wood carving by C. Keith Wilbur, M.D.
42, 43. University of Delaware Archives.
46. Unknown artist, *Mrs. Aaron Burr*. Bequest of Oliver Burr Jennings. Yale University Art Gallery.
48. LC.
49. PL.
52. Carl T. Julien.
57. UTS, VA.
60. *Historical Atlas of Religion in America*, by Edwin Scott Gaustad (New York, Harper & Row), ©1962 by Edwin Scott Gaustad. Used by permission.
61. All rights reserved, The Metropolitan Museum of Art.

Chapter III

Print no.:
1. UTS, VA.
2. © The National Galleries of Scotland.
4. University of Delaware Archives.

6. Courtesy of the Historical Society of Delaware.
7. LC.
11. Stanley P. Watson, Photographer. Courtesy of Pennsylvania Power & Light Co.
12. The Library Company of Philadelphia.
14, 15. Princeton University Archives.
16. PL.
17. Courtesy of the John Carter Brown Library at Brown University.
18. Hanover Presbytery, Executive Council.
19. Copyright Yale University Art Gallery. Used by permission.
21. Courtesy of Washington and Lee University, Lexington, VA.
24. Jones Rare Book Room, Hampden-Sydney College.
25. VASL.
27. Courtesy, The Henry Francis du Pont Winterthur Museum.
32. Courtesy of the New-York Historical Society, N.Y.C.
33. John Trumbull, Daniel Morgan (miniature). Copyright Yale University Art Gallery.
34. Wadsworth Atheneum, Hartford.
35. Courtesy of the New-York Historical Society, N.Y.C.
38. Courtesy, Tennessee State Museum.
42. Princeton University Archives.
47. Photograph by Iola Parker. Courtesy, Bethel Presbyterian Church, Bethel Park, PA.
48. Courtesy, Tennessee State Museum.
49. Hamilton College.
50. Carl T. Julien.
56. HF.
57. Carl T. Julien.
59, 61. HF.
62. PL.
65, 66. LC.
67. National Presbyterian Church, Washington, DC.

Chapter IV

Print no.:

1, 2. Photograph by Mary Elinor Eppler.
3. John R. Rogers.
4. Disciples of Christ Historical Society.
5. Whaling Museum, Old Dartmouth Historical Society, New Bedford, MA.
14. The Lilly Library, Indiana University, Bloomington, IN.
16. Carl T. Julien.
17. Courtesy of the Essex Institute, Salem, MA.
18, 19. From *A People Called Cumberland Presbyterians*, copyright © 1972 by Frontier Press, Cumberland Presbyterian Church. Used by permission.
20. The Historical Foundation of the Cumberland Presbyterian Church.
23. First Presbyterian Church, Baltimore, MD.
24. The Edward W. C. Arnold Collection. Lent by the Metropolitan Museum of Art. Photograph courtesy Museum of the City of New York.
25, 26. HF.
28. Frick Art Reference Library photograph.
30. UTS, VA.
31. Columbia Theological Seminary.
32. McCormick Theological Seminary.
34. Davidson College Communication Office.
35. Centre College.
37. Lafayette College.
40. Illinois College.
41. Muskingum College.
45. First Presbyterian Church, Detroit, MI.
47, 48. UTS, VA.
58, 59. LC.
60. Photograph by H. L. Broadbelt.
61. Photograph by William H. Patterson, Jr.
62. LC.
63. Courtesy, Tennessee State Museum.
66, 67. LC.
68. The Ladies Hermitage Association.
69. LC.
70. Oklahoma Historical Society, Photograph Archives.
71. Courtesy, Dwight Mission Agency.
73. Marjorie L. Barnhart.
74. Yale University Art Gallery, Gift of Dr. Parker about 1840.
77. Frick Art Reference Library photograph.
80. Frick Art Reference Library photograph.
81. Oberlin College Archives.
85. HF.
87, 88. Courtesy, Georgia Department of Archives and History.
89. © Mrs. Louise Bristol. Used with permission.
91. HF.
95, 96. HF.
98. Robert Tabscott.

Chapter V

Print no.:

1. RNS.
2. Hanover Presbytery, Executive Council.
3. UTS, VA.
6. From *Presbyterian Panorama* by Clifford M. Drury. Copyright, 1952, Board of Christian Education, Presbyterian Church in the United States of America. Reproduced and used by permission of The Westminster Press, Philadelphia, PA.
9, 10. The Evangelical and Reformed Historical Society.
12. HF.
13. LC.
16. LC.
17. Courtesy, Mrs. Marrion Blair Edmundson.
22. Erskine Clark.
24. HF.
25. The Historical Society of Pennsylvania.
28. Tompkins-McCaw Library, MCV Campus of Virginia Commonwealth University.
31. Second Presbyterian Church, Richmond, VA.
32. Courtesy of Tennessee State Museum.
33. Archives and Manuscript Section, Tennessee State Library and Archives.
34. HF.
35, 36. Paul Kane sketches. Courtesy of The Royal Ontario Museum, Toronto, Canada.
38. RNS.
39. Pacific University Library.
40. Protestant ladder drawn by Rev. & Mrs. Spalding, 1845-6. Neg. 627. Oregon Historical Society.
41. Courtesy, U.S. Postal Service.
43, 44, 45. San Francisco Theological Seminary Archives.
47, 48. The Hawaiian Mission Children's Society.
49. Courtesy of The Mariner's Museum of Newport News, VA.
50, 51, 52. University of Dubuque.
53. LC.

54. State Historical Society of Wisconsin.
55. HF.
61. National Portrait Gallery, Smithsonian Institution, Washington, DC.
62. University of Virginia Library.
69. U.S. Postal Service.
71, 72. LC.
79, 80. Photograph courtesy M. Knoedler & Co., collection unknown.
86. UTS, VA.
87, 88, 89. United States Military Academy Library, West Point, NY.
93. HF.
94. Carl T. Julien.

Chapter VI

Print no.:

3, 4. LC.
8. LC.
9. UTS, VA.
10. LC.
16. HF.
17, 18. Moorland-Spingarn Research Center, Howard University.
20. Georgia Department of Archives and History.
25, 26, 27. VASL.
29, 30, 31. HF.
33. Fourth Presbyterian Church. Ruins after 1871 fire. ICHi-02721. Chicago Historical Society.
34. HF.
35. Missouri Historical Society. Neg. Street Scenes #467.
38. By courtesy, Union Theological Seminary Archives, The Burke Library, NYC.
39. HF.
40. Historical Foundation of the Cumberland Presbyterian Church.
43. Cornelia P. Spencer Papers #P-683, selected picture, Southern Historical Collection, Library of the University of North Carolina at Chapel Hill.
45, 46. LC.
47. College of Wooster Archives.
49, 50. © Columbia University Press. Reprinted by permission of the publisher.
51. HF.
52. Manuscripts Department, University of Virginia Library.
53. Department of Rare Books, University of Virginia Library.
54, 55, 56. Courtesy, Mark Twain Home and Museum, Hannibal, MO.
63. University of Delaware Archives.
72, 73. VASL.
75. Moorland-Spingarn Research Center, Howard University.
77. Johnson C. Smith University.
79. HF.
83. LC.
90, 91. Department of Archives and Special Collections, Sandel Library, Northeast Louisiana University, Connor Photographic Collection.
94. Courtesy, South Park Community Church, Fairplay, CO.
96, 97. John H. Sinclair.
99, 100. Calvary Presbyterian Church, San Francisco, CA.
101. San Francisco Theological Seminary, San Anselmo, CA.
102, 103. HF.

Chapter VII

Print no.:

1, 2. Second Presbyterian Church, Chicago, IL.
5, 6. LC.
8. LC.
12. Courtesy of the United States Steel Corporation.
14. Westinghouse Historical Collection, Westinghouse Electric Corporation.
15. Mellon Historical File, Mellon Bank.
16. Ulster-American Folk Park.
18. Courtesy F. T. Weyerhaeuser.
19. Robert Dollar Company.
20. The Henry Morrison Flagler Museum, Palm Beach, FL.
21. Memorial Presbyterian Church, St. Augustine, FL.
22, 23. International Harvester Company.
26. University of Pennsylvania Archives.
28. VASL.
29. President Benjamin Harrison, picture no. 102276. Culver Pictures.
32. Indianapolis Museum of Art. Gift of the Session of the First Meridian Heights Presbyterian Church.
35. HF.
46. Chicago Historical Society. G. C. Cox, photographer.
47. McCormick Theological Seminary Archives.
48. UTS, VA.
49. Austin Presbyterian Theological Seminary.
50. Courtesy of the Presbyterian and Reformed Publishing Co.
53. Union Theological Seminary Archives, The Burke Library, NYC.
69, 70. HF.
71. Pearl S. Buck Foundation, Inc.
72. HF.
77. HF.
81. HF.
84. VASL.
87. PL.
91. LC.
95. National Board, YWCA Archives.
96. LC.
97. National Presbyterian Church, Washington, DC.
101, 102, 103. LC.
104. Courtesy H. W. Glenn, Jr.
109, 110. Waldensian Presbyterian Church, Valdese, NC.
111. First Armenian Presbyterian Church, Fresno, CA.
112. Menaul Historical Library of the Southwest, Albuquerque, NM.
113. Carolyn Atkins.
120. Union Theological Seminary Archives, The Burke Library, NYC.
121. LC.
122. Monmouth College.
123, 124. Trinity University Archives.
125. HF.

Chapter VIII

Print no.:

1. *Presbyterian Survey*.
2. San Francisco Theological Seminary, San Anselmo, CA.

253

8. Princeton University Archives.
10. American Red Cross, negative no. 54-100.
12. Second Presbyterian Church, St. Louis, MO.
14, 15, 16, 17, 18, 19. HF.
22. HF.
24. Courtesy, American Cast Iron Pipe Co.
26. HF.
29. Richard S. Kirkendall.
30. James W. Wallace.
31. *Presbyterian Survey*, October 1924.
32. HF.
33. Crossnore School, Inc., Crossnore, NC.
34. Jeffrey I. Meyers.
40. The Brick Presbyterian Church, NY, NY.
42. Used with permission of the Russell Sage Foundation.
43. Theodore Shaw Smylie.
44. Princeton University Library.
45, 46. LC.
47. Princeton University Library.
51. Eleanore Lansing Dulles.
52. The National Archives, picture no. 111-SC-62979.
54. Courtesy of the Billy Graham Center Museum.
55. Columbus Museum of Art, Ohio. Gift of Jeffrey Shedd.
56. *Home Mission Monthly*, July 1907.
57. *Ganado News Bulletin*, Nov. 1938.
60. Moorland-Spingarn Research Center, Howard University.
61, 62. HF.
64, 65, 66. HF.
68. Donaldina Cameron House, San Francisco, CA.
69. Courtesy of Westminster Theological Seminary.
71. G. Hall Todd.
77. UTS, VA.
78. VASL.
79. Valentine Museum, Richmond, VA.
82. From *Babbitt* by Sinclair Lewis, copyright 1922 by Harcourt Brace Jovanovich, Inc.; renewed 1950 by Sinclair Lewis. Reproduced by permission of the publisher.
83. Church of the Pilgrims, Washington, DC.
84. © National Geographic Society. Used by permission.
85, 86. Time Inc. Archives.
87. Macalester College Archives.
88. *Readers Digest*.
89. Westminster Choir College, Office of the President.
90. The Brick Presbyterian Church, NY, NY.
91. The College of Wooster Archives.
92. The National Conference of Christians and Jews.
93. *The Pittsburgh Press*.

Chapter IX

Print no.:
2. John D. Trotti.
4. Harry Fleischmann.
5, 6. Union Theological Seminary, The Burke Library, NY, NY.
7. Reinhold Niebuhr, title page from *Moral Man and Immoral Society* by Reinhold Niebuhr. Copyright 1932 Charles Scribner's Sons; copyright renewed 1960 Reinhold Niebuhr. Reprinted with permission of Charles Scribner's Sons.
8. T. Harry Blake.
9. UTS, VA.
10. East Liberty Presbyterian Church, Pittsburgh, PA.
11. U.S. Postal Service.
12. East Liberty Presbyterian Church, Pittsburgh, PA.
13. First Presbyterian Church, Kilgore, TX.
14. The Brick Presbyterian Church, NY, NY.
15. Pearl S. Buck Foundation, Inc.
16. Rosenbach Museum and Library. Photograph by Arthur Steiner. Used by permission of Clive E. Driver, Literary Executor of the Estate of Marianne C. Moore.
17. © 1974 Columbia Pictures Industries, Inc. Used by permission of Stone Public Relations Associates, Inc.
19. *Re-thinking Missions. . . ,* by William E. Hocking (New York: Harper Brothers, 1932). Copyright 1932. Reprinted by permission, Harper & Row, Publishers.
20. Robert E. Speer, Re-Thinking Missions Examined . . . (New York: Fleming H. Revell Company). Used with permission Fleming H. Revell Company.
21. Mrs. Umeko K. Momii.
25. LC.
26. PL.
30. HF.
31. Mary Agnes Brown Groover, Lt. Col., USAR Ret'd.
33. RNS.
34. PL. Stephen Deutch photograph.
35. Used by permission of Oxford University Press and John J. Compton.
36. The Brick Presbyterian Church, NY, NY.
37, 38. Westminster College, Fulton, MO.
39. John Leighton Stuart, Jr.
40, 41. First Presbyterian Church, Pittsburgh, PA.
42. PL.
43. RNS.
44. PL.
45. HF.
46. LC.
47. RNS.
48. First Presbyterian Church, Hollywood, CA.
50, 51. PL.
52. A Christian Ministry in the National Parks.
53. George E. Sweazey.
54. *Effective Evangelism: The Greatest Work in the World* by George E. Sweazey. (New York: Harper & Brothers, copyright 1953). Used with permission Harper & Row, Publishers, Inc.
55. PL.
56. RNS.
60. First Presbyterian Church, Hollywood, CA.
61. PL.
62. RNS.
64. Used with permission of Westminster Press.
65, 66. McCormick Theological Seminary.
67. UTS, VA.
70. PL.
71. HF.
72. Seward Hiltner.
73. RNS.
74. Courtesy of The Menninger Foundation.
75. A Hawthorne Book. Reprinted by permission of E. P. Dutton, Inc.
76. UTS, VA.
77. National Council of the Churches of Christ Archives.
78. RNS.
79. National Council of the Churches of Christ Archives.
80. PL. Seth Muse photograph.
81. "You Sure Everything's All Right, Foster?"—from *Herblock's Here And Now* (Simon & Schuster, 1955). Used with permission Herblock Cartoons.

82. PL.
84. Copyright 1954 Time Inc. All rights reserved. Reprinted with permission from TIME.
85. PL.
86. First Presbyterian Church, Stamford, CT.
88. Used by permission Presbyterian Publishing House.
89. Robert D. Miller.
90. HF.
91. Pittsburgh Theological Seminary.
92. Princeton Theological Seminary. Photograph by Menzies.
95. Menual Historical Library of the Southwest, Albuquerque, NM.
98. HF.
99. PL.
100. Margaret E. Towner.
101. *Presbyterian Survey.*
102. PL.

Chapter X

Print no.:

1. "The Presbyterian Pyramid," Drawing by St. Clair McKelway. © 1952, 1980 *The New Yorker Magazine, Inc.* Used with permission.
2. PL. Fred Kaplan photograph.
4, 5. PL.
6. Photo: *Houston Chronicle.* This photo may not be used for advertising purposes. This photo may not be resold. Copyright © *Houston Chronicle.*
7. PL.
8. Princeton Theological Seminary.
9. AD.
10. PL. Henry L. McCorkle photograph.
11. Collection of the United States Supreme Court.
13. Presbyterian News Service.
14. Frank P. Graham Papers, #P-1819, selected picture, Southern Historical Collection, Library of the University of North Carolina at Chapel Hill.
15. Jerry R. Tompkins, President, Presbyterian Children's Home and Service Agency of Texas.
16. National Aeronautics and Space Administration.
17. PL.
18. Letty Russell.
19. PL. W. Artin Haig photograph.
20. Presbyterian News Service.
21. *Presbyterian Survey.*
23. Presbyterian News Survey.
24. *Presbyterian Survey.*
25. AD.
27. Cook Christian Training School.
28. *Indian Quest.*
29. Sumio Koga.
30. Presbyterian School of Christian Education, Richmond, VA.
31. Fred Rogers.
32. D. Patrick McGeachy III.
33. PL. Les Bland photograph.
34. Westminster College, New Wilmington, PA.
35. © 1968 by The New York Times Company. Reprinted by permission.
36. W. Guy Delaney.
37. St. Andrews College.
38. Davidson College Communications Office.
39. Reprinted by permission of *The Philadelphia Inquirer.*
40. Westminster Towers, Orlando, FL.
41. *the bonus years. . . ,* by Thomas Bradley Robb (Valley Forge: Judson Press, 1968). Used by permission of Judson Press.
42. PL.
43. Edward L. DuPuy photograph.
44. PL. Bruce McAllister photograph.
45. PL.
46, 47. Central Presbyterian Church, Houston, TX. Fred L. Jinkins photographs.
48. Presbyterian Church (U.S.A.), Office of the General Assembly, Atlanta, GA. Alan W. Richards photograph.
49. UTS, VA Archives.
50. Princeton Theological Seminary.
51. Used by permission of Richard K. Avery and Donald Marsh.
52. Carl C. McIntire.
53. Used by permission of Presbyterian Publishing House.
54. Louisville Presbyterian Theological Seminary, Office of Information.
55. Used with permission of Spottswood Studios, Mobile, AL.
56. The *News-Star-World,* Monroe, LA.
57. PL.
58. Presbyterian Charismatic Communion.
59. Leonard E. LeSourd.
60. *Christy,* by Catherine Marshall (New York: McGraw Hill Book Company, 1967). Reproduced with permission.
61. Hanover Presbytery, Executive Council.
62. PL.
63. Montreat Conference Center.
64. Collection of the United States Supreme Court.
68. HF.
69. Allen O. Miller.
71. *Presbyterian Journal.*
72. Presbyterian Lay Committee, Inc.
75. Mrs. John N. Somerville.
76. National Council of the Churches of Christ Archives.
78. Presbyterian Church (U.S.A.), Office of the General Assembly, Atlanta, GA.
80, 81. World Council of Churches. John Taylor photographs.
82. National Council of the Churches of Christ Archives.
83. Templeton Foundation, Inc.
84. Robert F. Smylie.
86. AD.
87, 88. Lucille L. Rieben photographs.
89, 90. *Presbyterian Survey.* Charles Rafshoon photograph.
91. Willet Studios, Philadelphia, PA.
92. Westminster Presbyterian Church, Minneapolis, MN.

Index

A

Adams, John Q., 71
An Address to the Rev. Dr. Alison. . . (1765), [t.p.] 36
Adopting Act (1729), 15; [illus.] 22
An Affirmation. . . Presbyterian Church. . . (1924), [t.p.] 188
Africa, Pby. mission, 122
Africo-American Presbyterian, [illus.] 185
Afro-American Presbyterian Council, 185
Agnew, D. Hayes, [illus.] 141
Ahmaogak, Roy, [illus.] 208
Aitken, Robert, 45
Alaska, 131
Alaska, Pby. mission, 146
Albany, NY, Italian evangelization conf. (1920), [illus.] 184
Alcohol, temperance movement, 67; [poster] 174
Alexander, Archibald, 63, 68; [illus.] 62
Alexander, Mary, [illus.] 93
Alexander, Samuel C., 127
Alexander, William P., [illus.] 93
Alexandria, VA, Old Pby. Mtg. Hse., [illus.] 47
Alison, Francis, 32, 36, 41; [illus.] 26, 34
Allahabad, India, Higginbottom agricultural mission, [illus.] 200
Allegheny Sem., 100
Allen, Dinarca, [illus.] 63
Alliance of Reformed Churches Throughout the World. . ., 107, 128, 243; 2d General Coun., Philadelphia (1880), [illus.] 129
Allison, Matilda, [illus.] 163
Alton, IL, Lovejoy riot, [illus.] 80
Amends, Marilyn, [illus.] 211
American Anti-Slavery Soc., 84f.
American Assoc. for the Advancement of Science, 87
American Bible Soc., 105; [logo] 67
American Board of Commissioners for Foreign Missions, 58, 74, 93
American Caste Iron Pipe Co., 175
American Colonization Soc., 69, 105
American Guild of Organists, 193
American Home Missionary Soc., 105
American Peace Soc., 60
American Presbyterian Congo Mission, 172f.
American Red Cross, 170
American Sunday School Union, 61, 104
American Temperance Soc., 67
American Tract Magazine, [illus.] 67
American Tract Soc., 105; publications, [illus.] 67
American Woman's Home, 95
Amethyst, [illus.] 171
Anderson, Emma, [illus.] 151
Anderson, Harrison R., [illus.] 226
Anderson, Isaac, [illus.] 65
Anderson, John, [illus.] 248
Andrews, James E., [illus.] 248
Andrews, Jedediah, 16
Anglicans, 14, 32; [cartoon] 35
Antonelli, Roland G., v
Apologia Verae Doctrinae. . . Waldenses. . . , 3
Apostles' Creed, [banner] 238
Appalachian Mts., Pby. mission, 177
Architecture, Egyptian revival, 87, 89; Gothic, 88; Greek revival, 58; Italian renaissance, 140; Romanesque, 98, 149; church designs, [illus.] 130
Arizona, 131
Armenian immigrants, 162
Army of the Potomac, 109
Asheville, NC, 176
Asheville, NC, Children's missinary band, [illus.] 172
Asheville, NC, First Pby. Ch., 195
Ashmun Institue, 126
Asian-Americans, Pby. Ch., 232
Assembly Herald, [t.p.] 156, 181
Associate Church/Associate Reformed Church, union (1858), [illus.] 100f.
Associate Presbytery, 29
Associate Reformed Church, 45, 62
Associate Reformed Church/Associate Church, union (1858), [illus.] 100f.
Athenagoras, Ecumenical Patriarch, [illus.] 246
Atlanta, GA, Central Pby. Ch., 175
Atlanta, GA, Presbyterian Center, [illus.] 245
Atomic Age, 195, 203
Atomic Bomb, A. H. Compton, 203
Auburn Affirmation, see: An Affirmation. . . Presbyterian Church
Augusta, GA, First Pby. Ch., [illus.] 106
Augusta, GA, Haines Normal Sch., 144
Aunt Polly [Tom Sawyer], 120
Aurah, [illus.] 152
Austin College, 89
Austin Presbyterian Theo. Sem., 240; [illus.] 147
Avery Institute, 112

B

Backus, J. Trumbull, [illus.] 114
Backus, John C., [illus.] 105
Bacon, Sumner, [illus.] 59
Baird, Charles W., [illus.] 98; Eutaxia, or the Presbyterian Liturgies. . . (1855), [t.p.] 98
Baird, Robert, 81, 157; [illus.] 82; Religion in America. . . , [t.p.] 82
Baker, Daniel, [illus.] 89
Baldwin, Matthias, [illus.] 70
Baltimore, MD, First Pby. Ch., 105; [illus.] 60
Baltimore, MD, Second Pby. Ch., 79
Baltimore, Snynod, 127
Baptists, 54
Barlow, Joel, Doctor Watts's Imitation of the Psalms. . . (1785), [t.p.] 49
Barnes, Albert, [illus.] 76; The Way of Salvation. . . (1829), [t.p.] 76
Barnes, Roswell, [illus.] 215
Barnhouse, Donald G., [illus.] 206
Barrows, John H., [illus.] 149
Barth, Karl, [illus.] 237
Bartlett, Clay, 135
Baton Rouge, LA, 229
Baxter, Richard, 98
Beard, Richard, [illus.] 117; Lectures on Theology, 117
Beecher, Catherine, 94f., 97; [illus.] 95
Beecher, Edward, 80; [illus.] 65
Beecher, Henry W., 84; [illus.] 99; [cartoon] 99
Beecher, Lyman, 81, 97, 99; [illus.] 63; Six Sermons on. . . Temperance (1827), [t.p.] 67
Beirut, Syria, American Mission, [illus.] 124
Beirut, Syria, American Sch. for Girls, 124
Beirut, Syria, Female Sem., 124
Belgic Confession, 8
Bell, Alexander G., 192
Bell, B. Clayton, [illus.] 244
Bell, L. Nelson, family, [illus.] 244
Bellows, George, 183

Bellows, George, 183
Beman, Nathan S. S., [illus.] 79
Bennett, John C., 19
Bennett, Katherine J., [illus.] 186
Benson, Louis F., [illus.] 157
Bethesda, MD, Pby. Ch., v, 202
Bethune, Joanna, 61
Beverly Hills, CA, Pby. Ch., 199
Beza, Theodore, 6; [illus.] 4
Bible, Geneva, [t.p.] 11; New Testament. . . , R. Aitken (1781), [t.p.] 45; Revised Standard Ver., printing, [illus.] 215; Westminster Study Ed., [t.p.] 212; higher criticism, 148; inerrancy, 189
Bible Presbyterian Church, 238
Biblical Theology movement, 212
Biddle, Henry J., [illus.] 127
Biddle, Mary D., 127
Biddle Mem. Institute, 127
Bierkemper, Alice, [illus.] 184
Bierkemper, Charles H., [illus.] 184
Big Lick, TN, 236
Birmingham, AL, 175
Birmingham, AL, Briarwood Pby. Ch., 243
Birmingham, AL, Third Pby. Ch., 197
Birney, James G., [illus.] 84; *The American Churches. . .* , [t.p.] 84
Bishop, Robert H., [illus.] 66
Bissell, Emily, [illus.] 170
Blacks, Pby. Ch., 68f., 85, 112, 126f., 231
Blackburn, Gideon, 68; [illus.] 57
Blaikie, W. G., 128
Blaine, James G., 136
Blair, Samuel, 28
Blake, Eugene C., [illus.] 221, 227, 231, 246
Bloomfield College, 119
Bloomfield, NJ, Pby. Ch., 228
Blythe, David G., [paintings] 102
Bonnell, John S., [illus.] 214; *Psychology for Pastor and People* (1948), 214
Book of Common Prayer, 11
Book of Common Worship. . . (1906), 167; [t.p.] 170
Book of Confessions (1967), 238
Book of Discipline, 49
Borland, Francis, 14
Boston, MA, 38
Boston, MA, South Ch., 20
Bott, Susan, [illus.] 81
Bottoms, Lawrence, [illus.] 231
Boudinot, Elias, 58; [illus.] 52
Bourne, George, *The Book and Slavery Irreconcilable. . .* (1818), [t.p.] 69
Bradford, George C., [illus.] 240
Bradley, Omar, [illus.] 202
Brainerd, David, conch shell, [illus.] 25
Brazil, Pby. mission, 123
Brazil, Synod, 123
Breckinridge, Robert J., [illus.] 79
Briggs, Charles A., 149; [illus.] 148; *Whither?. . .* , [t.p.] 148
Bright, John, [illus.] 212; *History of Israel* (1959), 212
Bright, William, 211
Brooklyn, NY, Central Pby. Ch., 142
Brooklyn, NY, Lafayette Pby. Ch., 199
Brooklyn, NY, Plymouth Cong. Ch., 99
Brooklyn, NY, Siloam Pby. Ch., 68
Brown, Arthur J., 164; [illus.] 223
Brown, Aubrey N., [illus.] 245
Brown, James A., [illus.] 240
Brown, Mary Agnes, [illus.] 202; see also: Groover, Mary Agnes
Brown, Robert M., [illus.] 225; *Spirit of Protestantism* (1961), 225
Brown, William A., [illus.] 165; *Christian Theology in Outline*, 165
Brownsville, TX, 123
Bryan, George, [epitaph] 52

Bryan, James A., statue, [illus.] 197
Bryan, Jeptha, tombstone, [illus.] 53
Bryan, William J., 135, 180, 182; [illus.] 160, 190; [cartoon] 160, 190; *In His Image* (1922), [t.p.] 190
Bryn Mawr, PA, Pby. Ch., 151
Buchanan, James, [illus.] 99; [cartoon] 99; Wheatland [stamp] 99
Buck, John L., 199
Buck, Pearl, [illus.] 199; *The Exile*, 199; *Fighting Angel*, 199; *The Good Earth* (1931), 199; see also: Sydenstricker, Pearl
Bullinger, Heinreich, [illus.] 8
Burbank, J. Maze, "Revival" [caricature] 54f.
Burchard, Samuel, [cartoon] 136
Burr, Aaron, [illus.] 27
Burr, Esther, [illus.] 27
Bushnell, Horace, [illus.] 96; *Christian Nurture* (1847), [t.p.] 96
Buttrick, George, [illus.] 206

C

Cable, George, [illus.] 159; *The Silent South. . .* , [t.p.] 159
Cajuns, 159
Caldwell, James, 242; Battle of Springfield, [illus.] 42; statue, [illus.] 156
Caldwell, NJ, Pby. Ch., 137
Caldwell, William, *Union Harmony. . .* , [t.p.] 79
California, Presbytery, 92
California, Univ., 87; LA, 211
Calvin, John, 2, 4ff., 35, 98; [illus.] 4f.; statue, [illus.] 237; *Institutio Christianae religionis. . .* , [t.p.] 6; *La Forme des Prieres. . .* (1542), [t.p.] 5
Cambridge, Univ., 11
Cameron, Donaldina, [illus.] 187
Camp Hanover, VA, [illus.] 241
Campbell, Alexander, 54
Campbellites, 54
Campus Crusade, 211
Cane Ridge, KY, Cane Ridge Mtg. Hse, [illus.] 55
Canterbury, Archbp., 35
Canton, China, 74
Cardozo, Francis L., [illus.] 112
Carncastle, Ireland, Mtg. Hse., [illus.] 14
Carnegie, Andrew, 174, 179; [illus.] 139; *The Gospel of Wealth. . .* (1900), [t.p.] 139
Carnegie, Louise, 139; [illus.] 179
Cartwright, Thomas, [illus.] 11
Castletown, Ireland, Mellon homestead, [illus.] 139
Catholic Presbyterian, [t.p.] 128
Cavert, Samuel M., [illus.] 215
Cayuga-Syracuse, Presbytery, 224
Cayuse Indians, 90
Centre College, 65, 93; [illus.] 64
Chamberlain, George W., [illus.] 123
Chamberlain, Mary, [illus.] 123
Chanceford, PA, Guinston United Pby. Ch., [illus.] 29
Chanceford, PA, Old Muddy Creek Ch., [illus.] 29
Chancellorsville, VA, Battle of, 109
Chapman, J. Wilbur, [illus.] 183
Charismatic movement, [illus.] 240
Charles I, King, beheading, [illus.] 13
Charles (slave), [illus.] 112
Charleston, SC, First (Scots) Pby. Ch., [illus.] 48
Charleston, SC, Independent Pby. Ch., 48
Charleston, SC, Second Pby. Ch., [illus.] 96
Charleston, SC, Zion Pby. Ch., [illus.] 85
Charlotte, NC, 38, 127
Charlotte, NC, Covenant Pby. Ch., Chapel on wheels, [illus.] 209

Charlotte, NC, Mecklenburg Declaration celebration (1876), [illus.] 125
Charlotte, NC, Myers Pk. Pby. Ch., 249
Chartiers, PA, Women's missionary soc., [illus.] 45
Cherokee Indians, 57, 68, 73
Chiang Kai-shek, Madame, [illus.] 204
Chicago, IL, First Pby. Ch., 149
Chicago, IL, Fourth Pby. Ch., 118, 178, 226; ruins, [illus.] 116
Chicago, IL, Haymarket Sq. riot, [illus.] 141
Chicago, IL, Palmer Hse., [illus.] 228
Chicago, IL, Second Pby. Ch., angel statue, [illus.] 135; baptismal font, [illus.] 135
Chicago, Presbytery, 118
Chicago, Univ., 203
Chicago Div. Sch., 214
Chicago White Sox, 183
Chidlaw, Benjamin W., [illus.] 144
Children's Friend, [masthead] 120
The Children's Missionary, [cover] 154
Chile, Pby. mission, 123
China, People's Republic, 246; Pby. mission, 152
China, Pby. mission, 152
Chinese, immigrants, 92
Christian Church [denomination], 54
Christian Endeavor, San Francisco rally, [illus.] 166
Christianity Today, 244
Christmas Seal, 170
Church Service Soc., 157
Churchill, Winston, [illus.] 204
Cincinnati, OH, 63
City Point, VA, U.S. Christian Commission station, [illus.] 110
Civil War, 107ff., 134
Clark, Abraham, 39
Clark, Tom, [illus.] 242
Clemens, Jane L., [illus.] 120
Clemens, Samuel L., [illus.] 107, 120; *Tom Sawyer*, [illus.] 120; see also: Twain, Mark
Cleveland, Grover, 135f.; [illus.] 137; [cartoon] 137; wedding, [illus.] 137
Cleveland, Richard, 137
Clinchy, Everett R., [illus.] 194
Coffin, Henry, [illus.] 197
Coffin, William S., Jr., [illus.] 234
Coffman, John N., v
Colcord, WV, baptism, [illus.] 177
Cold War, 195, 204f.
Coligny, Gaspar de, 10
Colorado, 161
Columba, St., 2
Columbia, SC, 63
Columbia, SC, First Pby. Ch., 88
Columbia Theo. Sem., 88, 134; [illus.] 63
Colwell, Stephen, [illus.] 97; *New Themes for the Protestant Clergy...* (1851), [t.p.] 97
Communion tokens, [illus.] 15
Communism, 205, 217
Compton, Arthur H., [illus.] 194, 203; *Atomic Quest...*, [t.p.] 203
Compton, Elias, [illus.] 194
Compton, Karl, [illus.] 194
Compton, Mary, [illus.] 194
Compton, Wilson, [illus.] 194
Conestoga Manor, PA, Paxton massacre, 36
Confederate Army, prisoners of war, [illus.] 111
Confession of 1967, [banner] 238
Congo, Pby. mission, 172f.
Congregationalists, 56, 64, 66
Constance, Council (1414-18), 3
Consultation on Church Union, 227
Continental Congress, 33, 37ff.; Nassau Hall meeting, 57, [illus.] 44
Converse, John H., 151
Coolidge, Calvin, 186
Cooper, Joseph T., [illus.] 100

Corbett, Cecil, [illus.] 232
Corbett, Hunter, 168; [illus.] 169
Cornbury, Lord, [illus.] 17
Cornish, Samuel, [illus.] 68
Corporation for the Relief of Poor & Distressed..., charter, [illus.] 32
Costen, James, [illus.] 248
Cotton, John, [illus.] 13
Covenant Life Curriculum, [illus.] 239
Covenanters, 29, 45, 100
Cram, Ralph A., 198
Crane, William H., [illus.] 223
Cranmer, Thomas, 11
Creoles, 159
Cromwell, Oliver, [illus.] 13
Cross, Celtic, [illus.] 2, 226; Maltese, [illus.] 1
Crossnore, NC, 177
Crossroads, [illus.] 210
Cumberland Presbyterian, 168
Cumberland Presbyterian Church, 53, 83
Cumberland Presbyterian Church, General Assembly, 147
Cumberland Presbyterian Church/Presbyterian Ch., U.S.A., reunion (1906), 167ff.
Cumberland, Prebytery, 59
Cupp, Paul, [illus.] 244

D

Dabney, Robert L., [illus.] 109, 117; *Systematic and Polemic Theology* (1871), 237
Danville, KY, 65
Danville Theo. Sem., 179
Darien Colony, 14
Darwin, Charles, 87, 134
Davidson College, 65, 234; [illus.] 64
Davies, Samuel, 15f., 27f., 30, 156, 242; [illus.] 28; *Miscellaneous Poems...*, [t.p.] 28
Davis, Varina H., 112
Dayton, OH, Westminster Pby. Ch., choir, [illus.] 193
"Dear Mom and Dad, Your silence is killing me," [billboard] 234
DeValois, Margaret, Queen of Navarre, [illus.] 10
Declaration of Independence, 33, 37; signing, [illus.] 39
Defence of the Scots Settlement at Darien... (1699), [t.p.] 14
Delaney, Guy, 234
Democratic Party, National Convention (1896), 160
Dendy, Marshall C., 239
Dennis, James, *Christian Mission and Social Progress*, 164
Depression, 1930s, 195ff.
Des Peres, MO, Pby. Ch., [illus.] 80
Detroit, MI, First Pby. Ch., 102; [illus.] 149
Dickens, Charles, *American Notes*, 84
Dickey, John M., 126
Dickinson, Clarence, [illus.] 193
Dickinson, Jonathan, 15, 27; [illus.] 22; *The True Scripture Doctrine...*, [t.p.] 22
Dickinson College, 99
Dickson, TN, Samuel McAdow's home, [illus.] 59
Directory for Worship, 49
Disciples of Christ Church, 54
Doak, Samuel, [illus.] 46
Dodge, Cleveland, [illus.] 158
Dodge, David L., [illus.] 60; *Observations on the Kingdom of Peace*, 60
Dodge, Grace H., [illus.] 158
Dodge, William E., [illus.] 158
Dollar, Robert, [illus.] 140
Dort, Synod, (1619) 8
Douglas, Julia, 228
Douglas, William, 228

Douglas, William O., [illus.] 228; *An Almanac of Liberty* (1954), 228
Douglass, Frederick, funeral, [illus.] 159
Dowey, Edward A., [illus.] 238
DuBose, Hampton, C., [illus.] 152
Dubuque, IA, Female Sem., [illus.] 94
Dubuque, IA, German Pby. Ch., [illus.] 94
Dubuque, Univ., 94
Dubuque Theo. Sem., [illus.] 94
Duffield, George, [illus.] 44; *A Sermon Preached. . . 1783* (1784), [t.p.] 44
Duffield, George, Jr., [illus.] 102; "Stand up, stand up, for Jesus," 102
Dulles, Eleanor, [illus.] 182
Dulles, John F., [illus.] 182, 203; [cartoon] 216
Dutch Reformed, 18f.
Dwight, Timothy, [illus.] 56; "I love thy Kingdom, Lord," 56
Dwight Indian Mission, see: Sallisaw Creek, OK

E

Eagan, John, J., statue, [illus.] 175
Eagleville, PA, Old Norriton Pby. Ch., [illus.] 18
Eakins, Thomas, "Dr. Agnew in Clinique," painting, [illus.] 141
East Coast Railway, 140
Eastburn, Joseph, [illus.] 75
Eastward, Presbytery, *Bath-Kol. A Voice. . .* (1783), [t.p.] 44
Eaton, John H., 72
Eaton, Peggy, [cartoon] 72
Ecumenical Conference, NY (1900), [illus.] 164
Eddy, Mary P., [illus.] 124
Edinburgh, Scot., Greyfriars Ch., [illus.] 12
Edinburgh, Scot., St. Giles Cathedral, [illus.] 7
Edinburgh, Treaty of, 7
Education, higher, Presbyterians, 62ff.; women, 95
Edwards, Jonathan, 27f.; [illus.] 25; *The Great Christian Doctrine of Original Sin Defended. . .* , [t.p.] 25; *A Treatise Concerning Religious Affections. . .* , [t.p.] 25
Edwards, Sarah, [illus.] 25
Egypt, United Pby. mission, 124
Eisenhower, Dwight D., [illus.] 216
Eisenhower, Mamie, [illus.] 216
Elder, John, 25, 36
Elder, ruling, 70
Eliot, T. S., 199
Eliza [*Uncle Tom's Cabin*], 84
Elizabeth, NJ, 27
Elizabeth, NJ, First Pby. Ch., 22, 86
Ellinwood, Frank F., [illus.] 150
Elson, Edward L. R., 222; [illus.] 216
Ely, Ezra S., 120; [illus.] 71; *The Duty of Christian Freemen. . .* , [t.p.] 71
Embudo, NM, Pby. Hospital, [illus.] 222
Engel, John, 198
Englewood, NJ, Pby. Ch., 247
English Empire in America, colonial America [map] 31
Erdman, Charles R., 178; [illus.] 189
Eternity Magazine, 206
Evangelical Alliance, 107, 113, 115; *History, Essays. . . Sixth General Conference. . . 1873,* [t.p.] 115
Evangelical Church, 197
Evans, Louis H., [illus.] 207
Evolution controversy, 107, 134
Ewing, Finis, [illus.] 59
Ewing, John, 34, 36, 52

F

Faggs Manor, PA, Blair Academy, 28
Fairplay, CO, Sheldon Jackson Chapel, [illus.] 131
Faith and Life Curriculum, Pres. Ch., U.S.A., [illus.] 210
Farel, William, [illus.] 4
Federal Council of Churches, 167, 175, 181, 215; organizational mtg. (1908), [illus.] 171; Commission on a Just and Durable Peace, 203; *Social Creed,* 171
Fellowship of Concern, 231
Filson, Floyd V., [illus.] 212
Fincastle Co., VA, 38
Finley, Robert, [illus.] 69
Finley, Samuel, [illus.] 27
Finney, Charles G., 84; [illus.] 77; *Lectures on Revivals. . .* (1835), [t.p.] 77
Fisher, Samuel W., [illus.] 79
Flagler, Henry M., [illus.] 140
Flagler, Lily, [illus.] 140
Florida, 58
Floyd, William, 39
Folson, Frances, [illus.] 137
Food for Lambs. . . Frankfort Sabbath School, [t.p.] 61
Footstove, coalpan, [illus.] 15
Ford, Henry, 197
Ford, Leighton, 244
Form of Government, 49
Forman, Charles W., [illus.] 151
Forman Christian College, [illus.] 151
Ft. Defiance, VA, Augusta Stone Pby. Ch., [illus.] 38
Fort Sumter, SC, 105, 108
Fort Wrangell, AK, 146
Fortune, 192
Forward, [masthead] 144
Fosdick, Harry E., *Shall the Fundamentalists Win?,* [t.p.] 188
Foster, John, 216
Foster, John W., [illus.] 182
Fox, Mr., 129
Foxfire, 236
Franklin, Benjamin, 26, 36
Frederick III, Elector, 9
Freedom's Journal, 68
Frelinghuysen, Theodore, 24
French and Indian War, 33
Fresno, CA, First Armenian Pby. Ch., [illus.] 162
Friendship (spaceship), [illus.] 229
Fundamentalist/modernist controversy, 167, 212
The Fundamentals, v. 1, [t.p.] 178

G

Ganado, AZ, Pby. mission, 184; Sage Mem. Hospital, 184; nurses' class, [illus.] 184
Garnet, Henry H., [illus.] 85; *The Past and the Present. . . the Colored Race. . .* , [t.p.] 85
Gellatly, Alexander, 29
The General Assembly Daily News, [masthead] 201
Geneva, Swit., 2, 4ff.
Geneva, Swit., Academy, [illus.] 6
Geneva, Swit., St. Peter's Cathedral, [illus.] 6
George III, King, 35
Georgia, Cherokee Indians, 63
German Immigrants, 94
German Presbyterian Theo. Sch. of the Northwest, [illus.] 94
German Reformed Church, 113
Gettysburg, PA, Battle of, 107
Ghost Ranch, AZ, [illus.] 241
Giddings, Salmon, [illus.] 57
Gillette, Gerald W., v

Girardeau, John L., 85
Glasgow, Univ., 26
Glenn, John, [illus.] 229
Gloucester, James, 68
Gloucester, Jeremiah, 68
Gloucester, John, [illus.] 68
Gloucester, Stephen, 68
Good Will Indian Mission, SD, [illus.] 132
The Gospel According to Peanuts, 212
Gospel Light curriculum, 210
Graham, Billy, [illus.] 244
Graham, Frank P., [illus.] 229
Graham, Isabella, [illus.] 61
Graham, Ruth, [illus.] 244
Graham, William, 40
Granlund, Paul T., 249
Grant, Edward D., [illus.] 229
Gray Panthers, 235
Great Awakening, 15, 21, 23ff.
Green, Ashbel, 58; [illus.] 57
Greensboro, NC, First Pby. Ch., 206
Grimke, Archibald, [illus.] 126
Grimke, Charlotte L., [illus.] 185
Grimke, Francis J., [illus.] 126, 185
Groover, Mary Agnes, v; see also: Brown Mary Agnes
Grosvenor, Gilbert H., [illus.] 192
Grosvenor, Gilbert, [illus.] 192
Grosvenor, Melville B., [illus.] 192
Grove City College, 119
Growing, [illus.] 210
Guerrant, E. O., [illus.] 177
Guideposts, 240
Gum Spring, VA, Providence Presbyterian Church, [illus.] 28
Gurley, Phineas D., [illus.] 108

H

Haines, Frances E. H., 144; [illus.] 161
Hall, Cameron P., [illus.] 215
Hall, Ralph, [illus.] 209
Hall, Warner, [illus.] 209
Halpin, Maria, 137
Hamilton, Alexander, 46
Hamilton College, 46
Hampden-Sydney College, 63, 225; [illus.] 40; Medical College of VA, [illus.] 87
Hampton, John, 16
Hancock, John, *The Danger of an Unqualified Ministry...* (1743), [t.p.] 24
Handy, Isaac W. K., [illus.] 111
Hanna, Sara F., [illus.] 121
Hannibal, MO, 107
Hannibal, MO, Pby. Ch., 120
Hanover, Presbytery, 28, 224; Memorial... (1776), [illus.] 40
Harding, Warren G., 198
Harlan, John M., 135, 165; [illus.] 159
Harnack, Adolf, 165
Harper's Weekly, 114, 118
Harrisburg, PA, Paxton Pby. Ch., [illus.] 36
Harrison, Benjamin, 135, 138, 164f., 182, 216; [illus.] 143; [cartoon] 143
Harrison, William H., 143
Hart, John, 39
Harvard, Univ., 87, 212
Hastings, Thomas, [illus.] 78; *Spiritual Songs for Social Worship* (1832), 78
Hastings College, 119
Hawaii, 92f.
Hawkins, Edler G., [illus.] 231
Hayes, John, [illus.] 145

Hays, George P., *May Women Speak?* (1889), 147
He Restoreth My Soul..., [t.p.] 202
Heckel, C. Willard, [illus.] 228
Heidelberg Catechism, 83; [t.p.] 9; [banner] 238
Heidelberg, Germany, [illus.] 9
Heidelberg, Univ., 9, 85
Hemphill, Charles W., 179
Henderlite, Rachel, [illus.] 224
Hendry, George S., [illus.] 237
Henry VIII, King, 11
Henry, Alexander, 61
Henry, Joseph, [illus.] 87
Hepburn, James C., [illus.] 153
Herblock, 216
Hicks, Sally, v
Higginbottom, Sam, [illus.] 200
Higginbottom, Jane, 200
Hiltner, Seward, [illus.] 214
Hispanics, Pby. Ch., 232
Historical Foundation of the Presbyterian and Reformed Churches, [illus.] 242
Hobbie, F. Wellford, 234
Hodge, Archibald A., [illus.] 148
Hodge, Charles, 62, 105; [illus.] 76, 88, 117; *Systematic Theology*, v. 1 (1871), [t.p.] 117
Hodge, Margaret, [illus.] 186
Hoge, Moses D., 88; [illus.] 128
Hollinshead, William, 48
Hollywood, CA, First Pby. Ch., 210; choir, [illus.] 207
Holy Spirit, 1, 240; *Westminster Confession*, 135, 165, 189
Hopkins, Samuel, [illus.] 56; *The System of Doctrines...*, v. 1, [t.p.] 56
Horton, Mildred M., [illus.] 215
Houston, TX, Central Pby. Ch., Chapel of the Reformation, statues, [illus.] 237
Houston, TX, Ministerial Assoc., 227
Houston, TX, St. Stephen's Pby. Ch., 227
Howland, Abby, 110
Hughes, John, Bp., 86
Huguenots, 19, 98; [illus.] 10; Florida massacre, [illus.] 10; St. Bartholomew's Day massacre, 10
Hull, Roger, [illus.] 244
Human Survival Issues..., [cover] 245
Hunt, George L., 210; [illus.] 245
Hunt, Timothy, 92
Huron College, 119
Hus, John, [illus.] 3
Hutchison, Stuart N., 198
Hyde, Edward, see: Cornbury, Lord
The Hymnal... (1895), [t.p.] 157
The Hymnbook (1955), [t.p.] 221

I

Ibis (riverboat), [illus.] 124
Ichthus, 218; [illus.] 1
Idaho, 131; First women's missionary soc., [illus.] 145
Illinois College, 65, 80
Immigration, Armenian, 162; German, 94; Italian, 162, 184; Scotch, 33
Independent Reflector... (1753), [t.p.] 35
India, Pby. mission, 151
Indianapolis, IN, First Pby. Ch., Harrison Mem. Window, [illus.] 143
Institute for the Training of Colored Ministers, Tuscaloosa, AL, [illus.] 127
International Business Machines, 198
International Congregational Council, 243
Interpretation, [cover] 213
Interpreter's Bible, 206
Interpreter's Dictionary of the Bible, 206
Iona Abbey, [illus.] 2
Italian immigrants, 162, 184

J

Jackson, Andrew, 70ff.; [illus.] 71f.; [cartoon] 72
Jackson, Rachel, [illus.] 71
Jackson, Sheldon, [illus.], 131, 146
Jackson, Stonewall, see: Jackson, Thomas J.
Jackson, Thomas J., [illus.] 109; statue, [illus.] 128
Jamaica, NJ, Pby. Ch., [illus.] 18
James, Mary E., [illus.] 131
Jefferson College, 46
Jefferson, Thomas, 39; *Act for Religious Liberty* (VA), 40
Jennings, Lena L., [illus.] 194
Jessup, Henry H., [illus.] 124
Jessup, Samuel, [illus.] 124
Jesus Christ, 1, 52, 91, 102, 104, 129, 217f., 225, 237, 249; Faith and Life Curriculum, 210; Federal Coun. of Churches, 171; Ichthus, 218; J. G. Machen, 188; carving, [illus.] 236
"Jesus loves me, This I know," 104
Jim Crow, 135
John Knox Press, 212
Johnson C. Smith Univ., 127, 185
Jones, Charles C., 97; [illus.] 78; *The Religious Instruction of the Negroes. . .* , [t.p.] 78
Jones, David H., [illus.] 221
"Joyful, joyful, we adore Thee," [illus.] 170
Judge, 137, 160; [cover] 136
Juneau, AK, First Pby. Ch., [illus.] 146
Junkin, George, 65; [illus.] 64

K

Kagawa, Toyohiko, family, [illus.] 200
Kansas, 99
Kasai Co., 173
Keckley, Elizabeth, [illus.] 112
Keezel, Jeffrey K., v
Keith, Isaac S., 48
Kelly, Balmer, 213
Kemper, John, [illus.] 57
Kennedy, John F., [illus.] 227
Kennedy, William B., *Into Covenant Life* (1963), 239
Kerr, Hugh T., 213
Kilgore, TX, First Pby. Ch., [illus.] 198
King, Martin L., 231
King, Samuel, 59
King College, 119
King's Mountain, Battle of, [illus.] 43
Kiowa, CO, camp mtg., [illus.] 236
Kirkland, Samuel, [illus.] 46
Kirkwood, MO, First Pby. Ch., 199
Kirwan, Walter B., 86
Knox, John, 98; [illus.] 4, 7; statue, [illus.] 237
Knoxville, TN, Fourth Pby. Ch., 205
Knoxville College, YMCA Cabinet, [illus.] 126
Korea, Pby. mission, 153
Korean War, veterans, [illus.] 214
Krey, Isabella, v
Kuhn, Margaret, [illus.] 235
Kurtz, Dorothy, v
Kuyper, Abraham, [illus.] 165

L

Labor Day Message for 1932, [t.p.] 196
Lac Leman, Swit., 8
Lafayette College, 65; [illus.] 64; World War I ambulance corp, [illus.] 181
Lake Mohonk Conf. (1956), [illus.] 223
Lamar, Robert C., 248
Lancaster Co., PA, 38
Lancaster, PA, 36
Landrith, Ira, 168; [illus.] 169
Lane Theo. Sem., 63
Laney, Lucy C., [illus.] 144
Lanier, Sidney A., [illus.] 107
Lansing, Robert, 216; [illus.] 182
Lapsley, Samuel, 172
Lapsley (mission boat), [illus.] 172
Larabraud, Jorge, [illus.] 232
Laurens, Martha, [illus.] 48
Layman's Bible Commentary, 212
LeConte, Joseph, [illus.] 87
League of Nations, 182
Leber, Charles T., [illus.] 215
Lee, Brenda, v
Lee, Robert, *Religion and Leisure in America* (1964), 241
Leopold, King, 173
A Letter to Presbyterians. . . (1953), 228; [cover] 217
Lewis, Sinclair, *Babbitt* (1922), [t.p.] 191
Lewis and Clark College, 119
Lewisburg, WV, Old Stone Ch., [illus.] 47; Pew & collection bag, [illus.] 49
Lexington, Presbytery, 69
Liberia, 85; [map] 69
Liberty Co., GA, Sunday sch. class, [illus.] 112
Liberty Hall Academy, VA, [illus.] 40
Liberty Party, 84
Library of Christian Classics, 212
Life, 192
Lincoln, Abraham, 99, 105; [illus.] 108; [cartoon] 109
Lincoln, Mary T., [illus.] 108, 112
Lincoln Theo. Sem., 211
Lincoln Univ., bldgs., [illus.] 126
Lindsley, Philip, [illus.] 66
Livingston, Philip, 39
Livingston, William, [illus.] 35
Lo Mo, see: Cameron, Donaldina
Locke, John, 35
Log College, Tennent's, 27; [illus.] 21
Logsdon, Helen B., [illus.] 194
London, Eng., Westminster Abbey, [illus.] 12
Londonderry, Ireland, [illus.] 14
Lookout Mountain, TN, PCUS youth mtg., [illus.] 166
Lord's Supper, American colonial, [illus.] 30; Bullinger, 8; Communion tokens, [illus.] 15; Communion ware, [illus.] 18, 30; J. Engel carving, [illus.] 198; Pres. Ch. (U.S.A.) organization (1983), [illus.], 284; Waldensians, [illus.] 3; Zwingli, 8
Louisville, KY, Bardstown Rd. Pby. Ch., 167
Louisville, KY, Harvey Browne Mem. Pby. Ch., Great Foyer window, [illus.] 249
Louisville, KY, Third Pby. Ch., picnic, [illus.] 134
Louisville, KY, Walnut St. Pby. Ch., [illus.] 115
Louisville, KY, Warren Mem. Pby. Ch., [illus.] 201
Louisville Presbyterian Theo. Sem., 173; Class of 1915, [illus.] 179
Lovejoy, Elijah P., [illus.] 80
Lowrie, John C., [illus.] 121
Lowrie, Walter, [illus.] 121
Luce, Henry, 217
Luce, Henry R., [illus.] 192
Luce, Henry W., [illus.] 192
Lucy (slave), [illus.] 112
Luther, Martin, 2, 4, 8; Ninety-Five Theses, 4; statue, [illus.] 237
Lutherans, 4, 8f.
Lyon, James, *Urania. . .* (1761), [t.p.] 33

M

McAdow, Samuel, 59; home, [illus.] 59
Macalester College, 140, 192, 225
McAlpine, Anna H., [illus.] 153
McAlpine, Robert E., [illus.] 153
Macartney, Clarence E., [illus.] 205; *Shall Unbelief Win?*, [t.p.] 188
MacArthur, Douglas, 202
McBeth, Susan L., [illus.] 145; School, [illus.] 145
McCague, Henrietta L., [illus.] 124
McCague, Thomas, 124
McCarthyism, 217
McClanahan, James S., Jr., v
McClellan, George B., [illus.] 109
McCloud, J. Oscar, [illus.] 231
McCloud, Robbie, [illus.] 231
McCluer, Franc, [illus.] 204
McCord, James I., [illus.] 237
McCormick, Cyrus H., 81, 147; [illus.] 141
McCormick, Nettie, 141; [illus.] 147
McCormick reaper, [illus.] 141
McCormick Theo. Sem., 212; Fowler Hall, [illus.] 147
McCosh, James, [illus.] 128; *Whither? O Whither?. . . ,* [t.p.] 148
McCoy, Albert B., [illus.] 208
McCrae, Jane, murder, [illus.] 42
McCullough, John, [illus.] 144
MacDonald, Flora, [illus.] 43
McDougall, Alexander, [illus.] 42
McFarland, Amanda, [illus.] 146
McGeachy, Pat, [illus.] 233
McGready, James, 54
McGuffey, William H., 107; [illus.] 120; *Eclectic Fourth Reader* (1837), 95; *McGuffey's New Second Eclectic Reader*, [t.p.] 120
Machen, J. Gresham, [illus.] 188; *Christianity and Liberalism,* 188
McIntire, Carl, 238
Mackay, Jane, [illus.] 217
Mackay, John A., 213; [illus.] 217
McKean, Thomas, [illus.] 39, 41
McKelway, Alexander, 225
McKelway, Alexander J., III, [illus.] 175
McKelway, St. Clair, "The Presbyterian Pyramid," [cartoon] 225
McLaren, Donald C., [illus.] 100
McLeod, Alexander, *A Scriptural View of the Character. . .* (1815), [t.p.] 60
McMillan, John, 156, 242; [illus.] 46, saddlebags, [illus.] 46
McNaugher, John, [illus.] 189
McNish, George, 16
McPheeters, Samuel B., [illus.] 111
McWhir, William, [illus.] 58
Makemie, Francis, 15ff., 156; desk, [illus.] 16; *A Narrative of a New and Unusual Imprisonment. . .* (1707), [t.p.] 17; statue, [illus.] 16, 242; Trial before Lord Cornbury, [illus.] 17
Mao De-Tung, 204
March on Washington (1963), [illus.] 231
Mark Twain, 107, see also: Clemens, Samuel L.
Marshall, Catherine, [illus.] 240; *Beyond Our Selves* (1961), 240; *Christy* (1967), [cover] 240; *A Man Called Peter* (1951), 206
Marshall, Peter, [illus.] 206
Mary Baldwin College, 95
Mary I (Mary Tudor), 7
Mary, Queen of Scots, 7
Maryville College, 65
Maryville, TN, 65, 79
Mason, George, 149
Mason, John M., 45
Mason, Lowell, *Spiritual Songs for Social Worhsip* (1832), 78
Matamoros, Mexico, 123

Matanzas, FL, 10
Mateer, Calvin W., [illus.] 152
Mateer, Julia, [illus.] 152
Matthews, Mark A., [illus.] 178
Mattoon, Mary L., 196; [illus.] 154
Mattoon, Stephen, 196; [illus.] 154
Maui, HA, 93
Mears, Henrietta, [illus.] 210
Medical College of VA, Hampden-Sydney College, [illus.] 87
Meeker, Rebecca, [illus.] 163
Mellon, Andrew W., (stamp), [illus.] 198
Mellon, Richard, 198
Mellon, Thomas, [illus.] 139
Menninger Foundation, 214
Menninger, Karl, [illus.] 214; *Whatever Became of Sin?* (1973), [cover] 214
Mercersburg, PA, 99
Mercersburg Theo. Sem., 83
Mercersburg Theology, 83
Merrill, William P., [illus.] 179
Methodists, 54
Mexican War, 89, 109
Meza, Herbert, [illus.] 227
Miami, FL, First Pby. Ch., Bryan Sunday sch. class, [illus.] 190
Miami, Presbytery, 99
Miami, Univ., OH, 66, 120
Michigan, Univ., 66
Midway, GA, 107
Midway, GA, Pby. Ch., [illus.] 78
Miller, Donald, 213
Miller, Francis P., family, [illus.] 220
Miller, James R., [illus.] 110
Miller, Samuel, 58, 62; [illus.] 70; *An Essay on the. . . Ruling Elder. . .* (1831), [t.p.] 70
Miller, William B., v, 242
Miller, Willis L., 127
Mills, Caleb, [illus.] 65
Minneapolis, MN, Westminster Pby. Ch., sculpture, [illus.] 249
Miraji, India, Wanless Hospital, [illus.] 151
Mister Rogers' Neighborhood, [illus.] 233
"Mr. Smith Goes to Washington" (motion picture), [illus.] 199
Mobile, AL, Central Pby. Ch., [illus.] 239
Mobile, AL, Government St. Ch., [illus.] 58
Modernist/Fundamentalist controversy, 167, 212
Mohegan Indians, 66
Momii, Umeko, 200
Monmouth College, baseball team, [illus.] 166
Monroe, LA, First Pby. Ch., [illus.] 239
Montana, 131
Monteith, John, [illus.] 66
Monterey, Mexico, 123
Montgomery, WV, Bryan campaign, [illus.] 160
Monticello, AR, First Pby. Ch., 229
Montreat, NC, Bible Conf., [illus.] 207
Montreat Conference Center, Assembly Inn, [illus.] 241
Moody, Dwight L., 125, 138
Moody-Sankey Revival, Philadelphia, PA (1876), [illus.] 125
Moomaw, Donald, [illus.] 211
Moore, John W., 199
Moore, Marianne, [illus.] 199; *Selected Poems,* 199
Moore, Walter, W., 147
Morgan, Daniel, [illus.] 42
Mormons, Pby. mission, 164
Morning Star (packet ship), [illus.] 93
Morrison, Robert, 74
Morrison, William M., [illus.] 173
Morse, Hermann, [illus.] 215
Moseley, Sara B., [illus.] 230
Mountaineer Mountain Mission, WV, 208
Murray, Nicholas, [illus.] 86; *Kirwan's Letters,* [t.p.] 86
Muskingum College, 229; [illus.] 65
Mutual Life Insurance Co., 244

N

Nantes, Edict, 10
Nashville, TN, First Pby. Ch., 71; [illus.] 89
Nassau, Ann P., [illus.] 122
Nassau, Charles W., [illus.] 122
Nassau, Robert H., [illus.] 122
Nassau, William L., [illus.] 122
Natchez, MS, Pine Ridge Pby. Ch., [illus.] 130
National Academy of Science, 87
National Anti-Opium League, 152
National Asian Presbyterian Council, Assembly (1982), [illus.] 232
National Conference of Christians and Jews, [illus.] 194
National Congress of Colored Americans, 85
National Council of Churches, 195, 215, 221, 228, 232, 242, 246; Dept. of Church and Economic Life, [illus.] 215
National Council of Presbyterian Men, Chicago mtg. (1958), [illus.] 228
National Council of Presbyterian Women's Organizations, 1
National Geographic Magazine, 192
National Child Labor Comm., 175
Native American Consulting Comm., [logo] 232
Native Americans, see: particular tribal names
Nativist movement, 86
Navajo Indians, 184
Nehru, Jawaharlal, [illus.] 229
Neo-Orthodox theology, 237
Neo-Reformation theology, 237
Neshaminy, PA, Log College, [illus.] 21
Netherlands, 8
Nevin, Alfred, *Encyclopedia of the Presbyterian Church*... (1884), [t.p.] 136
Nevin, John W., [illus.] 83; *The Anxious Bench*... (1843), [t.p.] 83; *The Mystical Presence*... (1846), [t.p.] 83; *The Principle of Protestantism*... (1844), [t.p.] 83
Nevius, John L., [illus.] 152; *Methods of Mission Work*..., [t.p.] 152
New Brunswick, NJ, Pby. Ch., 24
New Caledonia, Darien Colony, 14
New Castle, DE, Pby. Ch., [illus.] 19
New Castle, Presbytery, 126
New Concord, OH, 229
New Edinburgh, Darien Colony, 14
New-England Primer, [illus.] 20
New Jersey, College of, 21, 25, 28, 33, 37, 44, 46, 56, 128; Nassau Hall, [illus.] 27, 37; see also Princeton Univ.
New London, PA, Alison's Academy, charter, [illus.] 26
New London, PA, Pby. Ch., 26
New Orleans, Battle of, 71
New Orleans, LA, Prytania St. Pby. Ch., 159
New School/Old School division, 53, 63, 76, 79, 81
New School/Old School reunion, 113; [illus.] 114
New Side/Old Side division, 15, 34
New York, NY, 35
New York, NY, 156 5th Ave., [illus.] 135, 150
New York, NY, Bleeker St. Pby. Ch., 78
New York, NY, Brick Pby. Ch., 105, 139, 170, 179, 193, 198; pulpit, [illus.] 203
New York, NY, Broadway Tabernacle, [illus.] 77
New York, NY, Ch. of the Covenant, 119
New York, NY, Ch. of the Master, 224
New York, NY, Collegiate Ref. Ch., [illus.] 103
New York, NY, Federal Hall, [illus.] 51
New York, NY, Female Soc. for the Promotion of Sabbath Schools, 61
New York, NY, First Colored Pby. Ch., 68, 85
New York, NY, First Pby. Ch., 188; [illus.] 56
New York, NY, Fulton St. revival, [illus.] 81, 103
New York, NY, Interchurch Center, [illus.] 245
New York, NY, Labor Temple, [illus.] 174
New York, NY, Lafayette Pby. Ch., 199
New York, NY, Madison Ave. Pby. Ch., 206
New York, NY, Madison Sq. Pby. Ch., [illus.] 155
New York, NY, Murray Hill Pby. Ch., 136
New York, NY, Orange St. Pby. Ch., 61
New York, NY, Presbyterian Hospital, [illus.] 119
New York, NY, Second Pby. Ch., 77
New York, NY, Tammany Hall, [cartoon] 155
New York, Presbytery, 148, 188
New York, Synod, 27f.
New York and Philadelphia, Synod, 33f.; *A Draught of the Form of the Government*... (1787), [t.p.] 49
New York Life Insurance Co., 244
New York Observer, 86, 103
New York Peace Soc., 60
New York Times, 188
New York Times Magazine, [cover] 234
New Yorker, 225
Newark, DE, Academy, 34
Newark, NJ, 27
Newark, NJ, First Pby. Ch., [illus.] 47
Newburyport, MA, First Pby. Ch., [illus.] 23
Nez Perce Indians, Pby. mission, 145
Niccolls, Samuel J., [illus.] 171
Nicene Creed, 1; [banner] 238
Nichols, James H., [illus.] 227; *History of Christianity, 1650-1950* (1956), 227
Niebuhr, Reinhold, [illus.] 197; *Moral Man and Immoral Society*... (1932), [t.p.] 197; *Nature and Destiny of Man*, 197
Nobel Prize, Literature, 199; Physics, 194
Noble, W. F. P., *A Century of Gospel Work*..., [t.p.] 125
North American Review, 139
North Carolina, Synod, 63
North Carolina Presbyterian, 118
North Carolina, Univ., 229
North Dakota, Synod, 132
Northampton, MA, 25
Noyon, France, 4

O

Oberlin College, 77
Occum, Samson, [illus.] 32
Oglesby, William B., Jr., [illus.] 214
Oglethorpe College, 107
Oklahoma, 73, 213
Old Buttonwood, see: Philadelphia, PA, First Pby. Ch.
Old Ironsides (locomotive), [illus.] 70
Old One Hundred, [illus.] 60
Old Quarterman (slave), [illus.] 78
Old School/New School division, 53, 63, 76, 79, 81
Old School/New School reunion, 113; [illus.] 114
Old Side/New Side division, 15, 34
Olevianus, Kaspar, [illus.] 9
Olyphant, David W. C., 74
"One in Love," American Pby. churches, [map] 219
Oneida Indians, 46
Operation Crossroads Africa, 224
Ordination, laying on of hands, [illus.] 11
Oregon, 89
Oregon Territory, [stamp] 91
Oregon Trail, 90
Orlando, FL, Westminster Towers, [illus.] 235
Orthodox christians, 221, 225, 246
Ost, Warren, [illus.] 208

P

Pacific Sch. of Religion, 225
Paden, William M., 164

Palmer, Benjamin M., [illus.] 106
Pan-Presbyterian Convention (1867), 113
Pan-Presbyterian Council, Philadelphia, 1880 mtg., 109
Parker, Peter, [illus.] 74
Parkesburg, PA, Upper Octorara Pby. Ch., 240; communion ware, [illus.] 249
Parkhurst, Charles, [illus.] 155; [cartoon] 155
Parliament, Great Britain, 33, 38, 173
Pasadena, CA, First Pby. Ch., 221
Pastoral Counseling, 214
Patiotick Barber of New York, [cartoon] 38
Patterson, Mary J., [illus.] 231
Patton, Francis L., [illus.] 118
Paul VI, Pope, [illus.] 246
Paxton Boys, 36
Paxton, William, 129
Payne, Paul C., [illus.] 210, 215
Peace demonstration, NY (1982), [illus.] 247
Peacemaking: The Believer's Calling (1980), [cover] 247
Peacemaking, United Pres. Ch., U.S.A./Pres. Ch., U.S., 247
Peel, Maria, [illus.] 167
Peking, China, Forbidden City, [illus.] 246
Pennington, James W. C., [illus.] 85; *The Fugitive Blacksmith. . .* , [t.p.] 85; *Text Book of the Origin, and History. . . of the Colored People*, 85
Pennsylvania, Presbytery (Assoc.), 45
Pennsylvania, Univ., 155; Dept. of Medicine, [illus.] 141
Petersburg, VA, Tabb St. Pby. Ch., 81
Pew, J. Howard, [illus.] 228
Phelps Dodge Corp., 158
Philadelphia, College of, 34
Philadelphia, PA, 34, 68
Philadelphia, PA, Academy, [illus.] 26
Philadelphia, PA, "Alarm in Philadelphia," [illus.] 36
Philadelphia, PA, Assoc. Ch., 45
Philadelphia, PA, Bethany Pby. Ch., 183; [illus.] 138; Session, [illus.] 138; Sunday school hall, [illus.] 138
Philadelphia, PA, Bible Soc., 75
Philadelphia, PA, First African Pby. Ch., [illus.] 68
Philadelphia, PA, First Pby. Ch., 26, 43; [illus.] 16, 76; lamp, [illus.] 49
Philadelphia, PA, Mariner's Pby. Ch., [illus.] 75
Philadelphia, PA, Nativist riot (1844), [illus.] 86
Philadelphia, PA, Pennsylvania Railroad freight warehouse, [illus.] 125
Philadelphia, PA, Presbyterian Home for Aged Couples and Aged Men, [seal] 136
Philadelphia, PA, Seaman's Chapel, see: Philadelphia, PA, Mariner's Pby. Ch.
Philadelphia, PA, Second Pby. Ch., 24, 52, 75; [illus.] 50
Philadelphia, PA, Sunday and Adult School Union, 61
Philadelphia, PA, Tenth Pby. Ch., 206
Philadelphia, PA, Third Pby. Ch., 44, 71; [illus.] 34
Philadelphia, PA, Witherspoon Building, 135; [illus.] 156
Philadelphia, PA, Wylie Mem. Ch., [illus.] 113
Philadelphia, PA, Presbytery, 15f.; 18f.; minutes (1706), [illus.] 16
Philadelphia, PA, Second Presbytery, 34
Philadelphia, Synod, 15, 22, 32
Philadelphia School for Christian Workers of the Presbyterian and Reformed Churches, [illus.] 187
Phoenix, AZ, Brush Ch., [illus.] 132
Pierson, Abraham, 18
Pike, James A., [illus.] 227
Pittsburgh, PA, City Hall, 100
Pittsburgh, PA, East Liberty Pby. Ch., [illus.] 198
Pittsburgh, PA, First Pby. Ch., 188; [illus.] 114; outdoor pulpit, [illus.] 205; Tuesday Noon Club [illus.] 205
Pittsburgh, PA, First Ref. Ch., [illus.] 129
Pittsburgh, PA, Second Pby. Ch., 74
Pittsburgh, PA, Third Pby. Ch., 114
Pittsburgh-Xenia Theo. Sem., 189, 226; [illus.] 220
Plan of Union (1801), 53, 56, 79
Plumer, William S., [illus.] 79, 115
Pocomoke River, MD, [illus.] 19

Police Gazette, 129
Polk, James K., 89, 99
Polk, Sarah C., [illus.] 89
Porcupine, SD, Pby. manse, [illus.] 132
Pt. Clarence, AK, reindeer landing, [illus.] 146
Port Gibson, MS, Pby. Ch., [illus.] 81
Portsmouth, VA, First Pby. Ch., 111
Practice of Piety. . . (1620), [t.p.] 11
Prentiss, Elizabeth, [illus.] 118; *Stepping Heavenward* (1869), 118
Presbyterian Church in America, General Assembly, organizing, 243
Presbyterian Church, C.S.A., General Assembly 1861, "Address of the Southern General Assembly. . . ," 106; organization (1861), 106
Presbyterian Church, U.S., Board of Christian Education, 229, 239
Presbyterian Church, U.S., Colored Women's Conference, Tuscaloosa (1916); 187
Presbyterian Church, U.S., Comm. of Publication, [illus.] 190
Presbyterian Church, U.S., Coun. on Theology and Culture, 232
Presbyterian Church, U.S., "A Declaration of Faith," 239
Presbyterian Church, U.S., General Assembly, 1883, 134; 1962, 229; 1972, 244; 1974, 231; 1978, 230; 1983, 248; Comm. on Moral and Social Welfare, 197; General Assembly Mission Board, 245; restructure, 245
Presbyterian Church, U.S., Men's parade, [illus.] 220
Presbyterian Church, U.S., spirituality, 106, 197
Presbyterian Church, U.S./United Pres. Ch., U.S.A., reunion (1983), [illus.] 248
Presbyterian Church, U.S., Women's mtg., Atlanta (1912), [illus.] 186
Presbyterian Church, U.S.A., Board of Christian Education, 235
Presbyterian Church, U.S.A., Board of Church Erection, 130
Presbyterian Church, U.S.A., Board of Education, 96
Presbyterian Church, U.S.A., Board of Foreign Missions, 74, 92, 150f., 164, 200, 223; Lake Mohonk Conf. (1956), [illus.] 223; Missionary conf. (1898), [illus.] 154
Presbyterian Church, U.S.A., Board of Home Missions, Dept. of Rural Church, 176; Dept. of Workingmen, 174
Presbyterian Church, U.S.A., Board of Missions, 57
Presbyterian Church, U.S.A., Board of National Missions, 222; Dept. of Work With Colored People, 208
Presbyterian Church, U.S.A., Board of Pensions, 156
Presbyterian Church, U.S.A., Board of Publications and Sabbath School Work, 161; building, [illus.] 96
Presbyterian Church, U.S.A., Expansion, 1837-1870, [map] 82
Presbyterian Church, U.S.A., General Assembly, 1789, 33, 37, 50f.; 1802, 57; 1818, 69; 1828, 71; 1837, 79; (N.S.) 1838, Minutes, [t.p.] 79; (O.S.) 1838, Minutes, [t.p.] 79; (O.S.) 1846, 88; (O.S.) 1847, 88; (O.S.) 1849, 86; (O.S.) 1852, 96; (O.S.) 1855, 130; (O.S.) 1861, [illus.] 105; 1883, 134; 1897, 146; 1907, [illus.] 168f.; 1910, 189; 1925, Special Commission, [illus.] 189; 1930, 167, 194; 1931, women commissioners, [illus.] 194; 1932, 200; 1953, 217; 1958, 226; Board of Trustees, 52; Centennial medallion (1888), [illus.] 143; Comm. on Missions, 57; Comm. for Revision of the Creed (1903), [illus.] 165; Comm. on Evangelism, 183; General Council (1925), [illus.] 186; New Life Movement Comm., [illus.] 209
Presbyterian Church, U.S.A., National Service Commission, *Presbyterians at Work for Their Boys. . .* , 181
Presbyterian Church, U.S.A., Presbyterian Foundation, 228
Presbyterian Church, U.S.A., Woman's Board of Foreign Missions, Saratoga mtg. (1879), [illus.] 121
Presbyterian Church, U.S.A., Woman's Board of Home Missions, 179, 186

Presbyterian Church, U.S.A., Woman's Executive Comm. of Home Missions, [illus.] 161
Presbyterian Church, U.S.A./Cumberland Pres. Ch., reunion (1906), 167f.
Presbyterian Church, U.S.A./United Pres. Ch., N.A., union, 225f.; [illus.] 226
Presbyterian Church, (U.S.A.), General Assembly, 1983, [illus.] 248
Presbyterian churches, 1750, American, [map] 31; 1837-70, [map] 82; 1950s, [map] 219
Presbyterian Family Almanac, 1858, [t.p.] 102
Presbyterian Family Connections, [chart] 250
Presbyterian Historical Society, 90, 96, 156; building, [illus.] 242
Presbyterian Lay Comm., 228, 244
Presbyterian Layman, [masthead] 244
Presbyterian Life, [cover] 213
Presbyterian Minister's Fund, 32
Presbyterian Outlook, 245
Presbyterian Review, v. 1, [t.p.] 148
Presbyterian Sch. of Christian Educ., [illus.] 233
Presbyterian Standard, 175
Presbytery, The, see: Philadelphia, Presbytery
Pressly, John T., [illus.] 100
Prime, Samuel I., [illus.] 103; *The Power of Prayer...* [t.p.] 103
Princeton, NJ, 44
Princeton, NJ, First Pby. Ch., 37, 50
Princeton Theo. Sem., 68, 70, 76, 88, 93, 126, 148, 154, 165, 178, 188f., 200, 212, 214, 217, 237f.; [illus.] 62; touring choir (1948), [illus.] 221
Princeton Univ., 154, 170, 180; see also: New Jersey, College of
Psalms and Hymns Adapted to Social... Worship... (1843), [t.p.] 97
Puck, 142, 155
Puerto Rico, Presbytery, [illus.] 163
Pugh, William B., [illus.] 201
Puritans, 13

Q

Quakers, 36
Quarryville, PA, Middle Octorara United Pby. Ch., [illus.] 29
Quebec Act (1774), 33

R

Rabun-Gap Napoochee Sch., 236
Ralston, Robert, [illus.] 75
Ramsay, David, [illus.] 48; *The History of the American Revolution...* (1789), [t.p.] 48
Ramsay, John G., [illus.] 205
Ramsay, Martha L., [illus.] 48
Randall, Claire, [illus.] 246
Rankin, John, family, [illus.] 84
Rankin, Melinda, [illus.] 123
Rauschenbusch, Walter, 171
Read, Thomas, [illus.] 34
Reader's Digest, 192
Reconstruction, 107, 134
Redhead, John A., Jr., [illus.] 206
Redman, John, [cartoon] 32
Reed, Isaac, [illus.] 57; *The Christian Traveler*, 57
Reformation, 2ff.
Reformation, England, 11
Reformation Wall, Geneva, Swit., [illus.] 4

Reformed Church of America, 8
Reformed Presbytery of America, 45
Reformed World, 243
Rehoboth, MD, Pby. Ch., [illus.] 19
Reindeer, Alaskan introduction, [illus.] 146
Religion and Labor Fellowship, 205
Restoration Fund, Pres. Ch., U.S.A., [illus.] 202, 209
Re-Thinking Missions: A Layman's Inquiry (1932), 200
Revolution, American, 33, 38ff.
Rice, John H., [illus.] 63
Rice, Zachariah, 149
Richardson, Henry H., 149
Richmond, VA, All Souls Pby. Ch., 224
Richmond, VA, First Pby. Ch., 79
Richmond, VA, Second Pby. Ch., 128; [illus.] 88
Rio de Janeiro, Brazil, 123
Rittenhouse, David, orrery, [illus.] 37
Robb, Thomas B., *The Bonus Years...* (1968), [t.p.] 235
Roberts, O. G., [illus.] 194
Roberts, William H., 168, 171; [illus.] 157, 169
Robinson, James, [illus.] 224
Robinson, Stuart, [illus.] 115
Rochester, NY, Central Pby. Ch., F. Douglass funeral, [illus.] 159
Rochester, NY, St. Peter's Pby. Ch., [illus.] 98
Rockefeller, John D., 140
Rocky Mountain College, 119
Rocky Mountain Presbyterian, [masthead] 131
Rodgers, John, [illus.] 50
Roe, E. P., [illus.] 116; *Barriers Burned Away* (1872)
Rogers, Fred, [illus.] 233
Roman Catholics, 10, 14, 81f., 136, 225, 227 246; Canada, 33; Nativist movement, 86
Romanticism, 88
Rome, Italy, St. Peter's Cathedral, [illus.] 227
Romney, WV, Pby. Ch., funeral bier, [illus.] 107
Roosevelt, Franklin D., 196, 228
Ross, Edward A., *Sin and Society...* (1907), [t.p.] 175
Rous, Francis, *Psalms of David in English Meeter...* (1646), [t.p.] 30
Royal Geographic Soc., 172
Rush, Benjamin, 39; [illus.] 41
Rusk, Dean, [illus.] 215, 234
Rusk, Robert H., 234
Russell, Letty M., [illus.] 230; *Human Liberation in a Feminist Perspective* (1974), 230
Russia, NCC visit (1956), [illus.] 221
Rutgers Univ., 228
Rutherford, Samuel, [illus.] 12; *Lex Rex*, 12

S

Safford, Anna, [illus.] 152
Sage, Margaret O., [illus.] 179
Sage, Russell, 179
St. Andrews College, [illus.] 234
St. Augustine, FL, First Pby. Ch., 58
St. Augustine, FL, Mem. Pby. Ch., [illus.] 140
St. John's River, FL, 10
St. Louis, MO, 57; [cityscape] 116
St. Louis, MO, First Pby. Ch., [illus.] 116
St. Louis, MO, Pine St. Pby. Ch., 111
St. Louis, MO, Second Pby. Ch., 171, 203
St. Louis Observer, 80
St. Paul, MN, House of Hope Pby. Ch., 140
Sallisaw Creek, OK, Dwight Indian Mission, [illus.] 73
Salt Lake City, UT, First Pby. Ch., 164
San Antonio, TX, Ch. of the Divine Redeemer, 233
San Francisco, CA, Benicia Pby. Ch., [illus.] 92
San Francisco, CA, Calvary Pby. Ch., [illus.] 133
San Francisco, CA, Chinatown, prostitution, 187
San Francisco, CA, earthquake (1906), [illus.] 167

San Francisco, CA, Grace Episc. Cathedral, 227
San Francisco, CA, Japanese Pby. Ch., 133
San Francisco, CA, YMCA, 133
San Francisco Theo. Sem., 140, 241; [illus.] 133, 167
Sanford, NC, Barbecue Pby. Ch., 43
Sankey, Ira, 125
Santa Fe, NM, Allison-James School, 163
Santa Fe, NM, First Pby. Ch., [illus.] 236
Saroyan, William, 162
Savannah, GA, Independent Pby. Ch., 39; [illus.] 47
Saxony, 4
Schaff, Philip, 107, 113, 128, 149; [illus.] 83, 148; *The Creeds of Christendom. . .* , v. 1, [t.p.] 113
Schenectady, NY, First Pby. Ch., 114
Schureman, William H., [illus.] 161
Scotch-Irish, 43
Scotland, Free Church, 128
Scots Confession (1560), 7; [banner] 238
Scots, immigration, 29, 33, 43, 45, 47f., 51
Scott, John M., 35
Scott, William A., [illus.] 133
Seattle, WA, First Pby. Ch., [illus.] 178
Seceders, 29, 45, 100
Second Great Awakening, 54, 59
Second Helvetic Confession (1566), 8; [banner] 238
See, Ruth, v
Seoul, Korea, Severance Hosp., [illus.] 153
Servetus, Michael, memorial, [illus.] 6
Service Theo. Sem., [illus.] 62
Severance, Louis H., 153; [illus.] 140
Shantung Christian Univ., 152
Shaull, Richard, 223
Shedd, William G. T., [illus.] 117; *Dogmatic Theology*, 117
Sheldon Jackson College, 119
Sheppard, Lucy J., [illus.] 172
Sheppard, William H., 172f.; [illus.] 127, 172
Shippen, Edward, [illus.] 43
Shriver, Donald, [illus.] 247; *The Unsilent South. . .* , [t.p.] 220
Silliman, B. J., [illus.] 194
Simonton, Ashbel G., [illus.] 123
Slavery, controversy, 49, 53, 68f., 80f., 84f., 88, 97
Sloop Eustace, [illus.] 177
Sloop, Mary T. M., [illus.] 177
Smathers, Eugene, [illus.] 236
Smith, Henry B., [illus.] 113
Smith, James, 39
Smith, Jane B., [illus.] 185
Smith, John B., [illus.] 40
Smith, Richard C., [illus.] 208
Smith, Samuel S., [illus.] 40
Smith, William, 35; [illus.] 43
Smithsonian Institution, 87
Smylie, Elizabeth R., v
Smylie, James, 97
Socialist Party, 196
Society for the Reformation of Morals, 67
Society of Soul Winners, 177
Somerville, John N., [illus.] 244
Sons of Liberty, 33, 38, 42
South Carolina, Univ., 134
South Dakota, Synod, 132
Southampton, NY, Pby. Ch., [illus.] 18; communion cups, [illus.] 18
Southern Presbyterian Journal, 244
Spalding, Eliza, 90; "Presbyterian Stairway to Heaven and Hell," [chart] 91
Spalding, Henry H., [illus.] 90
Sparta, NJ, Pby. Ch., 53
Speer, Robert E., 178, 181; [illus.] 154, 200; "Re-Thinking Missions" *Examined. . . .* , [t.p.] 200
Speer, William, [illus.] 92
Spencer, Cornelia, [illus.] 118
Spitzer, Julian, [illus.] 202
Sprague, William B., *Lectures on Revivals. . .* (1832), [t.p.] 77

Spring, Gardiner, 226; [illus.] 105
Spring Resolution (1861), 105
Springfield, NJ, Battle of, [illus.] 42
Stair, Lois H., [illus.] 230
Stamford, CT, First Pby. Ch., [illus.] 218
"Stand up, stand up for Jesus," 102
Standard Oil, OH, 140
Staunton, VA, Augusta Female Sem., [illus.] 95
Staunton, VA, Pby. Ch., 95
Steele's Tavern, VA, 141
Stelzle, Charles, [illus.] 174; *A Son of the Bowery*, 174; *The Gospel of Labor* (1912), [t.p.] 174
Stevenson, Arthur, *Chicago Pre-Eminently a Presbyterian City. . .* , [t.p.] 141
Stewart, James, [illus.] 199
Stewart, Lyman, [illus.] 178
Stewart, Milton, [illus.] 178
Stillman, Charles A., [illus.] 127
Stillman College, 127, 172
Stillman Institute, 127; [illus.] 187
Stillwater, OK, First Pby. Ch., [illus.] 201
Stimson, Henry, [illus.] 201
Stockton, Julia, [illus.] 41
Stockton, Presbytery, 162
Stockton, Richard, 39, 41
Stone, Barton W., [illus.] 54
Stone, John T., 178
Stonites, 54
Stowe, Calvin, 97; [illus.] 63
Stowe, Harriet B., 95; [illus.] 97; *Uncle Tom's Cabin*, 84, [t.p.] 97
Strong, William, 135; [illus.] 158
Stuart, George H., 110; [illus.] 113
Stuart, Jane, 110
Stuart, John L., [illus.] 204
Student Christian Movement, 211
Sun Oil Co., 228
Sunday, Billy, see: Sunday, William A.
Sunday, William A., [illus.] 183; [cartoon] 183
Sunderland, Byron, 137
Sweazey, George E., *Effective Evangelism. . .* (1953), [t.p.] 209
Swift, Elijah P., [illus.] 74
Swift, Elizabeth B., [illus.] 74
Swing, David, [illus.] 118
Sydenstricker, Absalom, [illus.] 152, 199
Sydenstricker, Carrie, [illus.] 152, 199
Sydenstricker, Pearl, [illus.] 152; see also: Buck, Pearl
Syracuse, NY, First Pby. Ch., 224
Syria, Pby. mission, 124

T

Talmage, Thomas D., [illus.] 142; [cartoon] 142
Tappan, Arthur, 77; [illus.] 70
Tappan, Lewis, 77; [illus.] 70
Tarkio College, 119
Taylor, Bruce L., v
Taylor, George, 39
Taylor, J. Randolph, [illus.] 231, 248
Taylor, Nathaniel, 16
Taylor, Theophilus M., [illus.] 226
Templeton, John, [illus.] 247
Templeton, Prize, 247
Tennent, Gilbert, 15, 33; [illus.] 24; *The Danger of an Unconverted Ministry. . .* (1740), [t.p.] 24; *Irenicum Ecclesiasticum. . .* , [t.p.] 34
Tennent, NJ, Old Tennant Pby. Ch., [illus.] 24
Tennent, William, 15, 24; [illus.] 21
Tennessee, Univ., 66
Teresa, Mother, [illus.] 247
Texas, 89

Texas, Presbytery (CPC), 59
Thailand, Pby. mission, 152, 154
Theological Declaration of Barmen, [banner] 238
Theological Medium, [illus.] 83
Theology Today, [cover] 213
Thirty Nine Articles, 11
Thomas, Emma, [illus.] 196
Thomas, Norman M., [illus.] 196
Thomas, Welling, family, [illus.] 196
Thompson, Charles L., [illus.] 160
Thompson, Ernest T., [illus.] 197, 245
Thompson, Robert E., [illus.] 155; *De Civitate Dei. . .* (1891), [t.p.] 155
Thompson, William P., [illus.] 247
Thomson, Charles, [illus.] 41
Thornton, Matthew, 39
Thornwell, James H., 106; [illus.] 88
Time, 192; [cover] 217
Today, [cover] 235
Topeka, KS, First Pby. Ch., 214
Towner, Margaret E., [illus.] 224
Trail of Tears, 73
Trinity College, TX, 119; football team, [illus.] 166; cheerleader, [illus.] 166
Tron, Charles A., [illus.] 162
Troy, NY, First Pby. Ch., 79
Troy, Presbytery, 84
Truchas, NM, Pby. mission, [illus.] 163
Truman, Harry S., [illus.] 204
Trumbull, David, [illus.] 123
Trumbull, John, Declaration of Independence, [illus.] 39
Tuscaloosa, AL, First Pby. Ch., 127
Twain, Mark, 173; see also: Clemens, Samuel L.

U

Underground railroad, 84
Underwood, Horace G., [illus.] 153
Underwood, Lillas, [illus.] 153
Union College, revival, [illus.] 66
Union Oil Co., 178
Union Theo. Sem., NY, 83, 113, 117, 128, 158, 165, 196f., 217, 225, 247; [illus.] 63; faculty (1888), [illus.] 148; Sch. of Sacred Music, 193
Union Theo. Sem., VA, 63, 190, 197, 212ff., 237; [illus.] 147
United Nations, 195, 203, 229; Disarmament Conf., 247
United Presbyterian Church, N.A., 29; organization, 81
United Presbyterian Church, N.A., General Assembly, 1858, [illus.] 100f.; 1958, 226
United Presbyterian Church, N.A., Women's General Missionary Soc.; 121; Board, [illus.] 150
United Presbyterian Church, N.A., Young People's Christian Union, 166
United Presbyterian Church, N.A./Pres. Ch., U.S.A., union, 225f., [illus.] 226
United Presbyterian Church, U.S.A., General Assembly, 1964, 231; 1967, 238; 1972, 228, 230; 1983, 248; General Assembly Mission Council, 245; reorganization, 245
United Presbyterian Church, U.S.A., organization (1958), [illus.] 226
United Presbyterian Church, U.S.A./Pres. Ch., U.S., reunion (1983), [illus.] 248
United Presbyterian Church, U.S.A., Program Agency, 231
United Presbyterian Women, Meeting (1958), [illus.] 230
U.S. Capitol, 90
U.S. Christian Commission, Headquarters, [illus.] 110; City Point, VA, Station, [illus.] 110
U.S. Constitution, 135; Bill of Rights, 51; Thirteenth Amendment, 85
U.S. House of Representatives, 85, 99
U.S. Military Academy, Warner Bible Class, [illus.] 104

U.S. Sanitary Commission, 110
U.S. Senate, 99, 173, 206
U.S. Supreme Court, 158f., 220, 228, 242; Plessy v. Ferguson (1896), 159; Walnut St. Ch. case, 115
U.S.S. Baltimore (ship), [illus.] 202
United Steelworkers of America, CIO, 205
Ursinus, Zacharias, [illus.] 9
Utah, 131
Utah Gospel Mission, wagons, [illus.] 164

V

Valdese, NC, Waldensian Ch., [illus.] 162
Valparaiso, Chile, 123
Van Dusen, Henry P., [illus.] 170, 217; "Joyful, joyful, we adore Thee," [illus.] 170
Van Dyke, Henry, 157; [illus.] 170
Van Rensselaer, Cortlandt, [illus.] 96
Van Vliet, Adrian, [illus.] 94
Vatican Council II, 227
Vietnam War, antiwar movement, [illus.] 234
Virginia, Synod, 63
Visser 't Hooft, Willem A., [illus.] 216
Vredenburgh, Jacob, [cartoon] 38

W

Wabash College, 65
Wagoner, Harold, 222
Waldensians, 3; North Carolina, 162
Waldo, Peter, [illus.] 3
Walker, John M., 236
Walker, William H., 180
Wallace, DeWitt, [illus.] 192
Wallace, Henry, [illus.] 176
Wallace, Henry A., [illus.] 176
Wallace, Henry C., [illus.] 176
Wallace, James, [illus.] 192
Wallace, Lila B., [illus.] 192
Wallaces' Farmer, [masthead] 176
Wanless, William J., [illus.] 151
Wanamaker, John, 135, 138, 183
War of 1812, 60
Ward, Levi A., [illus.] 98
Warfield, Benjamin B., 178; [illus.] 148
Warner, Anna B., [illus.] 104; "Jesus loves me, this I know. . .," 104; *Say and Seal* (1859), 104
Warner, John R., 199
Warner, Susan B., [illus.] 104; *The Wide, Wide World* (1851), 104
Warren, John B., 58
Warren Wilson College, [illus.] 176
Washington, DC, Ch. of the Covenant, 222
Washington, DC, Ch. of the Pilgrims, [illus.] 191, 231
Washington, DC, F St. Pby. Ch., 108
Washington, DC, 15th St. Pby. Ch., 126; [illus.] 185
Washington, DC, First Pby. Ch., 51, 137, 221
Washington, DC, National Pby. Ch., 192, 201, 216, 242; [illus.] 222
Washington, DC, New York Ave. Pby. Ch., [illus.] 108
Washington, DC, White House, carpenters' shop, [illus.] 51
Washington, George, 33, 42ff., 143; [illus.] 51
Washington and Lee Univ., 173
Washington Univ., 203
Watson, Thomas J., [illus.] 198
Watts, Isaac, 42, 49

Weber, Herman C., *Presbyterian Statistics...* (1927), [graphs] 191
Weld, Theodore D., [illus.] 84; *American Slavery As It Is...*, [t.p.] 84
West Point, NY, 104
Western Foreign Missionary Soc., 74
Westinghouse, George, [illus.] 139
Westinghouse, Marguerite W., [illus.] 139
Westinghouse Electric Co., 139
Westminster Assembly of Divines, 12
Westminster Choir College, 193
Westminster College, MO, Churchill Mem. and Library, [illus.] 204
Westminster College, PA, [illus.] 234
Westminster College, UT, 119
Westminster Confession of Faith, 15, 22, 34, 49, 60, 167, 188; (1647), [t.p.] 12; [banner] 238; revision (1903), 135, 158, 165, 168; UPCNA, 189
Westminster Larger Catechism, 15, 22, 49
Washington Post, 216
Westminster Press, 212
Westminster Shorter Catechism, 15, 20, 22, 49, 175; [t.p.] 12; [banner] 238
Weyerhaeuser, Frederick, [illus.] 140
Wheelock, Eleazer, 32
Whiskey Rebellion, 51
Whitefield, George, 23f.; [illus.] 23
Whitman, Marcus, 90, 156, 242; [illus.] 90; statue, [illus.] 90
Whitman, Narcissa, [illus.] 90
Willard, Samuel, [illus.] 20; *A Compleat Body of Divinity...* (1726), [t.p.] 20
Willet, Henry L., 1
Willet Stained Glass Studio, 1, 249
William the Silent, [illus.] 8
Williams, Albert, [illus.] 92
Williams, J. Rodman, [illus.] 240; *The Era of the Spirit* (1967), 240
Williams College, 58
Williamson, John F., [illus.] 193
Williamson, Lamar, *...And A Time To Laugh*, [cover] 229
Williamson, Rhea, 193
Wilmore, Gayraud, [illus.] 211
Wilson, Eleanor, [illus.] 180
Wilson, Ellen A., [illus.] 180
Wilson, James, 39; [illus.] 41
Wilson, Jane E., [illus.] 122
Wilson, Jessie, [illus.] 180
Wilson, John, 16
Wilson, John L., [illus.] 122
Wilson, Joseph R., 95; family, [illus.] 157
Wilson, Margaret, [illus.] 180
Wilson, Warren H., [illus.] 176
Wilson, Woodrow, 95, 134, 181, 195, 216; [illus.] 157, 180, 182; Cabinet, [illus.] 180; [cartoon] 180; Fourteen Points, 182
Wilson College, 119
Winn, Albert C., [illus.] 239
Winsborough, Hallie P., [illus.] 186
Winter, R. Milton, v
Winthrop, John, [illus.] 13
Wirt, William, [illus.] 73
Wisconsin, Univ., Pby. Student Center, 211
Witherspoon, John, 33, 39, 41, 44, 48, 50; [illus.] 37; clock, [illus.] 37; statue, [illus.] 156, 242

Wolfe, Thomas, *Look Homeward, Angel* (1929), 195; *You Can't Go Home Again* (1934), 195
Women, clergy ordination, M. Matthews, 178; elder ordination, 167; General Assembly moderators, 230; status, Pres. Ch., U.S.A., 186; women's suffrage, W. Wilson, 180
Women's Army Corp, 202
Woodbridge, Sylvester, [illus.] 92
Woodrow, James, 107; [illus.] 134
Woods, James, [illus.] 92
Woolsey, Georgeanna, 110
Woolsey, Jane S., [illus.] 119
Woosley, Louisa M., [illus.] 147; *Shall Woman Preach?...* (1891), [t.p.] 147
Wooster, College of, 194; Old Main, [illus.] 119
Worcester, Erminia, [illus.] 73
Worcester, Samuel A., [illus.] 73
World Alliance of Reformed Churches, Nairobi mtg. (1970), [illus.] 243
World Anti-Slavery Convention, 84
World Council of Churches, 195, 203, 246; 2d Assembly, Evanston (1954), 217; Div. of World Mission and Evangelism, 223
World Parliament of Religion, [illus.] 149
World Student Christian Federation, 220, 223
World War II, 195, 201ff.
World's Columbian Exposition, 149
Worms, Diet of, 4
The Worshipbook (1970), [t.p.] 243
Wright, George E., [illus.] 212
Wright, Theodore, 68
Wyclif, John, 3
Wycliffites, 3

X

Xenia, OH, Pby. Ch., Women's temperance mtg., [illus.] 119

Y

Yale College, 25, 56
Yale Univ., 230, 234
Yenching Univ., 204
Yielding, Mary A., [illus.] 194
Young Men's Christian Assoc., 138
Young Women's Christian Assoc., 158
Youth, Pby. Ch., 166, 233

Z

Zubly, John J., 47; *The Law of Liberty...* (1775), [t.p.] 39
Zurich, Swit., 8
Zwingli, Huldreich, [illus.] 8